BARRON'S

D1538986

TOEIC®
BRIDGE TEST
WITH AUDIO CDs

TEST OF ENGLISH FOR
INTERNATIONAL COMMUNICATION

2ND EDITION

DISCARD

Lin Lougheed
Ed.D., Teachers College
Columbia University

BARRON'S

Photo Credits
The author gratefully acknowledges the following institutions and companies
that granted permission to reproduce the respective photos.

Educational Testing Service
Photos on pages 24, 93, 235, and 265.

Instructional Design International, Inc.
Photos on pages 30 (4), 41 (3), 42 (4), 94 (2), 95 (3), 97 (8), 99 (12), 100 (14), 101, 238 (5),
239 (7–8), 240 (9), 241 (11–12), 242 (14), and 266 (1).

Shutterstock Corporation
Photos on pages 28 (5), 32 (1–2), 34 (5), 35 (3), 94 (1), 96 (5), 243 (15), 270 (9), and 271 (11).

Corbis Corporation
All other photos not identified above.

All inquiries should be addressed to:
Barron's Educational Series, Inc.
250 Wireless Boulevard
Hauppauge, New York 11788
www.barronseduc.com

Library of Congress Catalog Card No. 2009044803

ISBN-13: 978-0-7641-4417-2 (Book only)
ISBN-10: 0-7641-4417-0 (Book only)
ISBN-13: 978-0-7641-8785-8 (Audio 1)
ISBN-10: 0-7641-8785-6 (Audio 1)
ISBN-13: 978-0-7641-8786-5 (Audio 2)
ISBN-10: 0-7641-8786-4 (Audio 2)
ISBN-13: 978-0-7641-9711-6 (Book w/audio CDs package)
ISBN-10: 0-7641-9711-8 (Book w/audio CDs package)

Library of Congress Cataloging-in-Publication Data
Lougheed, Lin, 1946–
    [Barron's TOEIC]
    TOEIC® bridge test: test of English for international communication / Lin Lougheed.—2nd ed.
       p. cm.
    Includes bibliographical references and index.
    ISBN-13: 978-0-7641-4417-2 (alk. paper)
    ISBN-10: 0-7641-4417-0 (alk. paper)
    ISBN-13: 978-0-7641-9711-6 (alk. paper)
    ISBN-10: 0-7641-9711-8 (alk. paper)
    1. Test of English for International Communication—Study guides. 2. English language—Textbooks for foreign
speakers. 3. English language—Examinations—Study guides. I. Barron's Educational Series, Inc. II. Title.
III. Title: Test of English for International Communication.
    PE1128.L644 2010
    428.0076—dc22

                                                                            2009044803

PRINTED IN THE UNITED STATES OF AMERICA
9 8 7 6 5 4 3 2 1

Contents

Introduction

CHAPTER 1

> ## WHAT TO LOOK FOR IN THIS CHAPTER
>
> - Overview of the TOEIC Bridge Test
> - For the Teacher
> - For the Student
> - Frequently Asked Questions About the TOEIC Bridge Test

OVERVIEW OF THE TOEIC BRIDGE TEST

There are two sections on the TOEIC Bridge test: Listening Comprehension and Reading. You will be given a test book and an answer sheet. You will need a pencil to take the test. All of the questions are multiple-choice. Here is an outline of the TOEIC Bridge test.

TOEIC Bridge Test

Section 1 (25 minutes)	Listening Comprehension	
	Part I Photographs	15 questions
	Part II Question-Response	20 questions
	Part III Short Conversations and Short Talks	15 questions
Section 2 (35 minutes)	Reading	
	Part IV Incomplete Sentences	30 questions
	Part V Reading Comprehension	20 questions

You will find detailed information about each section in this book. In each chapter you will study the type of questions asked in each section of the TOEIC Bridge test. You will learn how to use strategies to improve your score in each section. In addition, you will study vocabulary in contexts commonly used on the TOEIC Bridge test.

FOR THE TEACHER

Rationale for a TOEIC Bridge Test Preparation Course

Barron's *TOEIC Bridge Test* guide may be used either as a self-study book or as a class text. In a class situation, this text will provide an excellent structure for helping students develop their English language skills and at the same time improve their test-taking skills.

The TOEIC Bridge test is designed for students who are just beginning to study English. The English-language level of these students could be classified as beginning or low-intermediate. The test is often given for placement in language courses as well as to measure achievement in these courses. The test is used for students of all ages.

This text is ideal for such a varied audience. It provides the foundation for many types of language learning courses. It gives the basics of English and the basics of test preparation. This text gives the students a streamlined approach to English. They can practice items and prepare for the test. This text gives you, the teacher, what you want for your students: a solid English preparation course with a lot of practice.

Timetable for a TOEIC Bridge Test Preparation Course

It is a challenge in every language teaching course to meet the needs of the students within the time limits of a course. There is never enough time. Here is a suggested approach. It gives you a basic outline that you can expand as time allows. Each suggestion is based on a 45-minute period.

FIRST CLASS PERIOD

Take the Mini-Test. This is a short test that will give the students an idea of how the TOEIC Bridge test works. Students really want to know about the test through experience, not by reading about it. This will give them in 30 minutes an opportunity to learn how the test works. Take the remaining time in the class to ask the class these questions. If you start with *yes/no* questions, you will get more class participation. Once the students are ready to talk, you can switch to *why* questions. Asking these questions will help you determine the curriculum for the rest of the course.

Was the test easy?

Did you understand the directions?

Did you finish each section?

Do you think you did well?

Could you hear the audio?

Were there many words you didn't know? Can you remember them?

Which section was easier—Listening Comprehension or Reading? Why?

In the Listening Comprehension section, which part was easier—Photographs or Question-Responses? Why?

Which part was easier—Question-Responses or Short Conversations and Short Talks? Why?

In the Reading section, which part was easier—Incomplete Sentences or Reading? Why?

SECOND CLASS PERIOD

Review the Mini-Test. Go over each item and discuss why it was wrong. The explanatory answers are in the back of the book. This will help the students become aware of the tricks in the test. Once they study each chapter, they will understand why they must learn to recognize these tricks.

SUBSEQUENT CLASS PERIODS

Alternate each class period with a chapter on vocabulary and a chapter on a test part. If you are short on time, have the students do the vocabulary work as homework.

Halfway through your course, give the students a model test. When you give a model test, you will need at least one class period to review the test with the students. You will probably need two class periods to cover the test thoroughly.

Teaching Listening Comprehension

The more opportunities students have to listen to English, the better their English comprehension will be. To this end, you should try to have an "English-only" classroom. When the students have a question, ask them to phrase the question in English. See if another student can rephrase the question or repeat it correctly. Have the students work in pairs and small groups so everyone has an opportunity to speak English and thereby listen to English.

Besides exposing the students to English, they must learn to develop their test-taking skills. In a multiple-choice test like the TOEIC Bridge test, students must pick one correct answer from several choices. The wrong choices or distracters are traps. Students must learn to avoid these traps.

The activities in the Listening Comprehension section of this book will help students improve their listening skills, develop their test-taking skills, and practice their communication skills. The ideas below will give you options to expand the exercises in the book to make them relevant and personal to your own students.

PHOTOGRAPH EXERCISES

Word Identification

In pairs or small groups, have the students name everything they can see in the picture. Have them identify possible actions.

True or False

Tell the students to write sentences that describe the photos. Have them also make up sentences that are false. Mix up the sentences and read them to another group or the class. Can the students tell which statements are true and which are false? Have them correct the statements that are false.

A Short Description

Have the students in pairs or small groups write a short description of the picture. Once they have the vocabulary and structure, have them repeat the description aloud without using their notes.

Personalize

Have the students describe a setting or action similar to the one in the photograph that they are familiar with.

QUESTION-RESPONSE EXERCISES

This is a very demanding section. The students are forced to choose an answer based on very little information. There is no context. The answer is based on what is grammatically and logically possible.

Establish a Context

Have the students in pairs or small groups establish a context for each statement. The students hear one line and choose one correct response. What do they think the speakers would say before? What would they say next?

Personalize

The students can create a short skit based on the one line of dialog. This skit will center on their own lives. See how different each group's interpretation will be.

SHORT CONVERSATIONS AND SHORT TALKS EXERCISES

There is more of a context in the short conversations and short talks; therefore the expansion activities can be richer.

Skits for Short Talks

Have the students add more dialog before and after the short talk.

Personalize

Have the students create a similar short conversation or short talk but change the context. If it is a weather report for Chicago, have them do a weather report for their own country.

Teaching Reading

If you want your students to learn how to listen, they must hear a lot of English. If you want your students to be good readers, they must read a lot. Reading will improve their vocabulary and their knowledge of English sentence structures. Both skills will help them on the TOEIC Bridge test.

INCOMPLETE SENTENCES

Have the students analyze the grammar of the sentence. Where is the subject? Where is the verb? Is there an object? Is there a prepositional phrase? Are there time markers? What is the tense of the sentence?

Have the students identify the part of speech for the blank. For the word choice items, have the students identify the part of speech of the answer options.

If the word choice is a verb, have the students look for time markers. What is the tense of the sentence?

When the students have filled in the blank, have them paraphrase the item.

READING COMPREHENSION

The skills taught in the Reading Comprehension section can be applied to all readings that the students do outside of class. These skills can be practiced in the students' native language as well as English.

Have the students bring in examples of signs, advertisements, forms, charts, graphs, tables, notices, and any other printed material. All of these types of readings can be found in an English news magazine. Have the students in small groups scan a magazine to find examples of these types of readings. Have them write their own questions about the readings and then give the readings and questions to other groups to answer.

Teaching Vocabulary

All students want to know words. To satisfy this desire, there is a lot of vocabulary practice in this book. Each unit begins with words at a variety of language levels. The sentences that follow are almost mini-definitions. Have the students create additional sentences with each word.

Recognizing word families is an important skill. Show the students the importance of suffixes and prefixes. Have them make sentences using the different grammatical forms of a word family.

After the Reading Review section, there is a Vocabulary Plus Review. Some of the words that were introduced previously are brought back for review. In addition there are other words in the same context and even new words in new contexts. All of these activities should satisfy your students' desire to know "words and more words!"

FOR THE STUDENT

You can study this book with a teacher or you can study it on your own. Either way, you must make a commitment to study English. Sign a contract with yourself. This will help you keep your commitment to study English.

TOEIC Bridge Test Study Contract

- Print your name below on the first line.
- Write the time you will spend each week studying English on the following lines. Think about how much time you have to study every day and every week, and make your schedule realistic.
- Sign your name and date the contract on the last line.
- At the end of each week, add up your hours. Did you meet the requirements of your contract?

> **TOEIC BRIDGE TEST STUDY CONTRACT**
>
> I, _____, promise to study for the TOEIC Bridge test. I will begin my study with Barron's *TOEIC Bridge Test*, and I will also study English on my own.
>
> I understand that to improve my English I need to spend time on English.
>
> I promise to study English _____ hours a week.
>
> I will spend _____ hours a week listening to English.
> I will spend _____ hours a week writing English.
> I will spend _____ hours a week speaking English.
> I will spend _____ hours a week reading English.
>
> This is a contract with myself. I promise to fulfill the terms of this contract.
>
> _____   _____
> Signed   Date

Self-Study

Here are some ways you can study English on your own. Check the ones you plan to try. Add some of your own ideas.

Internet-Based Self-Study Activities

Listening

____ Podcasts on the Internet
____ News websites: CNN, BBC, NBC, ABC, CBS
____ Movies in English
____ YouTube
____ _____
____ _____

Speaking

____ Use Skype to talk to English speakers
____ _____
____ _____

Writing

____ Write e-mails to website contacts
____ Write a blog

___ Leave comments on blogs
___ Post messages in a chat room
___ Use Facebook and MySpace

___ _____

___ _____

Reading

___ Read news and magazine articles online
___ Do web research on topics that interest you
___ Follow blogs that interest you

___ _____

___ _____

Other Self-Study Activities

Listening

___ Listen to CNN and BBC on the radio
___ Watch movies and TV in English
___ Listen to music in English

___ _____

___ _____

Speaking

___ Describe what you see and do out loud
___ Practice speaking with a conversation buddy

___ _____

___ _____

Writing

___ Write a daily journal
___ Write a letter to an English speaker
___ Make lists of the things you see every day
___ Write descriptions of your family and friends

___ _____

___ _____

Reading

___ Read newspapers and magazines in English
___ Read books in English

___ _____

___ _____

Examples of Self-Study Activities

You can use websites, books, newspapers, movies, and TV programs to practice reading, writing, speaking, and listening in English.

- Read about it.
- Write about it.
- Give a talk about it.
- Record or make a video of your talk.
- Listen to or watch what you recorded. Write down your words.
- Correct your mistakes.
- Do it all again.

Plan a Trip

Go to *www.concierge.com.*
Choose a city, choose a hotel, go to that hotel's website and choose a room, and then choose some places to visit (*reading*). Write a report about the city. In your report, answer these questions:

- Why do you want to go there?
- What is the hotel like?
- What places will you visit in the city?
- Where will you eat?

Now write a letter to someone recommending this place (*writing*). Pretend you have to give a lecture about your trip (*speaking*). Make a video of yourself talking about this place. Then watch the video and write down your words. Correct any mistakes you made and record the talk again. Then choose another city and do all of this again.

Shop for an Electronic Product

Go to *www.cnet.com.*
Choose an electronic product and read about it (*reading*). Write a report about the product. In your report, answer these questions:

- What is this product for?
- What will you do with it?
- How is it better than other similar products?
- How much does it cost? Is this a fair price?

Now write a letter to someone recommending this product (*writing*). Pretend you have to give a talk about this product (*speaking*). Make a video of yourself talking about this product. Then watch the video and write down your words. Correct any mistakes you made and record the talk again. Then choose another product and do all of this again.

Discuss a Book or a CD

Go to *www.amazon.com*.
Choose a book, a CD, or another product. Read the product description and reviews (*reading*). Write a report about the product. In your report, answer these questions:

- Why do you like it?
- What will you do with it?
- How much does it cost? Is this a fair price?

Now write a letter to someone recommending this product (*writing*). Pretend you have to give a talk about this product (*speaking*). Make a video of yourself talking about this product. Then watch the video and write down your words. Correct any mistakes you made and record the talk again. Then choose another product and do all of this again.

Discuss Any Subject

Go to *http://simple.wikipedia.org/wiki/Main_Page*.
This website is written in simple English. Pick any subject and read about it (*reading*). Write a short essay about the topic (*writing*). Give a talk about it (*speaking*). Record the talk. Then watch the video and write down your words. Correct any mistakes you made and record the talk again. Choose another topic and do all of this again.

Discuss Any Event

Go to *http://news.google.com*.
Google News has many links. Pick one event and read the articles about it (*reading*). Write a short report about the event (*writing*). In your report, answer these questions:

- What happened?
- Where did it happen?
- When did it happen?
- Who was there?

Now give a talk about the event (*speaking*). Record the talk. Then watch the video and write down your words. Correct any mistakes you made and record the talk again. Then choose another event and do all of this again.

Report the News

Listen to an English language news report on the radio or watch a news program on TV (*listening*). Take notes as you listen. Write a summary of what you heard (*writing*). In your summary, answer these questions:

- What happened?
- Where did it happen?
- When did it happen?
- Who was there?

Pretend you are a news reporter. Use your notes to report the news (*speaking*). Record the report. Then watch the video and write down your words. Correct any mistakes you made and record the report again. Then listen to another news program and do all of this again.

Express an Opinion

Read a letter to the editor in the newspaper (*reading*). Write a letter in response. Explain your own opinion. Do you agree or disagree with the first letter? Why? Pretend you have to give a talk explaining your opinion (*speaking*). Record yourself giving the talk. Then watch the video and write down your words. Correct any mistakes you made and record the talk again. Then read another letter to the editor and do all of this again.

Review a Book or Movie

Read a book (*reading*). Pretend you are a book reviewer for a newspaper. Write a review of the book (*writing*). In your review, answer these questions:

- What did you like about the book?
- What didn't you like about it?
- Who would you recommend it to and why?

Give a talk about the book. Explain what the book is about. Explain your opinion (*speaking*). Record yourself giving the talk. Then watch the video and write down your words. Correct any mistakes you made and record the talk again. Then read another book and do all of this again.

You can do this same activity after watching a movie (*listening*).

Summarize a TV Show

Watch a TV show in English (*listening*). Take notes as you listen. After watching, write a summary of the show (*writing*). In your summary, answer these questions:

- What is the show about?
- Who are the characters?
- Where does the story take place?
- Do you like the show? Why or why not?

Use your notes to give a talk about the show (*speaking*). Record yourself speaking. Then watch the video and write down your words. Correct any mistakes you made and record the talk again. Then watch another TV show and do all of this again.

FREQUENTLY ASKED QUESTIONS ABOUT THE TOEIC BRIDGE TEST

What Is the Difference Between the Format of the TOEIC Test and the TOEIC Bridge Test?

The TOEIC Bridge test is much easier than the TOEIC test. There are fewer questions and fewer parts. There are 200 questions and 7 parts in the TOEIC test. There are 100 questions and 5 parts in the TOEIC Bridge test. The type of item in each part is similar on both tests.

TOEIC Test		TOEIC Bridge Test	
Section I *Listening*	*Number of Questions*	**Section 1** *Listening Comprehension*	*Number of Questions*
Part 1 Photographs	10	Part I Photographs	15
Part 2 Question-Response	30	Part II Question-Response	20
Part 3 Conversations	30	Part III Short Conversations and Short Talks	15
Part 4 Talks	30		
Section II *Reading*		**Section 2** *Reading Comprehension*	
Part 5 Incomplete Sentences	40	Part IV Incomplete Sentences	30
Part 6 Text Completion	12	Part V Reading Comprehension	20
Part 7 Reading Comprehension	48		
TOTAL Questions	200 questions		100 questions
TOTAL Time	120 minutes		60 minutes

Where Can I Take the TOEIC Bridge Test?

Contact the TOEIC representative in your country to see if the test is offered near you. The list of representatives follows this section.

Who Takes the TOEIC Bridge Test?

The TOEIC Bridge test is for beginning and intermediate level students of English. The test is for any student who wants to know his or her level of English proficiency. The usual test-taker is still in school and studying English.

What Skills Are Measured on the TOEIC Bridge Test?

The TOEIC Bridge test measures a student's proficiency in listening and reading. It measures his or her knowledge of grammar and vocabulary.

What Content Is Covered on the TOEIC Bridge Test?

The TOEIC Bridge test uses everyday English vocabulary. The type of words used on the TOEIC Bridge test is found at the start of every chapter in this book. Here are some of the topics covered in this book and on the TOEIC Bridge test:

Directions	Activities
Clothing	Feelings and Emotions
Nature	Sports
Daily Routines	Entertainment
Culture	Groceries
Weather	Geography
Family and Friends	Furniture and Furnishings
News and Newspapers	Dining Out
Office	School
Travel	Housing
Dates and Time	Shopping
Measurement and Numbers	Health
Money	

How Is It Scored?

A test-taker receives a separate listening and reading score. These scores are added together. A possible score is 20 to 180 points.

Diagnostic information is included in the official Score Report. This information rates your proficiency in five areas: functions, listening skills, grammar, vocabulary, and reading skills. You will receive a rating from 1 to 3. For example, a score of "1" in functions means you should pay more attention to the way vocabulary and structure combine to express meaning. Understanding the functions of English means you understand the particular vocabulary and grammar used to make requests, make recommendations, offer opinions, express satisfaction, ask about someone's health, and so forth.

What Do the Test Scores Mean?

There is no passing grade. An institution determines the value of the scores.

Is a TOEIC Bridge Practice Test Available?

A practice test can be downloaded from the TOEIC website. *www.toeic.com.*

How Can I Find a TOEIC Bridge Representative in My Region?

You can locate a representative in your region by contacting a local ETS Preferred Network Office. Offices by geographic location can be found at *www.ets.org.*

Listening Comprehension

WHAT TO LOOK FOR IN THIS CHAPTER

- Vocabulary Building Activities for Part I—Photographs
- Skill Building Activities for Part I—Photographs
- Vocabulary and Skill Building Activities for Part II
- Vocabulary and Skill Building Activities for Part III
- Mini-Test for Listening Comprehension Review—Parts I, II, and III

Part I: Vocabulary Building Activities

In this section, you will learn words that could be used in any part of the TOEIC Bridge test. Studying the words here will also prepare you for the vocabulary used in other parts of the TOEIC Bridge test.

VOCABULARY FOCUS

- Directions
- Clothing
- Nature
- Daily Routines
- Culture

DIRECTIONS

WORDS IN CONTEXT

Directions: Use one of the words in the box to complete each sentence.

map   drive   straight   block   corner

1. I _____ the car to work because it is too cold to walk.

2. At the intersection of Main and Elm, you'll see a signpost on the southwest _____.

3. The road runs _____ through the desert without any curves or turns.

4. Before starting on a trip, check the _____ for the shortest routes.

5. The library is in the middle of the _____ , halfway between Jarvis Street and Mary Avenue.

> lane   direct   short cut   behind   entrance

6. The road sign says that slower traffic must stay in the right-hand _____.

7. The side doors are locked so use the front _____ to enter the auditorium.

8. I know a _____ that will get us to the recreation center much faster.

9. Use your rearview mirror to check for cars _____ you.

10. I wanted to take the most _____ route, but I got lost and wandered all over the city looking for your office.

> construction   follow   exit   pass   traffic light

11. When the _____ turns green you may drive through the intersection.

12. _____ me and I'll lead the way to the train station.

13. You have to drive slowly in the _____ zone because they are fixing the road.

14. Take the #2 _____ northbound to get off the highway and find a gas station.

15. You might want to _____ the truck in front of you because it's going so slowly.

WORD FAMILIES

Directions: Choose the correct form of the word to complete the sentence.

noun	continuation
verb	continue
adverb	continually

16. You won't have to change roads because Highway #2 is a _____ of Highway #1.

17. If he _____ drives this fast he will eventually get a ticket.

18. _____ down this street until you find the shopping center.

noun	direction
verb	direct
adverb	directly

19. Could you point us in the _____ of the beach?

20. The police officer will _____ you to a safer route.

21. The convenience store is _____ across from the bank so you can't miss it.

noun	driver
noun	driveway
verb	drive

22. You should hire a car and _____ to take you to the airport.

23. We had our _____ done in the same kind of brick as our sidewalk.

24. I never _____ to the shopping center because it is too difficult to find a parking spot.

CLOTHING

WORDS IN CONTEXT

Directions: Use one of the words in the box to complete each sentence.

> scarf   shoes   comfortable   pocket   secondhand

1. You ought to wear a _____ to cover up your neck in this weather.

2. I'm going to put some longer laces in my new _____.

3. I wish this shirt had a side _____ for my keys.

4. I buy my clothes at a _____ shop because I can't afford to buy new ones.

5. This dress is so _____ I could wear it for pajamas.

pants	expensive	bathing suit	wear	rings

6. I can't find one pair of _____ that doesn't have belt loops.

7. You will need to wear a _____ if you want to go swimming.

8. Why don't you _____ your new jacket over your T-shirt?

9. The bride and groom placed silver wedding _____ on each other's fingers.

10. The leather purse was too _____ so I bought a cheaper one.

tight	socks	boots	button	sew

11. I lost a _____ on my jacket so I'll have to sew the spare one on.

12. She didn't bring any _____ because she always wears sandals in the summer.

13. You will need a tall pair of _____ if you are going to be walking through deep snow.

14. Do you have a needle and thread so that I can _____ the hem on my dress?

15. I must have gained some weight because these shorts are too _____.

WORD FAMILIES

Directions: Choose the correct form of the word to complete the sentence.

noun	comforter
noun	comfort
adjective	comfortable

16. I bought a new _____ for my bed to keep me warm in the winter.

17. Put an insole in your shoe for added _____.

18. You will feel more _____ if you take off your coat.

noun	dress
noun	dresser
verb	dress

19. If you can't find a long _____ , then just wear a skirt and blouse.

20. Please fold your clothes and put them in the _____.

21. You should _____ in something formal such as a tuxedo.

noun	tights
verb	tighten
adjective	tight

22. In the winter we wear long black _____ under our skirts and dresses.

23. I can't breathe because this shirt is too _____ around my neck.

24. You should _____ your belt or your pants will fall down.

NATURE

WORDS IN CONTEXT

Directions: Use one of the words in the box to complete each sentence.

| plants | air | environment | sunlight | insects |

1. You will find that you breathe cleaner _____ when you get away from the city.

2. It is important to wear eye protection if you are going to be looking into the _____.

3. Mosquitoes and other _____ carry diseases such as malaria.

4. Could you water my indoor _____ while I'm on vacation?

5. We must protect the _____ so future generations can enjoy the plants and animals.

recycle   natural   minerals   biologists   ocean

6. Humans need small amounts of _____ such as iron and zinc.

7. Thousands of marine mammals live in the _____ and feed on other fish.

8. Animals have a _____ instinct to protect their young.

9. _____ study living things such as plants and animals.

10. We _____ any containers that are made of glass or tin so don't throw them in the garbage.

leaves   oxygen   pollute   desert   season

11. Human beings require _____ to breathe as do plants and animals.

12. In autumn the _____ on the trees change from green to yellow, red, and orange.

13. Only certain kinds of plants, such as a cactus, can survive with little water in the _____.

14. Cars and boats _____ the world's air and water by releasing harmful toxins.

15. My favorite _____ is winter because I love to cross-country ski.

WORD FAMILIES

Directions: Choose the correct form of the word to complete the sentence.

noun	recycling
verb	recycle
adjective	recyclable

16. Please put the _____ out with the garbage.

17. Are these milk bags _____ , or should I throw them out?

18. By law we have to _____ all of our plastic bags and tin cans.

noun	pollution
noun	pollutants
verb	pollute

19. Two _____ that cause acid rain are oxide and sulfur.

20. Air _____ is a problem in cities with smokestack factories.

21. We _____ the environment every time we drive a car.

noun	desert
adjective	deserted
verb	deserts

22. The _____ is a region that has very little precipitation.

23. They were shipwrecked on a _____ island so they had to build a life raft.

24. When a mother shark _____ her babies they are at risk of being eaten by other sharks.

DAILY ROUTINES

WORDS IN CONTEXT

Directions: Use one of the words in the box to complete each sentence.

brush   kitchen   education   dream   sleepy

1. Always _____ your teeth at least twice a day to keep them clean.

2. Take a short nap if you are _____.

3. It is important that you get a good _____ but you don't always need an advanced degree.

4. The _____ is my favorite room because I love to cook.

5. Many people say if you _____ about gold you will wake up rich.

bathe	read	television	breakfast	ready

6. Nutritionists suggest that you start the day with a balanced _____ such as fruit and cereal.

7. I'll keep the lights on so that you will still be able to _____ your book.

8. I hope you are _____ to go because the taxi is waiting out front.

9. What kind of soap do you usually _____ with?

10. Please put the _____ on channel 3 because I want to watch the news.

homework	clean up	take part in	bathroom	laundry room

11. I put the dirty clothes on top of the washing machine in the _____.

12. I have to be at work an hour early today to _____ a conference call.

13. Please _____ the mess in your bedroom before you go outside.

14. The teacher gives us _____ do every evening.

15. If you are looking for the tissue paper, it is in the cabinet next to the bathtub in the _____.

WORD FAMILIES

Directions: Choose the correct form of the word to complete the sentence.

noun	education
noun	educator
verb	educate

16. I want you to get an _____ from a good college.

17. The nurse will _____ the children about nutrition.

18. I think Mr. Jones is a good _____ because he takes the time to listen to his students.

verb	sleep
adjective	sleepy
adverb	asleep

19. I can't _____ on airplanes or buses unless I am really tired.

20. He fell _____ on his pillow as soon as we got on the highway.

21. I am _____ because I was awake all night working on this assignment.

noun	bath
noun	bather
verb	bathe

22. The _____ forgot his shampoo and his towel.

23. You have to take a _____ or a shower before you go to school.

24. I will _____ with soap in the river because the water is clean.

CULTURE

WORDS IN CONTEXT

Directions: Use one of the words in the box to complete each sentence.

instruments   beliefs   stories   festival   customs

1. It is common for grandparents to tell bedtime _____ to their grandchildren.

2. Local performers, artists, and musicians come to the folk _____.

3. One of our family's _____ is to be together for evening meals.

4. In the folk orchestra there are musical _____ made of bamboo or ivory.

5. What we believe, that is our _____ , give us our reason for living.

| tribe | ancestors | costumes | songs | legend |

6. The story of Bigfoot, the giant who lives in the forest, is a _____ that gets passed on from generation to generation.

7. My great-great grandfather, a Cheyenne Indian, belonged to a _____ that painted their faces and hands.

8. The traditional _____ we sing were taught to us by our grandparents.

9. On national days, some people wear _____ that represent their countries.

10. Looking at a family tree is a great way to teach children about their _____ .

| tradition | prepare | folktales | ancient | fireworks |

11. The _____ display lit up the sky on the final day of the celebration.

12. We visited the pyramids of _____ Egypt, which were built thousands of years ago.

13. For the holiday feast we _____ a special type of rice.

14. It is a _____ in some cultures to exchange gifts on New Year's Day.

15. Children learn valuable lessons from hearing their parents tell _____ and other stories.

WORD FAMILIES

Directions: Choose the correct form of the word to complete the sentence.

noun	beliefs
verb	believe
adjective	believable

16. Do you _____ in ghosts and goblins?

17. Witches and doctors had very different _____ about medicine.

18. That story was not very _____ because horses can't fly.

noun	festival
noun	festivities
adjective	festive

19. July is a month full of _____ such as fireworks and parades.

20. I am going to play my trumpet at the music _____ this weekend.

21. All of the decorations make this room look very _____.

noun	preparation
verb	prepare
adjective	preparatory

22. My mother will _____ the desserts so we won't have to buy any.

23. The required _____ year before we started college helped us prepare for academic life.

24. A big wedding requires a lot of _____ , such as sending invitations and choosing a cake.

Part I: Photographs—Skill Building Activities

There are 15 questions in Part I of the TOEIC Bridge test. You will see a picture in your test book and you will hear four short statements.

Look at the picture in your test book and choose the statement that best describes what you see in the picture. Then mark your answer on your answer sheet.

Look at this example.

EXAMPLE

You will see:

You will hear:
- (A) The boys are laughing.
- (B) The boys are reading.
- (C) The boys are fighting.
- (D) The boys are painting.

Statement (B), "The boys are reading," best describes what you see in the picture. Therefore, you should choose answer (B).

The TOEIC Bridge test uses these kinds of statements when describing a photograph.

> - Location   - Actions
> - People

In this section, you will learn the words often used to describe locations, people, and actions in TOEIC Bridge photographs. You will learn to ask the questions:

Where is the photograph being taken?

Who is in the photograph?

What is happening in the photograph?

LOCATION

Statements that describe location can be of two types:

- Name
- Description

NAME

Locations can be identified by their name. Look for clues that can help you identify the location. All of these answers are possible.

Possible Answers: (A) They're dining at an outdoor café.
(B) They're eating in a restaurant.
(C) They're ordering dinner from a menu.
(D) They're stopping to eat at a café. Ⓐ Ⓑ Ⓒ Ⓓ

DESCRIPTION

Locations can be identified by their description. Look for clues that can help you identify the location. All of these answers are possible.

Possible Answers: (A) The waiter is standing by the table.
(B) The customers are sitting at a table.
(C) The café has many tables outdoors.
(D) The chairs are placed at the tables. Ⓐ Ⓑ Ⓒ Ⓓ

Clues: waiter in uniform standing by customers at table; tables and customers.

Choose the statement that matches the photograph. Note the clues that help identify the location.

1.

(A) They're at a campsite.
(B) They're at a used car lot.
(C) They're in a parking lot.
(D) They're in a circus tent.

Ⓐ Ⓑ Ⓒ Ⓓ

Clues:_____

2.

(A) The net is full of fish.
(B) The waterfall runs over the rocks.
(C) Everyone is playing pool.
(D) The swimming pool is crowded.

Ⓐ Ⓑ Ⓒ Ⓓ

Clues:_____

3.

(A) The street is made of wood.
(B) The road runs through the trees.
(C) The trees are across the path.
(D) The highway goes near the forest.

Ⓐ Ⓑ Ⓒ Ⓓ

Clues:_____

4.

(A) They're cleaning out the drain.
(B) They're waiting for a plane.
(C) They're standing on a train platform.
(D) They're watching the rain.

Ⓐ Ⓑ Ⓒ Ⓓ

Clues:_____

5.

(A) The people are biking through the city.
(B) The cyclists are riding through the countryside.
(C) The commuters are driving to work.
(D) The bikers are racing across the bridge.

Ⓐ Ⓑ Ⓒ Ⓓ

Clues:_____

Listening Practice: Location

CD 1
Track
1

Look at the picture and choose the statement that best describes what you see in the picture.

1.

2.

Ⓐ Ⓑ Ⓒ Ⓓ

3.

Ⓐ Ⓑ Ⓒ Ⓓ

4.

(A) (B) (C) (D)

5.

(A) (B) (C) (D)

PEOPLE

Statements that describe people can be of two types:

- Description
- Occupation

DESCRIPTION

People can be identified by their descriptions. Look for clues that can help you identify the people.

Possible Answers: (A)   Three firefighters are holding a hose.
                                (B)   Two men are wearing hard hats.
                                  (C)   The hose is on their right sides.
                                  (D)   They're all looking at the sky.   Ⓐ Ⓑ Ⓒ Ⓓ

OCCUPATION

People can be identified by their occupations. Look for clues that can help you identify the people.

Possible Answers: (A)   The firefighters are putting out a fire.
                                  (B)   The gardeners are watering the grass.
                                  (C)   The attendants are washing the car.
                                  (D)   The cleaners are hosing the streets.   Ⓐ Ⓑ Ⓒ Ⓓ

Clues: Three men in uniform and hard hats are holding a large hose and spraying water on a brush fire.

Choose the statement that matches the photograph. Note the words that describe the people.

1.

(A) The teacher is reading a story

(B) The librarian is talking to a patron.

(C) The bookseller is painting the shelves.

(D) The student is looking for a book.   Ⓐ Ⓑ Ⓒ Ⓓ

Clues:_____

2.

(A) The customers are waiting to be seated.

(B) The cook is writing the menu.

(C) The waiter is serving the meal.

(D) The diners are picking their table.   Ⓐ Ⓑ Ⓒ Ⓓ

Clues:_____

3.

(A) The composers are taking a break.
(B) The musicians are performing on stage.
(C) The audience is enjoying the show.
(D) The players are hitting the ball.

Ⓐ Ⓑ Ⓒ Ⓓ

Clues:_____

4.

(A) The artist is painting in the garden.
(B) The gardener is planting some flowers.
(C) The carpenter is fixing the drawer.
(D) The grass cutter is mowing the lawn.

Ⓐ Ⓑ Ⓒ Ⓓ

Clues:_____

5.

(A) The buyers are inspecting shirts.
(B) The shoppers are looking at shoes.
(C) The cowboy is wearing boots.
(D) The customers are paying for footwear.

Ⓐ Ⓑ Ⓒ Ⓓ

Clues:_____

CD 1 Track 2 *Listening Practice—People*

Look at the picture and choose the statement that best describes what you see in the picture.

1.

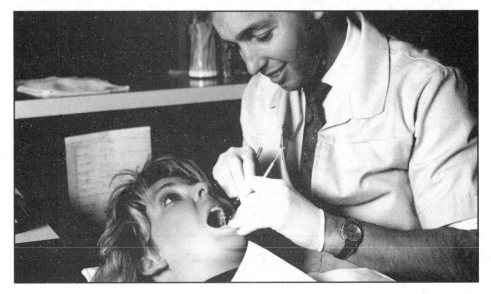

Ⓐ Ⓑ Ⓒ Ⓓ

2.

Ⓐ Ⓑ Ⓒ Ⓓ

3.

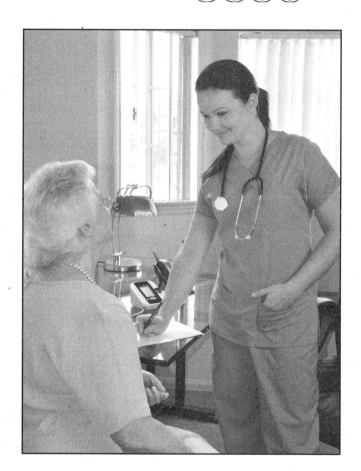

Ⓐ Ⓑ Ⓒ Ⓓ

4.

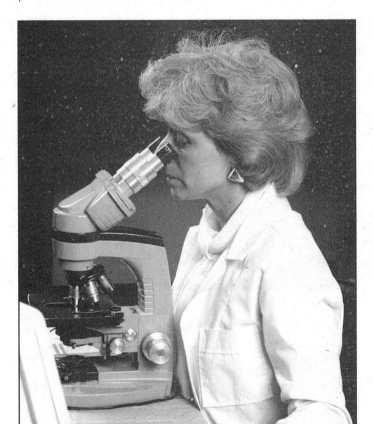

Ⓐ Ⓑ Ⓒ Ⓓ

5.

Ⓐ Ⓑ Ⓒ Ⓓ

ACTIONS

Statements that describe actions can be of two types:

- Actual
- Possible

ACTUAL

Some actions you can actually see. Look for clues that can help you identify actions that are happening now.

Possible Answers:
   (A) The group is sitting around the room.
   (B) The participants are looking at the front.
   (C) Two people are sitting at the head of the table.
   (D) The attendees are listening to the speaker.   Ⓐ Ⓑ Ⓒ Ⓓ

POSSIBLE

Some actions are possible. Based on the clues provided, you assume a particular action. Look for clues that can help you identify actions that are possible.

Possible Answers:
   (A) They're having a training session.
   (B) They're having a meeting.
   (C) They're discussing their business.
   (D) They're working on a problem.   Ⓐ Ⓑ Ⓒ Ⓓ

Choose the statement that matches the photograph. Note the words that describe the action.

1.

(A) The dog is getting a bath.
(B) The woman is giving her child a pet.
(C) They're washing their clothes.
(D) They're taking the dog for a walk.

Ⓐ Ⓑ Ⓒ Ⓓ

Clues:_____

2.

(A) She's pointing to her student.
(B) She's giving him a snack.
(C) She's writing a book.
(D) She's helping him with his schoolwork.

Ⓐ Ⓑ Ⓒ Ⓓ

Clues:_____

3.

(A) They're admiring the pictures.
(B) They're arranging the art on their walls.
(C) They're posing for an artist.
(D) They're attending a drawing class.

Clues:_____

4.

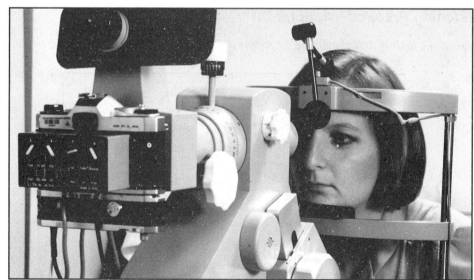

(A) The baker is checking the pies.
(B) The clerk is choosing her glasses.
(C) The woman is having her eyes examined.
(D) The driver is turning to the right.

Ⓐ Ⓑ Ⓒ Ⓓ

Clues:_____

5.

(A) He's making a note on the file.
(B) He's putting away a file.
(C) He's opening the file cabinet.
(D) He's rearranging the shelves.

Ⓐ Ⓑ Ⓒ Ⓓ

Clues:_____

Listening Practice—Actions

CD 1
Track
3

Look at the picture and choose the statement that best describes what you see in the picture.

1.

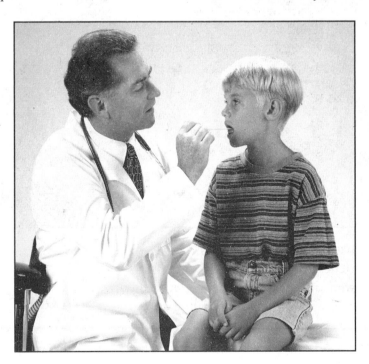

Ⓐ Ⓑ Ⓒ Ⓓ

2.

Ⓐ Ⓑ Ⓒ Ⓓ

3.

Ⓐ Ⓑ Ⓒ Ⓓ

4.

Ⓐ Ⓑ Ⓒ Ⓓ

5.

Ⓐ Ⓑ Ⓒ Ⓓ

Part II: Question-Response— Vocabulary Building Activities

In this section, you will learn words that could be used in any part of the TOEIC Bridge test. Studying the words here will also prepare you for the vocabulary used in other parts of the TOEIC Bridge test.

> **VOCABULARY FOCUS**
> - Weather
> - Family and Friends
> - News and Newspapers
> - Office
> - Travel

WEATHER

WORDS IN CONTEXT

Directions: Use one of the words in the box to complete each sentence.

> melt   freeze   thunder   lightning   temperature

1. The _____ is low today so you should wear a coat.

2. All this snow will _____ in today's bright sun.

3. I think the lake will _____ tonight because the weather will get very cold.

4. During the storm, the _____ was very loud.

5. The _____ hit a tree and made it fall down.

> warm   foggy   breeze   humid   predict

6. I _____ that the weather will be good this weekend.

7. The sun is shining so the air feels _____ .

8. There isn't a clear view today because the air is so _____ .

9. Everything feels wet today because the air is so hot and _____ .

10. I like to sit on the beach and feel the _____ blowing from the ocean.

blizzard	expect	cool	thermometer	flood

11. The water in the river is very high and it might _____ the streets.

12. The _____ is broken so I can't tell you the exact temperature.

13. The weather is bad today but we _____ it to improve tomorrow.

14. I don't want to go swimming because the water is too _____ .

15. Eighteen inches of snow fell during the _____ last week.

WORD FAMILIES

Directions: Choose the correct form of the word to complete the sentence.

noun	coolness
verb	cool
adjective	cool

16. The rainstorm will _____ the air.

17. This _____ feels nice after the long, hot day.

18. Put on a sweater because the air is _____ this evening.

noun	prediction
verb	predict
adjective	predictable

19. You can't _____ what the weather will be like a year in advance.

20. Our summer weather is easily _____ since it rains every afternoon.

21. You can read the daily weather _____ in the newspaper.

noun	warmth
verb	warm
adjective	warm

22. On _____ days, I like to go to the beach.

23. I like to feel the _____ of the sun.

24. All this sunshine will _____ the air.

FAMILY AND FRIENDS

WORDS IN CONTEXT

Directions: Use one of the words in the box to complete each sentence.

uncle	cousins	friendly	introduce	invite

1. James wants to meet new people so I plan to _____ him to some friends.

2. My father's brother is my _____.

3. Do you plan to _____ many people to your party?

4. Everybody likes Patricia because she is so _____.

5. My uncle's children are my _____.

get together	spouse	niece	divorced	married

6. My parents got _____ 25 years ago, and they are still very happy together.

7. Your _____ is your husband or wife.

8. My brother has a daughter and she is my _____.

9. Unfortunately, Bill and Maria got _____ after 30 years of marriage.

10. I like to _____ with my friends on the weekends.

| aunt | gets along | related | nephew | engaged |

11. Peter has a lot of friends because he _____ well with everyone.

12. My brother has a son, and he is my _____.

13. I am _____ to Martha; she is my aunt.

14. Susan and Ken are _____ , and they plan to get married next month.

15. My father's sister is my _____.

WORD FAMILIES

Directions: Choose the correct form of the word to complete the sentence.

noun	marriage
verb	marry
adjective	married

16. Sally is in love with Herbert and she wants to _____ him.

17. They will get _____ as soon as they can afford wedding rings.

18. I think they will have a very happy _____ because they make a great couple.

noun	invitation
verb	invite
adjective	inviting

19. That comfortable couch looks very _____.

20. They plan to _____ several people to dinner this weekend.

21. I received an _____ to Jonathan's party.

noun	relatives
noun	relationship
adjective	related

22. I have a good _____ with my parents; we get along very well.

23. I have a big family with a lot of _____.

24. Janet is a very close friend of mine, but we are not _____.

NEWS AND NEWSPAPERS

WORDS IN CONTEXT

Directions: Use one of the words in the box to complete each sentence.

> article   deliver   magazine   announce   advertisements

1. When I want to buy something, I look at the _____ in the newspaper.

2. They _____ the newspapers to the stores early every morning.

3. I read an interesting _____ in the newspaper this morning.

4. They will _____ the winner of the soccer game on TV tonight.

5. This movie _____ has stories about all my favorite actors.

> journalist   headlines   speech   live   subscribe

6. A _____ can work for a newspaper, a magazine, or a TV news program.

7. The president will make a _____ on television tonight.

8. A _____ news program shows news that is happening right now.

9. I don't _____ to the newspaper because I prefer to buy it at the store.

10. If you want to know the important news of the day, look at the _____ on the front page of the newspaper.

| report | interviews | comics | sections | international |

11. We watch the news _____ on television every evening.

12. I like to read both the sports and business _____ of the newspaper.

13. I am interested in other countries so I usually read the _____ news.

14. In magazines you can read _____ with famous people.

15. I read the _____ in the newspaper every day because I like to laugh.

WORD FAMILIES

Directions: Choose the correct form of the word to complete the sentence.

noun	speech
noun	speaker
verb	speak

16. Some famous people do not like to _____ to journalists.

17. I didn't hear the president give his _____ last night.

18. The _____ talked about the news of the week.

noun	advertisement
noun	advertisers
verb	advertise

19. If you want to sell something, _____ it in the newspaper.

20. _____ pay newspapers a lot of money.

21. I found my job through an _____ in the newspaper.

noun	announcement
noun	announcer
verb	announce

22. The _____ introduced the next speaker.

23. I heard the _____ on the radio.

24. They will _____ the winners of the competition on the radio.

OFFICE

WORDS IN CONTEXT

Directions: Use one of the words in the box to complete each sentence.

> supervisor   reply   due   meeting   salary

1. I got the letter today and I will _____ soon.

2. We have to finish this work quickly because it is _____ tomorrow.

3. We talk about our work at a _____ every Monday.

4. Because I don't make enough money, I want a bigger _____ .

5. My _____ gave me a lot of work to do this week.

> employees   turn in   hire   earn   in charge

6. We need more help at this office so we plan to _____ some new workers.

7. The _____ in this office all work very hard.

8. I will _____ a lot of money at my new job.

9. Ms. Warren is _____ of this work so she will explain it to you.

10. Please _____ your work before the end of the week.

assistant	raise	type	fire	discuss

11. I want to make more money so I plan to ask for a _____ .

12. I cannot do all this work alone; I need an _____ to help me.

13. Harry isn't doing well at work and I think they are going to _____ him.

14. I will _____ all of these letters now and mail them this afternoon.

15. We will _____ this work at the meeting tomorrow.

WORD FAMILIES

Directions: Choose the correct form of the word to complete the sentence.

noun	supervisor
noun	supervision
verb	supervise

16. In this office we _____ everybody's work carefully.

17. My _____ has 20 staff members under her.

18. Some people need a lot of _____ when they work.

noun	assistant
noun	assistance
verb	assist

19. I will be happy to _____ you with that work.

20. I needed some help so I hired an _____ .

21. I will need some _____ to finish this work on time.

noun	employer
noun	employees
verb	employ

22. We are very busy at this office and plan to _____ several new workers.

23. My _____ just gave me a raise in salary.

24. Ten _____ work in this office.

TRAVEL

WORDS IN CONTEXT

Directions: Use one of the words in the box to complete each sentence.

> passengers   depart   round-trip   arrive   return

1. John will _____ tomorrow evening, and I plan to meet him at the airport.

2. We will leave for our vacation tomorrow, and we plan to _____ in two weeks.

3. We should be at the train station by 9:45 because our train will _____ at 10:00.

4. This bus is very crowded so some of the _____ have to stand.

5. A _____ ticket is usually cheaper than two one-way tickets.

> flight   fares   luggage   reserve   check in

6. When you arrive at the hotel, _____ at the front desk.

7. Airplane _____ are usually lower in the winter when fewer people travel.

8. If you _____ a room at a hotel, you will be sure to have a place to sleep.

9. My _____ is very heavy and I can't carry it alone.

10. The _____ from Paris to New York takes about six hours.

delayed	subway	schedule	transportation	first class

11. Even though it costs more, I usually buy a _____ ticket.

12. The train was _____ because of the bad weather.

13. The _____ will tell you when the next bus leaves.

14. An airplane is the fastest form of _____ for long-distance travel.

15. A _____ runs underground and is faster than a bus.

WORD FAMILIES

Directions: Choose the correct form of the word to complete the sentence.

noun	delay
verb	delay
adjective	delayed

16. This bad weather will _____ us.

17. We arrived very late because our flight was _____ .

18. Many people travel on the weekend so there is usually a _____ at the train station.

noun	reservation
verb	reserve
adjective	reserved

19. Make your _____ early when you travel at a busy time.

20. Don't forget to _____ a hotel room before you start your trip.

21. You can't sit here because this is a _____ seat.

noun	transportation
verb	transport
adjective	transportable

22. Buses _____ thousands of people around the city every day.

23. Buses are an inexpensive form of _____ .

24. If you wrap that package well, it will be _____ .

Part II: Question-Response— Skill Building Activities

There are 20 questions in Part II of the TOEIC Bridge test. You will hear a question and three possible answers.

Question:	What day is it?
Possible Answers:	(A) Any day now.
	(B) Monday.
	(C) Yesterday. Ⓐ Ⓑ Ⓒ

The best possible answer to the question, "What day is it?" is (B) Monday.

When you see the question and answer written, it seems quite easy to answer it. But when you hear only the question and answer, it becomes more difficult.

The TOEIC Bridge test tries to trick your ears in several ways.

- Words Repeated
- Similar Sounds
- Associated Words
- Homonyms
- Same Sound and Spelling but Different Meaning
- Opposites
- Word Order

In this section, you will first read the questions and answers. This will help you learn the vocabulary and the tricks of the TOEIC Bridge test. You will then listen to the questions and answers just as you would on the actual TOEIC Bridge test.

WORDS REPEATED

Words in the answer options may be the same as those in the question.

Question: How long is this desk?

Possible Answers: (A) A long way.
                    (B) About 5 feet.
                    (C) A long time.

Answer: (B)

Answer the questions. Be careful of repeated words.

1. What did you do last weekend?

    (A) I played soccer.
    (B) It was last week.
    (C) That's the last one.   Ⓐ Ⓑ Ⓒ

2. Were there many people at the restaurant?

    (A) Yes, it's over there.
    (B) Yes, it was very crowded.
    (C) Yes, I like that restaurant.   Ⓐ Ⓑ Ⓒ

3. What time does the movie begin?

    (A) About two times.
    (B) I like movies sometimes.
    (C) At 8:30, I think.   Ⓐ Ⓑ Ⓒ

4. What month were you born in?

    (A) I'll go next month.
    (B) In December.
    (C) He was born last month.   Ⓐ Ⓑ Ⓒ

5. What would you like to eat?

    (A) I'd love to have a sandwich.
    (B) Let's eat at that restaurant.
    (C) I like to eat early.   Ⓐ Ⓑ Ⓒ

6. How often do you play tennis?

    (A) I play very well.
    (B) Let me show you how.
    (C) About twice a week.   Ⓐ Ⓑ Ⓒ

7. When will you call Jim?

    (A) I'll do it this evening.
    (B) This call's not for him.
    (C) He called last night.   Ⓐ Ⓑ Ⓒ

8. What day is the meeting?

   (A) It's warm today.
   (B) It's a week from tomorrow.
   (C) The meeting will be short.   Ⓐ Ⓑ Ⓒ

9. How long was the concert?

   (A) A long time ago.
   (B) It was a great concert.
   (C) About two hours.   Ⓐ Ⓑ Ⓒ

10. Whose glasses are those?

    (A) They belong to Mary.
    (B) I need new glasses.
    (C) Those are reading glasses.   Ⓐ Ⓑ Ⓒ

Listening Practice: Words Repeated

CD 1 Track 4

You will hear a question or statement followed by three responses. Choose the best response to each question or statement.

1. Ⓐ Ⓑ Ⓒ	6. Ⓐ Ⓑ Ⓒ	11. Ⓐ Ⓑ Ⓒ
2. Ⓐ Ⓑ Ⓒ	7. Ⓐ Ⓑ Ⓒ	12. Ⓐ Ⓑ Ⓒ
3. Ⓐ Ⓑ Ⓒ	8. Ⓐ Ⓑ Ⓒ	13. Ⓐ Ⓑ Ⓒ
4. Ⓐ Ⓑ Ⓒ	9. Ⓐ Ⓑ Ⓒ	14. Ⓐ Ⓑ Ⓒ
5. Ⓐ Ⓑ Ⓒ	10. Ⓐ Ⓑ Ⓒ	15. Ⓐ Ⓑ Ⓒ

SIMILAR SOUNDS

Words in the answer options may sound like those in the question.

Question: You were sick, weren't you?

Possible Answers: (A) Take your pick.
                   (B) Thick enough.
                   (C) Yes, but I'm better now.   Ⓐ Ⓑ Ⓒ

Answer: (C)

Answer the questions. Be careful of similar sounds.

1. Where does Theresa live?

   (A) In London, I think.
   (B) Don't leave until she does.
   (C) She wears what she wants.   Ⓐ Ⓑ Ⓒ

2. How much money did you spend?

   (A) I'll send those messages now.
   (B) There were too many.
   (C) About ten dollars.

   Ⓐ Ⓑ Ⓒ

3. It's really cold in here, isn't it?

   (A) Yes, put on a sweater.
   (B) Yes, she's very old.
   (C) Yes, she told me about it.

   Ⓐ Ⓑ Ⓒ

4. Do you think it'll rain tomorrow?

   (A) Yes, the train leaves every day.
   (B) Yes, don't forget your umbrella.
   (C) Yes, he'll come by plane.

   Ⓐ Ⓑ Ⓒ

5. Did you cut your hair?

   (A) Yes, it's over here.
   (B) Yes, I need fresh air.
   (C) Yes, it's shorter now.

   Ⓐ Ⓑ Ⓒ

6. Why did you open the door?

   (A) The pen was out of ink.
   (B) Because it's very warm in here.
   (C) It never happened before.

   Ⓐ Ⓑ Ⓒ

7. How long did you wait for her?

   (A) Only about 15 minutes.
   (B) It's a long way from here.
   (C) She doesn't weigh much.

   Ⓐ Ⓑ Ⓒ

8. What's the date today?

   (A) No, it's not too late.
   (B) It's April 15th or 16th.
   (C) I ate a sandwich for lunch today.

   Ⓐ Ⓑ Ⓒ

9. Where did you go on your walk?

   (A) We went to the park.
   (B) The chalk belongs to Hugo.
   (C) There wasn't time to talk.

   Ⓐ Ⓑ Ⓒ

10. When does your plane leave?

    (A) We'll plan a trip to Florida.
    (B) At two in the afternoon.
    (C) Where the mountain meets the plain.

    Ⓐ Ⓑ Ⓒ

Listening Practice: Similar Sounds

You will hear a question or statement followed by three responses. Choose the best response to each question or statement.

1. Ⓐ Ⓑ Ⓒ   6. Ⓐ Ⓑ Ⓒ   11. Ⓐ Ⓑ Ⓒ

2. Ⓐ Ⓑ Ⓒ   7. Ⓐ Ⓑ Ⓒ   12. Ⓐ Ⓑ Ⓒ

3. Ⓐ Ⓑ Ⓒ   8. Ⓐ Ⓑ Ⓒ   13. Ⓐ Ⓑ Ⓒ

4. Ⓐ Ⓑ Ⓒ   9. Ⓐ Ⓑ Ⓒ   14. Ⓐ Ⓑ Ⓒ

5. Ⓐ Ⓑ Ⓒ   10. Ⓐ Ⓑ Ⓒ   15. Ⓐ Ⓑ Ⓒ

ASSOCIATED WORDS

Words in the answer options may be similar in meaning to those in the question.

Question: What time does the movie start?

Possible Answers: (A) My watch is new.
           (B) In about ten minutes.
           (C) I'm out of film.   Ⓐ Ⓑ Ⓒ

Answer: (B)

Answer the questions. Be careful of associated words.

1. How fast can you type?

     (A) On a new keyboard.
     (B) About 75 words a minute.
     (C) Only a mile in an hour.   Ⓐ Ⓑ Ⓒ

2. Where did you go to school?

     (A) She works at a college.
     (B) I graduated from Harvard University.
     (C) I studied French at school.   Ⓐ Ⓑ Ⓒ

3. Would you like a glass of water?

     (A) Plastic is better.
     (B) It's very wet.
     (C) Yes, I'm very thirsty.   Ⓐ Ⓑ Ⓒ

4. Where did you buy those flowers?

     (A) I put them in the glass vase.
     (B) I got them from a local florist.
     (C) I planted roses in the garden.   Ⓐ Ⓑ Ⓒ

5. What kind of school is this?

(A) It's a high school.
(B) The teachers are very good.
(C) I take English classes.

Ⓐ Ⓑ Ⓒ

6. How far is the airport?

(A) Yes, the pilot's name is Howard.
(B) It's about ten miles from here.
(C) The plane is very big.

Ⓐ Ⓑ Ⓒ

7. Do you prefer coffee or tea?

(A) It's a hot drink.
(B) Yes, this one is my cup.
(C) Actually, I usually drink milk.

Ⓐ Ⓑ Ⓒ

8. Where is the telephone?

(A) It's on my desk.
(B) Phone me at home.
(C) I'll telephone you tonight.

Ⓐ Ⓑ Ⓒ

9. What time does the post office open?

(A) We get letters every day.
(B) Before eight o'clock.
(C) I just bought some stamps.

Ⓐ Ⓑ Ⓒ

10. That's Carol's desk, isn't it?

(A) No, hers is by the window.
(B) No, the chair is over here.
(C) No, it's not a new table.

Ⓐ Ⓑ Ⓒ

Listening Practice: Associated Words

CD 1
Track
6

You will hear a question or statement followed by three responses. Choose the best response to each question or statement.

1. Ⓐ Ⓑ Ⓒ	6. Ⓐ Ⓑ Ⓒ	11. Ⓐ Ⓑ Ⓒ
2. Ⓐ Ⓑ Ⓒ	7. Ⓐ Ⓑ Ⓒ	12. Ⓐ Ⓑ Ⓒ
3. Ⓐ Ⓑ Ⓒ	8. Ⓐ Ⓑ Ⓒ	13. Ⓐ Ⓑ Ⓒ
4. Ⓐ Ⓑ Ⓒ	9. Ⓐ Ⓑ Ⓒ	14. Ⓐ Ⓑ Ⓒ
5. Ⓐ Ⓑ Ⓒ	10. Ⓐ Ⓑ Ⓒ	15. Ⓐ Ⓑ Ⓒ

HOMONYMS

Words in the answer options may be homonyms of words in the question. Homonyms are words that sound exactly alike, but they are spelled differently and have different meanings. Some examples of homonyms are: *for* and *four*; *new* and *knew*; *some* and *sum*.

Question:	There are two of you for dinner, right?
Possible Answers:	(A) Yes, me and my friend Bob.
	(B) You got the right answer, too.
	(C) They're trying to find you. Ⓐ Ⓑ Ⓒ

Answer: (A)

Answer the questions. Be careful of homonyms.

1. Do you like my new red sweater?

   (A) It's very pretty.
   (B) I read that story.
   (C) They look alike.   Ⓐ Ⓑ Ⓒ

2. Did you write a letter to Herbert?

   (A) Yes, I sent it yesterday.
   (B) No, I don't think she's right.
   (C) Yes, she feels all right now.   Ⓐ Ⓑ Ⓒ

3. What should I wear to the party?

   (A) I don't know where it is.
   (B) Put on your new black dress.
   (C) I put it somewhere.   Ⓐ Ⓑ Ⓒ

4. Did your son call you on your birthday?

   (A) No, I didn't hear the bird call.
   (B) Yes, there's a lot of sun today.
   (C) No, but he sent me a card.   Ⓐ Ⓑ Ⓒ

5. Is your vacation next week?

   (A) No, he's feeling very weak.
   (B) No, it's the week after next.
   (C) No, this tea is too weak.   Ⓐ Ⓑ Ⓒ

6. Where did you buy your new pants?

   (A) I said good-bye to my parents.
   (B) It wasn't close by.
   (C) I got them at a department store.   Ⓐ Ⓑ Ⓒ

7. Who ate dinner with you?

   (A) We had it at eight.
   (B) I had eight cookies.
   (C) My parents did.

   (A) (B) (C)

8. What time does that store close?

   (A) At six in the evening.
   (B) It's not very close.
   (C) They sell only women's clothes.

   (A) (B) (C)

9. Did I leave my book in here?

   (A) It's too loud to hear.
   (B) Yes, it's on the table.
   (C) We booked you a room here.

   (A) (B) (C)

10. When can we meet?

    (A) I never eat meat.
    (B) That store sells meat.
    (C) After lunch is a good time.

    (A) (B) (C)

CD 1 Track 7 *Listening Practice: Homonyms*

You will hear a question or statement followed by three responses. Choose the best response to each question or statement.

1. (A) (B) (C)	6. (A) (B) (C)	11. (A) (B) (C)
2. (A) (B) (C)	7. (A) (B) (C)	12. (A) (B) (C)
3. (A) (B) (C)	8. (A) (B) (C)	13. (A) (B) (C)
4. (A) (B) (C)	9. (A) (B) (C)	14. (A) (B) (C)
5. (A) (B) (C)	10. (A) (B) (C)	15. (A) (B) (C)

SAME SOUND AND SPELLING BUT DIFFERENT MEANING

Words in the answer options may sound exactly like words in the question, and they may be spelled the same, but they have a different meaning.

Question: Can you give me a call tonight?

Possible Answers: (A) Call me Mary.
                                    (B) I'll phone you when I get home.
                                    (C) Call your brother to eat breakfast.

                                    (A) (B) (C)

Answer: (B)

Answer the questions. Be careful of words that have the same sound and the same spelling.

1. Do you go running every morning?

   (A) Yes, I go there.
   (B) Yes, it's running very well.
   (C) Yes, I want to stay in shape.

   Ⓐ Ⓑ Ⓒ

2. Mary didn't look well today, did she?

   (A) No, she seemed sick.
   (B) She'll look for it tomorrow.
   (C) She can look it up in the directory.

   Ⓐ Ⓑ Ⓒ

3. Where did you go on your trip?

   (A) Be careful, don't trip.
   (B) We went to the mountains.
   (C) I tripped on a rock.

   Ⓐ Ⓑ Ⓒ

4. How many students are in this class?

   (A) They're in a class by themselves.
   (B) We have two business class tickets.
   (C) I think there are 18.

   Ⓐ Ⓑ Ⓒ

5. That test was hard, wasn't it?

   (A) Yes, this seat is very hard.
   (B) Yes, it was really difficult.
   (C) Don't laugh so hard.

   Ⓐ Ⓑ Ⓒ

6. When do you play tennis?

   (A) I play the piano.
   (B) I enjoyed the play last night.
   (C) I play on Saturday afternoon.

   Ⓐ Ⓑ Ⓒ

7. Where did you park the car?

   (A) It's a very pretty park.
   (B) Right in front of the house.
   (C) Mr. Park is from Korea.

   Ⓐ Ⓑ Ⓒ

8. Where do you work?

   (A) My office is downtown.
   (B) My car doesn't work.
   (C) It worked out well.

   Ⓐ Ⓑ Ⓒ

9. Does Laura look like her sister?

    (A) The house had a new look.
    (B) No, they are very different.
    (C) No, she doesn't like cooking.

        Ⓐ Ⓑ Ⓒ

10. When will the movie be over?

    (A) The film ends at midnight.
    (B) Turn over or move over.
    (C) It's over the sofa.

        Ⓐ Ⓑ Ⓒ

CD 1 Track 8

Listening Practice: Same Sound and Spelling but Different Meaning

You will hear a question or statement followed by three responses. Choose the best response to each question or statement.

1. Ⓐ Ⓑ Ⓒ   6. Ⓐ Ⓑ Ⓒ   11. Ⓐ Ⓑ Ⓒ

2. Ⓐ Ⓑ Ⓒ   7. Ⓐ Ⓑ Ⓒ   12. Ⓐ Ⓑ Ⓒ

3. Ⓐ Ⓑ Ⓒ   8. Ⓐ Ⓑ Ⓒ   13. Ⓐ Ⓑ Ⓒ

4. Ⓐ Ⓑ Ⓒ   9. Ⓐ Ⓑ Ⓒ   14. Ⓐ Ⓑ Ⓒ

5. Ⓐ Ⓑ Ⓒ   10. Ⓐ Ⓑ Ⓒ   15. Ⓐ Ⓑ Ⓒ

OPPOSITES

Words in the answer options may be the opposite of words in the question. Such options may be the correct answer. Don't be confused by opposites.

Question: Why is she not very friendly?

Possible Answers: (A) She's very unfriendly.
                        (B) I don't have any friends.
                        (C) He's my best friend.

        Ⓐ Ⓑ Ⓒ

Answer: (A)

Answer the questions. Be careful of opposites.

1. Jane hardly ate her dinner.

    (A) She ate a lot.
    (B) She didn't eat much, it's true.
    (C) She was very hungry.

        Ⓐ Ⓑ Ⓒ

2. He's not usually on time, is he?

   (A) No, he's often late.
   (B) No, he's never late.
   (C) No, he's usually on time.

   Ⓐ Ⓑ Ⓒ

3. David's not a very careful driver.

   (A) I agree. He drives very carefully.
   (B) You're right. He's a very safe driver.
   (C) No, he's a careless driver.

   Ⓐ Ⓑ Ⓒ

4. I've read more interesting books.

   (A) Right. The book was very interesting.
   (B) Me too. This book was boring.
   (C) Let's read more books.

   Ⓐ Ⓑ Ⓒ

5. It wasn't an important message.

   (A) I'd better answer it right away.
   (B) True. The message was unimportant.
   (C) Yes, it's a very important message.

   Ⓐ Ⓑ Ⓒ

6. Lisa didn't look happy today.

   (A) No, she seemed very unhappy.
   (B) Yes, she's happy every day.
   (C) No, my birthday wasn't happy.

   Ⓐ Ⓑ Ⓒ

7. That wasn't the easiest test I've taken.

   (A) Yes, it was a very easy test.
   (B) I agree. The questions were easy to answer.
   (C) You're right. That test was difficult.

   Ⓐ Ⓑ Ⓒ

8. This chair is not very comfortable.

   (A) It is a very comfortable chair, isn't it?
   (B) I feel uncomfortable in this chair, too.
   (C) Yes, it's nice to sit in this chair.

   Ⓐ Ⓑ Ⓒ

9. This house is not very big.

   (A) No, it is small.
   (B) You're right. This house is big.
   (C) No, this house is not little.

   Ⓐ Ⓑ Ⓒ

10. This room is too noisy.

    (A) Yes. I like a lot of noise.
    (B) I agree. It's not very loud.
    (C) Yes, let's move to a place that's quieter.

    Ⓐ Ⓑ Ⓒ

Listening Practice: Opposites

You will hear a question or statement followed by three responses. Choose the best response to each question or statement.

1. Ⓐ Ⓑ Ⓒ   6. Ⓐ Ⓑ Ⓒ   11. Ⓐ Ⓑ Ⓒ

2. Ⓐ Ⓑ Ⓒ   7. Ⓐ Ⓑ Ⓒ   12. Ⓐ Ⓑ Ⓒ

3. Ⓐ Ⓑ Ⓒ   8. Ⓐ Ⓑ Ⓒ   13. Ⓐ Ⓑ Ⓒ

4. Ⓐ Ⓑ Ⓒ   9. Ⓐ Ⓑ Ⓒ   14. Ⓐ Ⓑ Ⓒ

5. Ⓐ Ⓑ Ⓒ   10. Ⓐ Ⓑ Ⓒ   15. Ⓐ Ⓑ Ⓒ

WORD ORDER

The word order of an item determines if it is positive or negative, a question or a statement.

Question: What a rainy day this is!

Possible Answers: (A) It's supposed to rain today.
                          (B) It's been raining all day.
                          (C) It's Thursday.   Ⓐ Ⓑ Ⓒ

Answer: (B)

Answer the questions. Be careful of word order.

1. How heavy the baby is!

     (A) About 10 pounds more.
     (B) I'll weigh it.
     (C) Yes, she likes to eat.   Ⓐ Ⓑ Ⓒ

2. What a beautiful day it is!

     (A) Yes, let's go to the beach.
     (B) It's Friday.
     (C) Yes, it's today.   Ⓐ Ⓑ Ⓒ

3. This is the house where I grew up!

     (A) In New York.
     (B) In a quiet neighborhood.
     (C) It's a beautiful house.   Ⓐ Ⓑ Ⓒ

4. How fast your car goes!

     (A) Yes, it has a great engine!
     (B) About 100 miles an hour.
     (C) I don't know how fast.   Ⓐ Ⓑ Ⓒ

5. What a good time we had!

   (A) It's 10:30, I think.
   (B) It was a very nice time.
   (C) I'm sorry, I don't have a watch.
                          Ⓐ Ⓑ Ⓒ

6. How long this movie is!

   (A) About two and a half hours.
   (B) Yes, I'm getting bored.
   (C) I think it's about three miles.
                          Ⓐ Ⓑ Ⓒ

7. What a big office this is!

   (A) Yes, it's an office.
   (B) It has a nice view, too.
   (C) Yes, it's my office.
                          Ⓐ Ⓑ Ⓒ

8. Never have I seen a cleaner house!

   (A) Yes, the house is very clean.
   (B) Yes, the house is very dirty.
   (C) No, I never clean the house.
                          Ⓐ Ⓑ Ⓒ

9. No one can sing as well as Tom.

   (A) No, nobody likes Tom.
   (B) Tom sings very badly.
   (C) Tom sings very well.
                          Ⓐ Ⓑ Ⓒ

10. How big your children are!

   (A) Yes, they've grown a lot.
   (B) About five feet tall.
   (C) Twelve years old.
                          Ⓐ Ⓑ Ⓒ

(CD 1 Track 10) *Listening Practice: Word Order*

You will hear a question or statement followed by three responses. Choose the best response to each question or statement.

1. Ⓐ Ⓑ Ⓒ	6. Ⓐ Ⓑ Ⓒ	11. Ⓐ Ⓑ Ⓒ
2. Ⓐ Ⓑ Ⓒ	7. Ⓐ Ⓑ Ⓒ	12. Ⓐ Ⓑ Ⓒ
3. Ⓐ Ⓑ Ⓒ	8. Ⓐ Ⓑ Ⓒ	13. Ⓐ Ⓑ Ⓒ
4. Ⓐ Ⓑ Ⓒ	9. Ⓐ Ⓑ Ⓒ	14. Ⓐ Ⓑ Ⓒ
5. Ⓐ Ⓑ Ⓒ	10. Ⓐ Ⓑ Ⓒ	15. Ⓐ Ⓑ Ⓒ

More Listening Practice

You will hear a question or statement followed by three responses. Choose the best response to each question or statement.

1. Ⓐ Ⓑ Ⓒ   6. Ⓐ Ⓑ Ⓒ   11. Ⓐ Ⓑ Ⓒ

2. Ⓐ Ⓑ Ⓒ   7. Ⓐ Ⓑ Ⓒ   12. Ⓐ Ⓑ Ⓒ

3. Ⓐ Ⓑ Ⓒ   8. Ⓐ Ⓑ Ⓒ   13. Ⓐ Ⓑ Ⓒ

4. Ⓐ Ⓑ Ⓒ   9. Ⓐ Ⓑ Ⓒ   14. Ⓐ Ⓑ Ⓒ

5. Ⓐ Ⓑ Ⓒ   10. Ⓐ Ⓑ Ⓒ   15. Ⓐ Ⓑ Ⓒ

Part III: Short Conversations and Short Talks—Vocabulary Building Activities

In this section, you will learn words that could be used in any part of the TOEIC Bridge test. Studying the words here will also prepare you for the vocabulary used in Part V and in other parts of the TOEIC Bridge test.

> ### VOCABULARY FOCUS
> - Dates and Time
> - Measurement and Numbers
> - Money
> - Activities
> - Feelings and Emotions

DATES AND TIME

WORDS IN CONTEXT

> **Directions:** Use one of the words in the box to complete each sentence.

> hours   clock   watch   early   afternoon

1. I wish there were more than 24 _____ in a day.

2. Our plane came in _____ because one of the stops was canceled.

3. I forgot my _____ today so I don't know what time it is.

4. The _____ on the wall says it's almost midnight.

5. We will be meeting for lunch this _____ at around 1:00 P.M.

| minutes | sunset | evening | time | month |

6. The recipe says to bake the cookies in the oven for 25 _____ .

7. September is the worst _____ because we have to go back to school.

8. What _____ do we have to be at the hockey rink?

9. I love to watch the _____ when the sky turns pink and orange.

10. I made a dinner reservation for this _____ at 7:00 P.M.

| later | calendar | week | seconds | midnight |

11. You can stay up a little _____ than 9:00 P.M. because the movie goes until 9:30 P.M.

12. Many people stay up until the clock strikes _____ to celebrate New Year's Day.

13. There are 60 _____ in a minute and 1440 minutes in a day.

14. My one- _____ vacation package includes five nights and seven days.

15. I'll have to check my _____ to make sure I am not busy on May 21.

WORD FAMILIES

Directions: Choose the correct form of the word to complete the sentence.

noun	time
noun	timer
verb	time

16. Excuse me, do you know what _____ the bus arrives?

17. I will _____ you to see how fast you go.

18. I need a _____ so that I know when the cake is ready to come out of the oven.

noun	week
noun	weekend
adverb	weekly

19. You will get paid _____ , or every seven days.

20. It is a long _____ so we get three days off instead of two.

21. There are seven days in the _____ .

noun	seconds
adjective	second
adjective	secondary

22. We start the countdown when there are ten _____ left in the final minute.

23. After primary school children go on to _____ school.

24. The winner beat me by one point so I came in _____ .

MEASUREMENT AND NUMBERS

WORDS IN CONTEXT

Directions: Use one of the words in the box to complete each sentence.

> plenty   subtract   measure   few   million

1. A person who has one _____ dollars is called a millionaire.

2. Only a _____ people are coming, which means about two or three.

3. We have to _____ your height so we can write down how much you grew.

4. _____ two guests from the list because Lisa and John can't come.

5. There will be _____ of food so everyone will get enough to eat.

feet	ruler	add	dozen	triple

6. Children have to be at least four _____ tall in order to go on this roller coaster.

7. Would you like a single, double, or _____ scoop of ice cream on your cone?

8. A set of twelve eggs is called a _____ .

9. Please _____ a little bit of sugar because it isn't sweet enough.

10. Use a _____ to check the length and to make sure the line is straight.

Mathematics	annual	kilometers	multiply	amount

11. _____ that by seven and you will find the total cost for one week.

12. An _____ event is something that happens once a year.

13. I hate studying _____ because I am not good with numbers.

14. The speed limit is 100 _____ per hour on this highway.

15. What is the total _____ of the bill after taxes?

WORD FAMILIES

Directions: Choose the correct form of the word to complete the sentence.

noun	measurement
verb	measure
adjective	measurable

16. There was a _____ distance between first and second place so we didn't have to watch the replay.

17. I have to take a _____ of your waist so I can find the right size for you.

18. The shoe salesman must _____ your feet before you try on any skates.

noun	addition
verb	add
adjective	additional

19. I have to make one _____ to the grocery list because I forgot to write down the butter.

20. You need to _____ two eggs to the mixture before you stir it.

21. There will be three _____ science courses offered next year, making a total of ten instead of seven.

noun	multiplication
verb	multiply
adjective	multiple

22. Children must memorize their _____ tables in Mathematics.

23. The fabric comes in _____ colors, including green, red, purple, blue, and yellow.

24. If you _____ that recipe by three, you will have enough dough for three pies.

MONEY

WORDS IN CONTEXT

Directions: Use one of the words in the box to complete each sentence.

count	lend	spend	free	borrow

1. _____ your money before you go shopping so that you know exactly how much you have.

2. I am going to _____ my birthday money on a new CD.

3. The pool is _____ for hotel guests, but visitors have to pay.

4. Could you _____ me some money until I get my paycheck?

5. I had to _____ a little bit of money from my parents and now I have to pay them back.

wallet	earn	tax	coin	expensive

6. This restaurant is more _____ than I can afford.

7. I keep my money and credit cards in a _____ in my purse.

8. You need to put a 25 cent _____ in the slot if you want to make a phone call.

9. Don't forget that you have to pay 15% sales _____ on anything you buy.

10. I will get a part-time job and _____ my own money.

check	currency	cheap	bank	poor

11. I need to find a _____ so that I can deposit my paycheck.

12. It was great how _____ that meal was after we used the coupon.

13. We need to exchange our _____ so that we can pay the taxi driver in American dollars.

14. I have to write a _____ for my landlord to pay for my rent.

15. There was a _____ man on the street begging for money.

WORD FAMILIES

Directions: Choose the correct form of the word to complete the sentence.

noun	freedom
adjective	free
adverb	freely

16. Jason is spending his money _____ because he is on vacation.

17. My parents have more _____ to go places now that they aren't working anymore.

18. Children under three years old are _____ because they don't take up an airplane seat.

noun	tax
verb	tax
adjective	taxable

19. These are not _____ items because they are for children.

20. The government must _____ the citizens in order to build roads and provide services.

21. Don't forget that you have to include the cost of the _____ and tip.

noun	bank
noun	banker
adjective	bankrupt

22. My father's company is going to go _____ this year because they don't have any money.

23. I love working with numbers and people so I should be a _____ .

24. She always asks for her account balance when she goes to the _____ .

ACTIVITIES

WORDS IN CONTEXT

Directions: Use one of the words in the box to complete each sentence.

> hobby   games   camp   join   groups

1. When we have a family party we always play _____ such as checkers and chess.

2. I would like to take up knitting as a new _____ this winter.

3. We need an extra person to _____ our soccer team this season.

4. He goes to summer _____ and learns survival skills from the counselors.

5. We prefer to travel in _____ of four people rather than in pairs.

| sport | park | exciting | family | teamwork |

6. We all have to work together because winning relies on _____ .

7. The children love to go on the swings and climb on the monkey bars at the _____ .

8. It is more _____ to jump out of a plane than to fly one.

9. Golf is the only _____ that I have never tried before.

10. Our dog is always in our group pictures because he is part of the _____ .

| club | kite | outdoor | competition | rink |

11. I am in a canoeing _____ that practices every other Wednesday.

12. It is best to fly a _____ on a windy day.

13. In the winter we go to the indoor skating _____ to play hockey.

14. There is a major _____ between the two best teams during the championships.

15. I prefer _____ activities such as hiking on a sunny day, rather than going to the gym.

WORD FAMILIES

Directions: Choose the correct form of the word to complete the sentence.

noun	camp
noun	camper
verb	camp

16. We set up _____ along the riverbank where all of the other tents were.

17. The _____ forgot to put out the campfire and lock away the food.

18. Let's _____ tonight instead of staying in a hotel.

noun	excitement
verb	excite
adjective	exciting

19. It was more _____ to watch the baseball game live than on TV.

20. There was so much _____ from the crowd that the security guards had to calm things down.

21. Try not to _____ the puppy too much or he will knock something over.

noun	competition
verb	compete
adjective	competitive

22. We keep score because we are very _____ when we play golf.

23. These two teams _____ against each other only once a year.

24. There is a sand castle _____ this Saturday and I am one of the judges.

FEELINGS AND EMOTIONS

WORDS IN CONTEXT

Directions: Use one of the words in the box to complete each sentence.

> frustrating   angry   tears   depressed   kind

1. I got _____ at my dog for chewing my brand new shoes.

2. Our new neighbor is so _____ that she baked us a loaf of bread.

3. Mark is _____ because his girlfriend broke up with him.

4. We shed a few _____ at the airport when it was time to say good-bye.

5. It is _____ when you can't get the thread through the eye of the needle.

smile	upset	cheer up	cry	embarrassed

6. I always _____ when I watch a sad film on TV.

7. She will _____ if you bring her some flowers and say you are sorry.

8. Please _____ for the picture to show that you are happy to be here.

9. The baby got _____ when his mother took away his toy.

10. John was _____ because so many people saw him trip and fall.

love	frown	kiss	argue	scared

11. I got _____ when the mouse jumped out of the cupboard and disappeared.

12. Mr. Greene had a _____ on his face when he read that the trip he arranged was canceled.

13. Give your grandma a _____ on the cheek before she gets on the train.

14. My brother and I always _____ about who is going to do the dishes.

15. A heart is a symbol of true _____ .

WORD FAMILIES

Directions: Choose the correct form of the word to complete the sentence.

noun	depression
verb	depress
adjective	depressed

16. I get _____ every time I read a sad book like this.

17. _____ is a serious mental health problem.

18. It will _____ me if I see that hungry dog on the street again.

noun	argument
verb	argue
adjective	argumentative

19. Mr. Morris and his wife _____ about money matters all the time.

20. The drivers were having an _____ about who caused the accident.

21. My parents become _____ when they disagree about directions.

verb	scare
adjective	scared
adjective	scary

22. You _____ me when you put those vampire teeth in your mouth.

23. I am _____ of spiders, mice, and snakes.

24. We watched a _____ movie last night and then I had nightmares.

Part III: Short Conversations and Short Talks—Skill Building Activities

There are 15 questions in Part III of the Bridge test. You will hear either a short conversation or a short talk, followed by a question. In your test booklet, you will see four possible answers.

Short conversation
Woman: Aren't you going to take an umbrella?
Man: Why? Is it going to rain?
Woman: There may be a shower this afternoon.

Question: What does the woman think will happen?
Possible Answers: (A) She'll take a shower this afternoon.
                     (B) It may rain later.
                     (C) The man will buy an umbrella.
                     (D) The man will take her with him.   Ⓐ Ⓑ Ⓒ Ⓓ

The best possible answer to the question, "What does the woman think will happen?" is (B) It may rain later.

Short talk
Woman: Please move away from the entrance. Will everyone with tickets for tonight's show stand on the right. All ticket holders on the right. If you need to buy a ticket, stand on the left. Those without tickets stand on the left. Please stand clear of the exits.

Question: Where do people with tickets stand?
Possible Answers: (A) On the left.
                     (B) On the right.
                     (C) By the entrance.
                     (D) By the exit.   Ⓐ Ⓑ Ⓒ Ⓓ

The best possible answer to the question, "Where do people with tickets stand?" is (B) On the right.

The Bridge test in Part III tries to trick your ears in several ways, just as in Part II.

> • Words Repeated   • Same Sound and Spelling but
> • Similar Sounds   Different Meaning
> • Associated Words   • Opposites
> • Homonyms   • Intonation

WORDS REPEATED

Words in the answer options may be the same as those in the short conversation or short talk.

Short conversation
Man: I have to leave the office early. Can you stay late and answer the phones?
Woman: I'm sorry, but I can't. I have a doctor's appointment after work.
Man: And I have to meet someone at that new restaurant for dinner.

Question: Where are the man and woman?
Possible Answers: (A) At a restaurant.
                     (B) At the doctor's.
                     (C) At the office.
                     (D) At a telephone booth.   Ⓐ Ⓑ Ⓒ Ⓓ

Answer: (C)

Listening Practice—Words Repeated

Answer the questions. Be careful of repeated words.

1. What's for dinner?

    (A) Chicken only.
    (B) Steak only.
    (C) Chicken and salad.
    (D) Chicken and steak.

    Ⓐ Ⓑ Ⓒ Ⓓ

2. What's the problem with the car?

    (A) It's red.
    (B) The headlights are on.
    (C) The door is open.
    (D) It's parked in front of the door.

    Ⓐ Ⓑ Ⓒ Ⓓ

3. What's on sale this week?

    (A) Women's dresses.
    (B) Men's shirts.
    (C) Children's shoes.
    (D) Sports jackets.

    Ⓐ Ⓑ Ⓒ Ⓓ

4. How does she go to work?

    (A) By plane.
    (B) Driving.
    (C) Walking.
    (D) By train.

    Ⓐ Ⓑ Ⓒ Ⓓ

5. Where does she want to go?

    (A) To the bus station.
    (B) Downtown.
    (C) To the train station.
    (D) To the park.

    Ⓐ Ⓑ Ⓒ Ⓓ

6. What will the woman do tonight?

    (A) Go to a soccer game.
    (B) Work late.
    (C) Go out with a friend.
    (D) Buy tickets.

    Ⓐ Ⓑ Ⓒ Ⓓ

7. How will the weather be this weekend?

    (A) Hot.
    (B) Clear.
    (C) Sunny.
    (D) Rainy.

    Ⓐ Ⓑ Ⓒ Ⓓ

8. What does the man like to do?

   (A) Read books.
   (B) Watch TV.
   (C) Play tennis.
   (D) Watch movies.

   Ⓐ Ⓑ Ⓒ Ⓓ

9. What describes Jane?

   (A) She has long, red hair.
   (B) She doesn't wear glasses.
   (C) She has long, black hair.
   (D) She has red hair and glasses.

   Ⓐ Ⓑ Ⓒ Ⓓ

10. Where will Susan meet John?

    (A) At the movies.
    (B) At the restaurant.
    (C) At the office.
    (D) At home.

    Ⓐ Ⓑ Ⓒ Ⓓ

SIMILAR SOUNDS

Words in the answer options may sound like those in the question.

Short Talk
Man: Today's high temperature will be in the 80s, probably around 84–85.
           It may even go as high as 86. There may be a chance of rain later in
           the day, but it will be clear this evening. You'll be able to see the full
           moon tonight.

Question: What is the man talking about?
Possible Answers: (A) The train number.
                   (B) The weather today.
                   (C) The number of dancers.
                   (D) The month of June.

                   Ⓐ Ⓑ Ⓒ Ⓓ

Answer: (B)

Listening Practice—Similar Sounds

Answer the questions. Be careful of similar sounds.

1. What is she going to do?

   (A) Write a long letter.
   (B) Clean the living room.
   (C) Help Gene paint.
   (D) Leave the room.

   Ⓐ Ⓑ Ⓒ Ⓓ

2. What will the woman do?

   (A) She'll get some shoes.
   (B) She'll eat a pear.
   (C) She'll choose a peach.
   (D) She'll buy a suit.   Ⓐ Ⓑ Ⓒ Ⓓ

3. What time is it now?

   (A) It's 9:00.
   (B) It's two minutes to 8:00.
   (C) It's after 8:00.
   (D) It's 9:04.   Ⓐ Ⓑ Ⓒ Ⓓ

4. What describes the plane to Miami?

   (A) All the seats are full.
   (B) It's at night.
   (C) It leaves at 9.
   (D) It's boring.   Ⓐ Ⓑ Ⓒ Ⓓ

5. What is the man going to do?

   (A) Pick up some baggage.
   (B) Get some stamps.
   (C) Eat a meal.
   (D) Mail a form.   Ⓐ Ⓑ Ⓒ Ⓓ

6. What describes John?

   (A) He's tall.
   (B) He's good at cooking.
   (C) He likes art.
   (D) He's very nice.   Ⓐ Ⓑ Ⓒ Ⓓ

7. What does the woman want to do?

   (A) Lend Mary a dress.
   (B) Return Mary's phone call.
   (C) Send Mary an invitation.
   (D) Show Mary her garden.   Ⓐ Ⓑ Ⓒ Ⓓ

8. Why doesn't she want soup?

   (A) She's in a hurry.
   (B) She already ate.
   (C) She's on a diet.
   (D) It's really late.   Ⓐ Ⓑ Ⓒ Ⓓ

9. When will the circus come to town?

    (A) Tonight.
    (B) On Monday.
    (C) On Thursday.
    (D) Next month.   Ⓐ Ⓑ Ⓒ Ⓓ

10. What does a pet bird need?

    (A) It needs to be careful.
    (B) It needs to take a walk.
    (C) It needs to eat fresh fish.
    (D) It needs to have clean water.   Ⓐ Ⓑ Ⓒ Ⓓ

ASSOCIATED WORDS

Words in the answer options may be similar in meaning to those in the short conversation or short talk.

Short conversation
Woman: What a big apartment. How many rooms does it have?
Man: Two bedrooms and a big kitchen.
Woman: You like to cook, don't you?
Man: Yes. Cooking is my hobby, you know.

Question: Why does the man like the apartment?
Possible Answers: (A) It's close to restaurants.
                  (B) It has a large kitchen.
                  (C) There's a bed in every room.
                  (D) His roommate is a chef.   Ⓐ Ⓑ Ⓒ Ⓓ

Answer: (B)

Listening Practice—Associated Words

Answer the questions. Be careful of associated words.

1. Where are they?

    (A) At a bookstore.
    (B) At a bank.
    (C) At a restaurant.
    (D) In a kitchen.   Ⓐ Ⓑ Ⓒ Ⓓ

2. What will they do this afternoon?

    (A) Take a rest.
    (B) Eat a meal together.
    (C) Play a game.
    (D) Go swimming.   Ⓐ Ⓑ Ⓒ Ⓓ

3. What does she need?

    (A) A cup of coffee.
    (B) A ride.
    (C) A pickup truck.
    (D) A telephone.

    Ⓐ Ⓑ Ⓒ Ⓓ

4. Why is he tired?

    (A) His bed is uncomfortable.
    (B) He worked late.
    (C) He went to a party.
    (D) His job is too difficult.

    Ⓐ Ⓑ Ⓒ Ⓓ

5. What is the announcement about?

    (A) The weather.
    (B) A restaurant.
    (C) A movie theater.
    (D) A store.

    Ⓐ Ⓑ Ⓒ Ⓓ

6. What is inside the building now?

    (A) A history museum.
    (B) Government offices.
    (C) A home for old people.
    (D) An art museum.

    Ⓐ Ⓑ Ⓒ Ⓓ

7. What will he do for Sam's birthday?

    (A) Invite Sam to a concert.
    (B) Take Sam to a restaurant.
    (C) Give Sam a soccer ball.
    (D) Buy Sam a new CD.

    Ⓐ Ⓑ Ⓒ Ⓓ

8. How does the woman feel?

    (A) Hot.
    (B) Cold.
    (C) Wet.
    (D) Thirsty.

    Ⓐ Ⓑ Ⓒ Ⓓ

9. What does the office need?

    (A) More space.
    (B) A better location.
    (C) A more comfortable chair.
    (D) A prettier desk.

    Ⓐ Ⓑ Ⓒ Ⓓ

10. What happened?

    (A) He fell down.
    (B) He dropped his plate.
    (C) He washed a dish.
    (D) He ate some soup. Ⓐ Ⓑ Ⓒ Ⓓ

HOMONYMS

Words in the answer options may sound exactly like words in the short conversation or short talk, but they are spelled differently and have a different meaning.

Short Talk
Woman: Attention, shoppers. There is a sale on sporting goods in progress.
            This is our first sale of the week and will be our biggest. You will find
            savings up to 40% on boating shoes and other marine wear.

Question: What is the talk about?
Possible Answers: (A) A sale on sporting goods.
                    (B) A new sailboat.
                    (C) A weak market.
                    (D) A kind of glassware. Ⓐ Ⓑ Ⓒ Ⓓ

Answer: (A)

 Listening Practice—Homonyms

Answer the questions. Be careful of homonyms.

1. What does the woman want to do?

    (A) Buy new clothes.
    (B) Get a TV on sale.
    (C) Go on a sailboat.
    (D) Buy a watch. Ⓐ Ⓑ Ⓒ Ⓓ

2. What is the announcement about?

    (A) A place to buy books.
    (B) A person who writes books.
    (C) A person who reads some books.
    (D) A place to buy meat. Ⓐ Ⓑ Ⓒ Ⓓ

3. What was the weather like yesterday?

    (A) It was windy.
    (B) The sky was blue.
    (C) It was freezing.
    (D) The sun was out. Ⓐ Ⓑ Ⓒ Ⓓ

4. What describes George?

    (A) He has a big nose.
    (B) He's overweight.
    (C) He understands computers.
    (D) He has a writing business.

    (A) (B) (C) (D)

5. What is the announcement about?

    (A) Hearing music in the park.
    (B) Things you can buy in the park.
    (C) Hours that the park is open.
    (D) Things you can do in the park.

    (A) (B) (C) (D)

6. What did he do at the party?

    (A) He met a new friend.
    (B) He talked to Robert.
    (C) He said hi to everyone.
    (D) He ran for a long time.

    (A) (B) (C) (D)

7. Why does the woman want to be careful?

    (A) The lock is made of steel.
    (B) She has two cars.
    (C) Somebody might take her bicycle.
    (D) The brakes don't work.

    (A) (B) (C) (D)

8. What did Janet do last week?

    (A) She stayed home.
    (B) She went to the sea.
    (C) She flew to a new place.
    (D) She came here.

    (A) (B) (C) (D)

9. What did they do?

    (A) They ate dinner.
    (B) They got the kitchen ready.
    (C) They got some flour.
    (D) They opened a can.

    (A) (B) (C) (D)

10. What happened?

    (A) They looked through the window.
    (B) They covered the window.
    (C) The wood fell off the window.
    (D) Someone broke the window.

    (A) (B) (C) (D)

SAME SOUND AND SPELLING BUT DIFFERENT MEANING

Words in the answer options may sound exactly like words in the short conversation or short talk, and they may be spelled the same, but they have a different meaning.

Short conversation
Woman: You're flying to Spain with your students?
Man: All night in coach.
Woman: What? Not first class?
Man: Not on a student budget.

Question: Where will the man be with the students?
Possible Answers: (A) In class.
                       (B) On a plane.
                       (C) On a train.
                       (D) On a bus.   Ⓐ Ⓑ Ⓒ Ⓓ

Listening Practice—Same Sound and Spelling but Different Meaning

Answer the questions. Be careful of words with the same sound and spelling but different meaning.

1. What is the woman going to do?

   (A) Write a check for the mechanic.
   (B) Run to work.
   (C) Pick out a new car.
   (D) Take the car to the mechanic.   Ⓐ Ⓑ Ⓒ Ⓓ

2. Why can't she read?

   (A) The book is too heavy.
   (B) There's not enough room.
   (C) She needs more light.
   (D) Her chair is too hard.   Ⓐ Ⓑ Ⓒ Ⓓ

3. What's the matter with the cake?

   (A) It's too sweet.
   (B) It made them laugh.
   (C) It's very expensive.
   (D) It's too little.   Ⓐ Ⓑ Ⓒ Ⓓ

4. Why didn't he call about the plane tickets?

   (A) The phone was out of order.
   (B) He was too busy.
   (C) He already got them.
   (D) He didn't have the right phone number.   Ⓐ Ⓑ Ⓒ Ⓓ

5. What will they do?

   (A) Walk to work.
   (B) Work outside.
   (C) Park the car.
   (D) Take a walk in the park.

   Ⓐ Ⓑ Ⓒ Ⓓ

6. What does she like about golf?

   (A) It's relaxing.
   (B) It's free.
   (C) It's good for her back.
   (D) It takes a lot of time.

   Ⓐ Ⓑ Ⓒ Ⓓ

7. What is the problem?

   (A) They need a watch.
   (B) The TV program is over.
   (C) They can't hear the movie.
   (D) The TV is too heavy to move.

   Ⓐ Ⓑ Ⓒ Ⓓ

8. What did he ask her to do?

   (A) Plant some flowers.
   (B) Water the plants.
   (C) Put the table outside.
   (D) Look at the kitchen.

   Ⓐ Ⓑ Ⓒ Ⓓ

9. Why can't you book a flight to Los Angeles?

   (A) All the agents have left.
   (B) There is no place to go.
   (C) The flights are full.
   (D) The line is too long.

   Ⓐ Ⓑ Ⓒ Ⓓ

10. Why is City College the school for working people?

    (A) It offers evening and weekend classes.
    (B) You can meet kind people there.
    (C) It offers typing classes.
    (D) Everybody at the school is interesting.

    Ⓐ Ⓑ Ⓒ Ⓓ

OPPOSITES

Words in the answer options may be the opposite of words in the short conversation or short talk. This may be the correct answer. Don't be confused by opposites.

Short Talk
Man: When you are finished eating, take your trays to the clean-up area. Please separate paper plates and plastic knives, forks, and spoons. Do not wash your tray. Please do not place glassware on the counter.

Question: What are customers asked NOT to do?
Possible Answers: (A) Wash their trays.
                   (B) Separate plates and cutlery.
                   (C) Finish eating.
                   (D) Put glassware in the trash.   Ⓐ Ⓑ Ⓒ Ⓓ

Answer: (A)

CD 1 Track 17   *Listening Practice—Opposites*

Answer the questions. Be careful of opposites.

1. Why is the woman upset?

    (A) The man wants to hear more.
    (B) The man is too busy cleaning.
    (C) The place is dirty.
    (D) The room is spotless.   Ⓐ Ⓑ Ⓒ Ⓓ

2. What's the problem?

    (A) He doesn't like the book.
    (B) The book isn't useful for his report.
    (C) The book has the information he needs.
    (D) He isn't used to writing reports.   Ⓐ Ⓑ Ⓒ Ⓓ

3. What are employees asked to do?

    (A) Keep the office clean.
    (B) Take drinks and food to their desks.
    (C) Make their desks dirty.
    (D) Stay out of the lounge.   Ⓐ Ⓑ Ⓒ Ⓓ

4. What do they think of the movie?

    (A) It was a bad movie.
    (B) It was the best movie.
    (C) It was a good movie.
    (D) It wasn't the worst movie.   Ⓐ Ⓑ Ⓒ Ⓓ

5. What's the matter with the hotel room?

    (A) It isn't crowded.
    (B) It's very long.
    (C) It's too big.
    (D) It's too small.   Ⓐ Ⓑ Ⓒ Ⓓ

6. What do they think of the test?

    (A) It was easy.
    (B) It was difficult.
    (C) It was short.
    (D) It took a long time.   Ⓐ Ⓑ Ⓒ Ⓓ

7. How was the day at the beach?

    (A) It was good.
    (B) It was cloudy.
    (C) It was sunny.
    (D) It was wonderful.   Ⓐ Ⓑ Ⓒ Ⓓ

8. What are you allowed to do in the theater?

    (A) Bring food from the outside.
    (B) Talk during the show.
    (C) Buy food and soda in the lobby.
    (D) Listen to the radio.   Ⓐ Ⓑ Ⓒ Ⓓ

9. What's the problem with the restaurant?

    (A) It's too expensive.
    (B) The food is bad.
    (C) The service is slow.
    (D) The desserts aren't good.   Ⓐ Ⓑ Ⓒ Ⓓ

10. What does she think of the kitchen?

    (A) It looks bad.
    (B) It looks good.
    (C) It looks hard.
    (D) It looked better before.   Ⓐ Ⓑ Ⓒ Ⓓ

INTONATION

The intonation can determine if a sentence is positive or negative, a question, or a statement.

Short conversation
Woman: What kind of a chair is this? Who's small enough to sit on this?
Man: You don't think it looks comfortable?
Woman: Comfortable? It doesn't even look safe to sit in.
Man: Try it. Sit down. You'll really like it. (sarcastic).

Question: What do they think about the chair?
Possible Answers: (A) It's comfortable.
                   (B) They think it's too large.
                   (C) It's unsafe.
                   (D) They like it.   Ⓐ Ⓑ Ⓒ Ⓓ

Answer: (C)

CD 2 Track 1

Listening Practice—Intonation

Answer the questions. Be careful of intonation.

1. What will the woman do?

    (A) Drive the car.
    (B) Ride in the car.
    (C) Stay home.
    (D) Think about it.

    Ⓐ Ⓑ Ⓒ Ⓓ

2. What does the woman think of Susan?

    (A) She's nice.
    (B) She's kind.
    (C) She's real.
    (D) She's not generous.

    Ⓐ Ⓑ Ⓒ Ⓓ

3. What did she like about the trip?

    (A) The food.
    (B) The plane ride.
    (C) The hotel.
    (D) The weather.

    Ⓐ Ⓑ Ⓒ Ⓓ

4. What did the woman do?

    (A) She ate too much.
    (B) She didn't eat enough.
    (C) She ate bad food.
    (D) She saved some food for later.

    Ⓐ Ⓑ Ⓒ Ⓓ

5. What will the man do?

    (A) Go swimming.
    (B) Stay home.
    (C) Go fishing.
    (D) Watch TV.

    Ⓐ Ⓑ Ⓒ Ⓓ

6. What did the man do?

    (A) He forgot to call Martha.
    (B) He sent an e-mail to Martha.
    (C) He answered Martha's message.
    (D) He left a message for Martha.

    Ⓐ Ⓑ Ⓒ Ⓓ

7. What does he think of the joke?

    (A) It was a good joke.
    (B) It was a bad joke.
    (C) It was a mean joke.
    (D) It was a funny joke.

    Ⓐ Ⓑ Ⓒ Ⓓ

8. What doesn't she like?

   (A) Rice.
   (B) Soup.
   (C) Fish.
   (D) Chicken.

   Ⓐ Ⓑ Ⓒ Ⓓ

9. What does the man think about the apartment?

   (A) It's not big enough.
   (B) He doesn't like the living room.
   (C) It's expensive.
   (D) It's too big.

   Ⓐ Ⓑ Ⓒ Ⓓ

10. What will the man do?

    (A) Get a birthday present.
    (B) Wear his tie to the office.
    (C) Buy a new suit.
    (D) Throw his tie away.

    Ⓐ Ⓑ Ⓒ Ⓓ

Mini-Test Answer Sheet
LISTENING COMPREHENSION REVIEW

Part I

1. Ⓐ Ⓑ Ⓒ Ⓓ
2. Ⓐ Ⓑ Ⓒ Ⓓ
3. Ⓐ Ⓑ Ⓒ Ⓓ
4. Ⓐ Ⓑ Ⓒ Ⓓ
5. Ⓐ Ⓑ Ⓒ Ⓓ

6. Ⓐ Ⓑ Ⓒ Ⓓ
7. Ⓐ Ⓑ Ⓒ Ⓓ
8. Ⓐ Ⓑ Ⓒ Ⓓ
9. Ⓐ Ⓑ Ⓒ Ⓓ
10. Ⓐ Ⓑ Ⓒ Ⓓ

11. Ⓐ Ⓑ Ⓒ Ⓓ
12. Ⓐ Ⓑ Ⓒ Ⓓ
13. Ⓐ Ⓑ Ⓒ Ⓓ
14. Ⓐ Ⓑ Ⓒ Ⓓ
15. Ⓐ Ⓑ Ⓒ Ⓓ

Part II

16. Ⓐ Ⓑ Ⓒ
17. Ⓐ Ⓑ Ⓒ
18. Ⓐ Ⓑ Ⓒ
19. Ⓐ Ⓑ Ⓒ
20. Ⓐ Ⓑ Ⓒ
21. Ⓐ Ⓑ Ⓒ
22. Ⓐ Ⓑ Ⓒ

23. Ⓐ Ⓑ Ⓒ
24. Ⓐ Ⓑ Ⓒ
25. Ⓐ Ⓑ Ⓒ
26. Ⓐ Ⓑ Ⓒ
27. Ⓐ Ⓑ Ⓒ
28. Ⓐ Ⓑ Ⓒ
29. Ⓐ Ⓑ Ⓒ

30. Ⓐ Ⓑ Ⓒ
31. Ⓐ Ⓑ Ⓒ
32. Ⓐ Ⓑ Ⓒ
33. Ⓐ Ⓑ Ⓒ
34. Ⓐ Ⓑ Ⓒ
35. Ⓐ Ⓑ Ⓒ

Part III

36. Ⓐ Ⓑ Ⓒ Ⓓ
37. Ⓐ Ⓑ Ⓒ Ⓓ
38. Ⓐ Ⓑ Ⓒ Ⓓ
39. Ⓐ Ⓑ Ⓒ Ⓓ
40. Ⓐ Ⓑ Ⓒ Ⓓ

41. Ⓐ Ⓑ Ⓒ Ⓓ
42. Ⓐ Ⓑ Ⓒ Ⓓ
43. Ⓐ Ⓑ Ⓒ Ⓓ
44. Ⓐ Ⓑ Ⓒ Ⓓ
45. Ⓐ Ⓑ Ⓒ Ⓓ

46. Ⓐ Ⓑ Ⓒ Ⓓ
47. Ⓐ Ⓑ Ⓒ Ⓓ
48. Ⓐ Ⓑ Ⓒ Ⓓ
49. Ⓐ Ⓑ Ⓒ Ⓓ
50. Ⓐ Ⓑ Ⓒ Ⓓ

Mini-Test for Listening Comprehension Review— Parts I, II, and III

In this section of the review, you will have the chance to show how well you understand spoken English. There are three parts to this section, with special directions for each part.

PART I: PHOTOGRAPHS

Directions: For each question, you will see a picture in your test book and you will hear four short statements. The statements will be spoken just one time. They will not be printed in your test book, so you must listen carefully.

When you hear the four statements, look at the picture in your test book and choose the statement that best describes what you see in the picture. Then, on your answer sheet, find the number of the question and mark your answer. Look at the sample below.

Now listen to the four statements.

Sample Answer

Ⓐ Ⓑ Ⓒ Ⓓ

Statement (B), "The boys are reading," best describes what you see in the picture. Therefore, you should choose answer (B).

1.

2.

3.

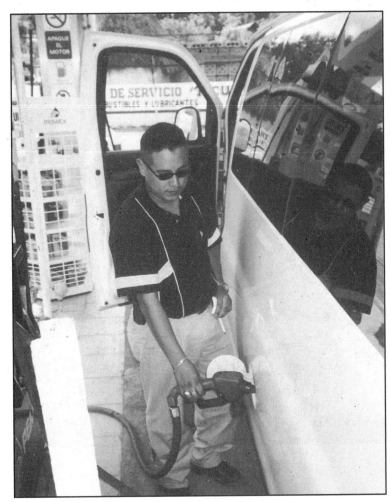

4.

5.

6.

7.

8.

9.

10.

11.

12.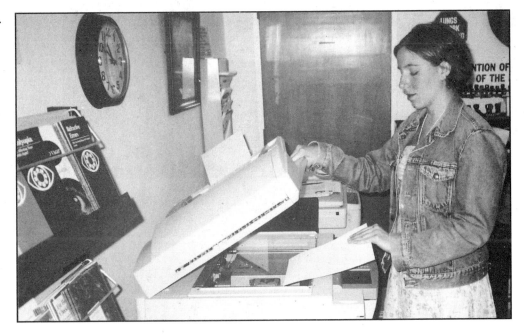

13.

14.

15.

PART II: QUESTION-RESPONSE

Directions: In this part of the test, you will hear a question or statement spoken in English, followed by three responses, also spoken in English. The question or statement and the responses will be spoken just one time. They will not be printed in your test book, so you must listen carefully. Choose the best response to each question.

[Narrator]   Now listen to a sample question.

[Narrator]   You will hear:
[Woman B]   Excuse me, where is the bus stop?

[Narrator]   You will also hear:
[Man A]   (A) It's across the street.
                 (B) It's underneath.
                 (C) It arrives in 10 minutes.

[Narrator]   The best response to the question *Where is the bus stop?* is Choice (A), *It's across the street.* Therefore, you should choose answer (A).

16. Mark your answer on your answer sheet.

17. Mark your answer on your answer sheet.

18. Mark your answer on your answer sheet.

19. Mark your answer on your answer sheet.

20. Mark your answer on your answer sheet.

21. Mark your answer on your answer sheet.

22. Mark your answer on your answer sheet.

23. Mark your answer on your answer sheet.

24. Mark your answer on your answer sheet.

25. Mark your answer on your answer sheet.

26. Mark your answer on your answer sheet.

27. Mark your answer on your answer sheet.

28. Mark your answer on your answer sheet.

29. Mark your answer on your answer sheet.

30. Mark your answer on your answer sheet.

31. Mark your answer on your answer sheet.

32. Mark your answer on your answer sheet.

33. Mark your answer on your answer sheet.

34. Mark your answer on your answer sheet.

35. Mark your answer on your answer sheet.

PART III: SHORT CONVERSATIONS AND SHORT TALKS

 Directions: In this part of the test, you will hear 15 short conversations or short talks only once, so you must listen carefully.

In your test book, you will read a question about each conversation or talk. The question will be followed by four short answers. Choose the best answer to each question and mark it on your answer sheet.

36. Why was the woman late?

    (A) The traffic was bad.
    (B) Her car broke down.
    (C) She walked.
    (D) The bus was slow.

37. Where would you hear this message?

    (A) At a travel agency.
    (B) At an airline office.
    (C) At a movie theater.
    (D) At a television station.

38. How is the weather?

    (A) Cloudy.
    (B) Warm.
    (C) Cold.
    (D) Snowy.

39. What does the man want to do this evening?

    (A) Go to the gym.
    (B) Go to the movies.
    (C) Go home.
    (D) Go to work.

40. What time will the plane arrive?

    (A) 1:30.
    (B) 10:00.
    (C) 8:00.
    (D) 12:45.

41. What is the woman doing?

    (A) Shopping for groceries.
    (B) Planning a party.
    (C) Cooking a meal.
    (D) Ordering food at a restaurant.

42. What will the woman do this weekend?

    (A) Go to a game.
    (B) Rest.
    (C) Eat at a restaurant.
    (D) Work.

43. How do the speakers feel about the new office?

    (A) Unhappy.
    (B) Tired.
    (C) Troubled.
    (D) Excited.

44. Who is the speaker?

    (A) A writer.
    (B) A teacher.
    (C) A doctor.
    (D) A librarian.

45. Where does this conversation take place?

    (A) At a park.
    (B) At a car repair shop.
    (C) At a parking lot.
    (D) At a bank.

46. What is this talk about?

    (A) Today's weather.
    (B) A travel agency.
    (C) Traffic conditions.
    (D) A car sale.

47. What is the speakers' opinion of the party?

    (A) It was boring.
    (B) The people were interesting.
    (C) It was fun.
    (D) The food was tasty.

48. What does the woman ask the man to do?

    (A) Weigh a package.
    (B) Carry a package.
    (C) Mail a package.
    (D) Deliver a package.

49. What does the man want to do?

    (A) Cash a check.
    (B) Return a shirt.
    (C) Get a credit card.
    (D) Buy a shirt.

50. What costs $20?

    (A) Breakfast.
    (B) Lunch.
    (C) Dinner.
    (D) Dessert.

STOP

This is the end of the Listening Comprehension portion of the test.
Turn to Part IV in your test book.

CHAPTER 3

Reading

WHAT TO LOOK FOR IN THIS CHAPTER

• Vocabulary and Skill Building Activities for Part IV
• Vocabulary and Skill Building Activities for Part V
• Mini-Test for Listening Comprehension Review—Parts IV and V

Part IV: Vocabulary Building Activities

In this section, you will learn words that could be used in any part of the TOEIC Bridge test. Studying the words here will also prepare you for the vocabulary used in Part V and in other parts of the TOEIC Bridge test.

VOCABULARY FOCUS

- Sports
- Entertainment
- Groceries
- Geography
- Furniture and Furnishings

SPORTS

WORDS IN CONTEXT

Directions: Use one of the words in the box to complete each sentence.

| win | finish | fast | cheered | basketball |

1. The swimmer was so _____ that he finished the race in record time.

2. The crowd _____ when the home team got the last goal.

3. In _____ the players have to shoot the ball into the hoop.

4. The runner was too tired to make it to the _____ line.

5. If we _____ this game we will be the semifinal champions.

coach	referee	field	scored	goalie

6. The _____ told his team to play fair and try their best.

7. The players argued with the _____ about the call he made on the goal.

8. The _____ let in two goals during the first period.

9. I can't believe Jonathan _____ on his own net and lost us the game.

10. Unfortunately the _____ is too wet to play ball on tonight.

whistle	safe	match	uniform	lose

11. Did anyone hear the referee blow the _____?

12. The last tennis _____ will be played by two of the top tennis players.

13. We have to wear a new team _____ with our logo on the front.

14. The umpire signaled that the hitter was _____ on second base.

15. If we _____ one more game we won't qualify for the next round.

WORD FAMILIES

Directions: Choose the correct form of the word to complete the sentence.

noun	winner
noun	winnings
verb	win

16. We will split the _____ equally so that we all get 50 dollars.

17. I think our team will _____ the trophy because we have the best players.

18. The _____ got a free scholarship for coming in first.

noun	safety
verb	safe
adverb	safely

19. You should always wear a helmet because _____ is important.

20. The race car driver got out of the burning car _____ and without any injuries.

21. It is not _____ to do water sports without a life jacket.

noun	loser
noun	loss
nverb	lose

22. It was a terrible _____ for the hockey club when the captain quit.

23. Don't be a sore _____ just because we lost one football game.

24. If we _____ this year, we will try to win the trophy next year.

ENTERTAINMENT

WORDS IN CONTEXT

Directions: Use one of the words in the box to complete each sentence.

actor	film	funny	laugh	circus

1. It was such a _____ movie that I couldn't stop laughing until the end.

2. My favorite part about the _____ was the clown in the fire truck.

3. I haven't seen a good _____ since that one we rented at Christmastime.

4. I had to _____ when the monkey took the man's banana right out of his hand.

5. I don't have a favorite _____ or actress because I rarely go to movies.

| clapped | applause | dance | theater | band |

6. We went to see a live jazz _____ last night at music night in the pub.

7. I will be doing ballet and tap at my _____ recital.

8. It is cheaper to rent a movie than to go to the _____ to see one.

9. The crowd's _____ was so loud that the musicians had to come back out on stage again.

10. We _____ for so long after the performance that my hands actually hurt.

| musician | movie | set | lighting | curtains |

11. The students built and painted the _____ for the high school musical.

12. The people at the back said they couldn't see because the _____ was poor.

13. As soon as they opened the _____ the show began.

14. This was the first _____ I have been to this year because we usually wait for the videos.

15. I always dreamed of being a _____, but I never picked up an instrument.

WORD FAMILIES

Directions: Choose the correct form of the word to complete the sentence.

noun	action
noun	actress
verb	act

16. I love to watch movies with a lot of _____ because they are fast paced and exciting.

17. She was a great _____, but not the best person for the part.

18. Some say it is harder to _____ like a bad guy than a good guy.

noun	music
noun	musician
adjective	musical

19. Julia grew up in a very _____ family so she can play the piano and the guitar.

20. I love to get in the car and listen to _____.

21. He used to be a professional _____, but now he only teaches music.

noun	lighting
verb	lighten
adjective	light

22. I think we should _____ up the background a little bit by adding some white.

23. It isn't _____ enough to do the play outside after 8:00 P.M.

24. Lisa and Mark did an excellent job on the stage _____ because we could see everything perfectly.

GROCERIES

WORDS IN CONTEXT

Directions: Use one of the words in the box to complete each sentence.

aisle   frozen   juice   pack   cart

1. You can borrow a grocery _____ to push your groceries around in.

2. I'm going to buy some orange _____ so we will have something to drink for breakfast.

3. The man at the checkout will _____ your groceries in bags for you.

4. I sometimes buy _____ vegetables if the fresh ones aren't on sale.

5. The pasta is in _____ three with the rice and spices.

| coupons | fruit | bags | cheese | list |

6. We always recycle our plastic grocery _____ for next time.

7. If the cheddar _____ is on sale, we should make a pizza.

8. Are there any _____ for half-priced bread to clip out of the flyer this week?

9. I made a long _____ of things we need, but I left it on the kitchen counter.

10. We always buy our strawberries and other _____ at the farmer's market.

| pick | grocer | weigh | dairy | butcher |

11. We can _____ some fresh grapes off the vines ourselves.

12. The clerk will _____ your fruit and tell you how many pounds you have.

13. Let's ask the _____ where to find the baking ingredients.

14. I would prefer to go to the _____ shop to buy fresh meat.

15. The butter and yogurt are in the _____ section.

WORD FAMILIES

Directions: Choose the correct form of the word to complete the sentence.

noun	freezer
verb	freeze
adjective	frozen

16. The ice cream is in the _____ foods section.

17. You should _____ the meat until you are ready to use it so that it stays fresh.

18. The ice cubes are in the _____ next to the popsicles.

noun	package
verb	pack
adjective	packed

19. Sorry, I brought a _____ lunch today so I don't need to go out.

20. I can't _____ anything else in this fridge; it's completely full.

21. It says on the _____ to add the sauce after the meat is cooked.

noun	grocer
noun	groceries
adjective	grocery

22. Take the _____ out of the trunk and put them in the refrigerator.

23. I went to the _____ store on the way home from school today to buy dinner.

24. The _____ packed the store's shelves with cereal and canned goods.

GEOGRAPHY

WORDS IN CONTEXT

Directions: Use one of the words in the box to complete each sentence.

island   equator   mountainous   terrain   continent

1. An _____ is a small section of land completely surrounded by water.

2. A _____ region is great for hiking or rock climbing.

3. The _____ is an imaginary circle around the middle of the earth.

4. The _____ varies from valleys to rocky peaks.

5. Asia is the largest _____ at 17,300,000 square miles.

| globe | population | valley | distance | far |

6. Over 6 billion inhabitants make up the world's _____ today.

7. A _____ is an area of lowland surrounded by hills or mountains.

8. The _____ between Africa and Australia is about 6,500 miles.

9. How _____ is it from Tokyo to New York?

10. A _____ is a model of the world that can be used like a map.

| volcano | planet | solar | atlas | altitude |

11. Many people use _____ heating to make good use of the sun's energy.

12. The _____ on Mount Etna erupted in 1964.

13. It is important to prepare for _____ change when hiking up a high mountain.

14. Pluto is the solar system's smallest _____ .

15. Turn to page 31 in your _____ for a map of the southern states.

WORD FAMILIES

Directions: Choose the correct form of the word to complete the sentence.

noun	equator
verb	equate
adjective	equatorial

16. This region of the continent is warm because of its _____ position.

17. You can _____ a river to a stream.

18. The _____ lies between the North and South Poles.

noun	globe
adjective	global
adjective	globular

19. Planet Earth is shaped like a _____.

20. A ball is _____ or spherical in shape.

21. _____ warming is an environmental concern about the earth's increase in temperature.

noun	population
verb	populate
adjective	populated

22. India is one of the most heavily _____ countries in the world and has over 1 billion people.

23. The high birth rate in China has made it the country with the greatest _____.

24. Human beings _____ the earth at a rate of about four babies per second.

FURNITURE AND FURNISHINGS

WORDS IN CONTEXT

Directions: Use one of the words in the box to complete each sentence.

couch	pillows	plastic	fabric	lift

1. If your back is sore you should let me _____ the heavy things.

2. _____ chairs are great for the patio because the weather won't damage them.

3. I sleep with two _____ under my head and one at my feet.

4. We need to find a strong _____ for the curtains so the light can't shine through.

5. Please don't put your feet up on the _____ when you have your shoes on.

paint	lamp	carpet	move	hang

6. The blue _____ in my bedroom is starting to chip off the walls.

7. We have only three days to _____ all of this furniture to the new house.

8. The old _____ needs to be replaced with floor tiles.

9. Do you think I should _____ that portrait over the fireplace?

10. The _____ in the dining room doesn't give off enough light.

wooden	furnish	carpenter	tablecloth	bedding

11. The _____ bed frame is made of either oak or pine.

12. I need to get a _____ that will cover up the stain on the table.

13. Would you mind getting out of bed so that I can change the _____?

14. I am going to _____ the living room with antiques.

15. A _____ made this wooden bookshelf by hand.

WORD FAMILIES

Directions: Choose the correct form of the word to complete the sentence.

noun	painting
noun	painter
verb	paint

16. My uncle is a famous _____ who uses water colors.

17. I bought that oil _____ at an auction last weekend.

18. Would you like to help me _____ the kitchen yellow?

noun	bed
noun	bedroom
noun	bedding

19. I had a really hard time getting out of _____ this morning.

20. You can sleep in the spare _____ down the hall.

21. I need new _____, including sheets and pillowcases.

noun	furniture
verb	furnish
adjective	furnished

22. I am renting a _____ apartment so I don't need my couch or my bed.

23. I'd like to buy some used _____, but it is very expensive.

24. We can _____ the dining room with a new table and chairs when we are finished painting.

Part IV: Incomplete Sentences— Skill Building Activities

This part of the test has incomplete sentences. Four words or phrases, marked (A), (B), (C), (D), are given beneath each sentence. You must choose the one word or phrase that best completes the sentence. Then, on your answer sheet, find the number of the question and mark your answer.

EXAMPLE: This soup doesn't _____ good.

    (A) tasteful
    (B) tasty
    (C) taste   Sample Answer
    (D) tasted   Ⓐ Ⓑ Ⓒ Ⓓ

The sentence should read, "This soup doesn't taste good." Therefore, you should choose answer (C).

The TOEIC Bridge test measures your general proficiency with English grammar. You should understand the following basic grammar.

Parts of Speech

Parts of speech are the different kinds of words we find in every language. Nouns, adjectives, verbs, adverbs, and prepositions are important parts of speech. You can identify a part of speech by (1) looking at the ending of a word, the *suffix*, or (2) by looking at the *word order* of a sentence.

SUFFIX

One way to recognize the part of speech of a word is to look at the suffix, the end of the word. For example, when you see *–ly* on the end of a word, it usually means this is an adverb (*happily, calmly, nicely*), and when you see *–tion* on the end, it usually means this is a noun (*caution, recognition, investigation*). There are many, many *exceptions*. Here are two exceptions: *friendly* looks like an adverb because it ends in *–ly*, but it's really an adjective; *sanction* can be a verb even though it ends in *–tion*.

WORD ORDER

Another way to recognize a part of speech is by looking at its position in a sentence. There are common word order patterns in English.

> *It was warm and the young children played noisily around the fountain.*
>   1   2   3   4   5   6   7

1. Because *warm* comes after *be*, *warm* is probably an adjective.
2. Because *young* is between the definite article *the* and another word *children*, *young* is probably an adjective.
3. Since *children* follows what we think is an adjective, we'd say this is a noun.
4. When we see the *–ed* on the end of *play*, we can assume play is a verb. We can also assume it's a verb because it follows a noun phrase (an article, an adjective, and a noun).
5. Since *noisily* comes after the verb play and ends in *–ly*, we think it's an adverb.
6. Since *around* is located after a verb and an adverb and before a noun phrase, we would guess that *around* is a preposition.
7. Since *fountain* comes after the definite article *the*, it must be a noun.

In this section, you will practice recognizing parts of speech by their suffixes and by their positions in sentences.

Circle the part of speech of the underlined word.

1. Mark swims very <u>quickly</u>.

    (A) noun
    (B) adjective
    (C) verb
    (D) adverb
    (E) preposition

2. Mary is a <u>fast</u> worker.

    (A) noun
    (B) adjective
    (C) verb
    (D) adverb
    (E) preposition

3. Kim's <u>concentration</u> is better than anybody's.

    (A) noun
    (B) adjective
    (C) verb
    (D) adverb
    (E) preposition

4. The children <u>walked</u> to school.

   (A) noun
   (B) adjective
   (C) verb
   (D) adverb
   (E) preposition

5. Mark <u>thoroughly</u> cleaned the house.

   (A) noun
   (B) adjective
   (C) verb
   (D) adverb
   (E) preposition

6. The students waited <u>at</u> the corner.

   (A) noun
   (B) adjective
   (C) verb
   (D) adverb
   (E) preposition

7. The woman's <u>curly</u> hair is attractive.

   (A) noun
   (B) adjective
   (C) verb
   (D) adverb
   (E) preposition

8. We will <u>leave</u> at noon.

   (A) noun
   (B) adjective
   (C) verb
   (D) adverb
   (E) preposition

9. The train <u>station</u> is near here.

   (A) noun
   (B) adjective
   (C) verb
   (D) adverb
   (E) preposition

10. There's been a lot of discussion <u>concerning</u> the new school.

   (A) noun
   (B) adjective
   (C) verb
   (D) adverb
   (E) preposition

SINGULAR AND PLURAL NOUNS

Nouns are either singular or plural.

Most nouns are regular. The plural form is made by adding –*s* or –*es* to the end of the noun.

table	tables	dish	dishes
street	streets	watch	watches
cat	cats	kiss	kisses

Some nouns are irregular. The plural form does not end in –*s*.

child	children	foot	feet
man	men	mouse	mice
woman	women	goose	geese
person	people	sheep	sheep
tooth	teeth	fish	fish

Words and phrases that begin with *each* or *every* are singular, even if the phrase includes a plural noun.

   Everyone is at the conference today.
   Every day flies by quickly.
   Each student has his own book.
   Each of the doors is locked.

Sometimes names contain plural nouns, but the name is still singular because it refers to a single unit.

   International Communications is the biggest company in this town.
   The Hotel Pink Sands offers excellent service.

Some nouns may look plural but are actually singular.

   The news was frightening.

Some nouns may look singular but are actually plural.

   The police visit this neighborhood regularly.

Choose the one word or phrase that best completes the sentence.

1. Every country _____ represented at the meeting.

   (A) are
   (B) is
   (C) be
   (D) being

2. All of my classes _____ interesting.

   (A) is
   (B) be
   (C) are
   (D) was

3. _____ has his own desk.

   (A) The employees
   (B) All employees
   (C) Every employee
   (D) Employees

4. We saw a lot of _____ at the park this afternoon.

   (A) younger
   (B) youngster
   (C) child
   (D) children

5. The _____ look very beautiful.

   (A) flowers
   (B) flower
   (C) flower pot
   (D) flower garden

6. I met a lot of interesting _____ on my vacation.

   (A) man
   (B) person
   (C) woman
   (D) people

7. The Hotel Palms _____ a private beach.

   (A) own
   (B) has
   (C) all own
   (D) have

8. The news _____ very exciting.

    (A) seem
    (B) is
    (C) are
    (D) sound

9. The _____ protect us from crime.

    (A) policewoman
    (B) police
    (C) police officer
    (D) policeman

10. Everybody _____ to pay attention.

    (A) needs
    (B) want
    (C) are
    (D) have

ARTICLES

A, *an*, and *the* are articles. They precede nouns. Sometimes an adjective is placed between the article and the noun.

A is used before singular count nouns:

> I read a book.
> I read a boring book.

An is used before words that begin with a vowel sound, either a singular count noun or an adjective followed by a singular count noun:

> It takes an hour to get there.
> An icy wind blew all night.

A and *an* are used to refer to a noun that is not specific. The speaker is not talking about a particular person, place, idea, or thing.

The is used before singular count nouns, plural count nouns, and non-count nouns.

> The movie was interesting.
> The apples tasted delicious.
> The old man walked slowly.

The specifies nouns. That means both the speaker and the listener know which thing, person, place, or idea is being discussed. Often a phrase or clause in the sentence specifies the noun:

> The movie <u>that John saw last night</u> was interesting.
> The questions <u>on this test</u> are easy to answer.

When speaking in general, *a* or *an* are used before singular count nouns:

A parrot is a smart bird.

When speaking in general, an article is not used before a plural count noun or a non-count noun:

Vegetables are good for your health.
Music is relaxing.

When speaking about a specific noun, an article is used before a plural count noun or a non-count noun:

The shoes in the shop window are on sale.
The milk in the refrigerator is spoiled.

Circle the one word or phrase that best completes the sentence.

1. _____ that I bought last week don't fit.

   (A) A shoe
   (B) New shoe
   (C) The shoes
   (D) Shoes

2. John gave Mary _____ on her birthday.

   (A) a present
   (B) nice present
   (C) present
   (D) any present

3. I received _____ from Arthur.

   (A) sad letter
   (B) a sad letter
   (C) letter
   (D) lettered

4. _____ John told us was very sad.

   (A) Story
   (B) The story
   (C) Stories
   (D) Long story

5. _____ in that store cost a lot of money.

   (A) Dress
   (B) A dress
   (C) Dresses
   (D) Dressing

6. _____ cause a lot of pollution.

    (A) A car
    (B) The car
    (C) Cars
    (D) Any car

7. _____ in that bottle isn't pure.

    (A) The water
    (B) A water
    (C) Waters
    (D) Watering

8. That's _____ that Elizabeth is carrying.

    (A) large umbrella
    (B) large umbrellas
    (C) umbrella
    (D) a large umbrella

9. I don't like _____ of their house.

    (A) color
    (B) colored
    (C) the color
    (D) coloring

10. _____ doesn't buy happiness.

    (A) Money
    (B) The money
    (C) Moneyed
    (D) Many

NOUNS—COUNT AND NON-COUNT

Count nouns are nouns that can be counted. They have both singular and plural forms.

    pencil—pencils
    bus—buses
    person—people
    vegetable—vegetables

Non-count nouns are usually not counted. They don't have a plural form.

    poultry   information
    machinery   health
    anger

Some nouns can be both count and non-count, but their meanings will change.

As Count Nouns	**As Non-Count Nouns**
a chicken/chickens = live bird(s)	chicken = a food
a paper/papers = newspaper(s), document(s)	paper = material made from wood pulp
a beauty/beauties = someone or something	beauty = the quality or qualities that is beautiful in a person or thing that gives pleasure to the senses
a work/works = individual creations, e.g.,	work = activity in which one books, operas exerts strength or faculties to do or perform something

DETERMINERS WITH COUNT NOUNS

Singular:

	A	I need a computer.
	An	He ate an orange.
	The	The plane is enormous.

Plural:

	The	The students are late.
	Some	Rick bought some shoes.
	Any	I don't see any clouds in the sky. (negative)
		Are there any cookies left? (question)
	Many	Many people work downtown.
	A lot of	A lot of movies are boring.
	A few	I have a few days for vacation.
	Few	They have few friends in this town. (negative idea)

Numbers are also used with count nouns.

There are three cars in the parking lot.
I read ten books last month.

DETERMINERS WITH NON-COUNT NOUNS

The	The food here is delicious.
Some	He gave me some information.
Any	They didn't drink any coffee.
	Did you drink any coffee?
Much	We don't have much time. (*much* is usually used after negative, not affirmative verbs)

A lot of	Jim spent a lot of money on his vacation.
A great deal of	He has a great deal of patience.
Little	I need a little advice.

Don't use *a/an* or numbers with non-count nouns.

Choose the one word or phrase that best completes the sentence.

1. We saw _____ children in the park.

   (A) some
   (B) much
   (C) a
   (D) any

2. Paul doesn't earn _____ money.

   (A) few
   (B) an
   (C) a
   (D) much

3. Do you have _____ cold drinking water?

   (A) many
   (B) any
   (C) few
   (D) an

4. Mary has _____ friends in Seoul.

   (A) much
   (B) any
   (C) a lot of
   (D) a little

5. Did you read _____ article in the newspaper?

   (A) few
   (B) some
   (C) little
   (D) the

6. We had _____ rain last spring.

   (A) many
   (B) ten days
   (C) a lot of
   (D) a

7. Did you meet _____ interesting people at the party?

   (A) any
   (B) an
   (C) much
   (D) little

8. The test was very hard so _____ students passed it.

   (A) little
   (B) few
   (C) much
   (D) any

9. George was really hungry so he ate _____ sandwiches.

   (A) much
   (B) a
   (C) three
   (D) a little

10. We bought _____ new equipment for our office.

   (A) many
   (B) any
   (C) some
   (D) few

PRONOUNS

Pronouns take the place of nouns. There are three basic types of pronouns—subject, object, and possessive pronouns.

Subject	Object	Possessive
I	me	mine
you	you	yours
he	him	his
she	her	hers
it	it	its
we	us	ours
they	them	theirs

SUBJECT

He took a train to Paris.
It's on the table.

OBJECT

John taught me how to drive.
Show us the money.

POSSESSIVE

That's Mary's homework, not yours.
Is this Robert's sandwich or mine?

1. _____ lives in Tokyo.

   (A) Me
   (B) Him
   (C) She
   (D) Your

2. Tom saw _____ on the bus yesterday.

   (A) you
   (B) you're
   (C) your
   (D) you've

3. _____ my math book.

   (A) He's
   (B) She's
   (C) It's
   (D) I'm

4. That's not Susan's homework, it's _____ .

   (A) my
   (B) mine
   (C) me
   (D) I

5. We sent _____ a present for his birthday.

   (A) she
   (B) him
   (C) his
   (D) her

6. This can't be your car because you parked _____ over there.

   (A) yours
   (B) your
   (C) you
   (D) you're

7. Sam and Sally got married last month and _____ are still very happy.

   (A) he
   (B) she
   (C) it
   (D) they

8. Please pick up your books and put _____ on the shelf.

   (A) they
   (B) their
   (C) it
   (D) them

9. Maria has a serious problem so I really want to help _____ .

   (A) she
   (B) her
   (C) he
   (D) his

10. Are these your keys, or are they _____ ?

    (A) our
    (B) you
    (C) us
    (D) ours

DEMONSTRATIVE ADJECTIVES

The demonstrative adjectives *this, that, these,* and *those* precede a noun or an adjective and a noun and are used to identify the noun.

This and *That* are used before singular count nouns and non-count nouns. *This* usually refers to something that is close to you. *That* usually refers to something that is far from you.

> This book here is yours.
> That umbrella by the door is wet.

This and *that* can also be used to show contrast.

> This seat is mine; that one is yours.

These and *Those* are used before plural nouns. *These* usually refers to things that are close to you. *Those* usually refers to things that are far from you.

> I have to mail these packages today.
> Would you hand me those pencils, please?

This, *that*, *these*, and *those* are also used as pronouns.

> This is my car.
> Those are expensive.

This and *that* can be used with the pronoun *one*.

> I want that one.
> This one is the best.

Choose the one word or phrase that best completes the sentence.

1. Harold saw _____ movie you told him about.

   (A) that
   (B) these
   (C) those
   (D) them

2. _____ shoes are too big for me.

   (A) This
   (B) That
   (C) Then
   (D) These

3. Look at _____ beautiful flowers.

   (A) those
   (B) this
   (C) than
   (D) that

4. _____ is delicious cake.

   (A) Those
   (B) These
   (C) Their
   (D) This

5. We've lived in _____ house for several years.

   (A) this
   (B) those
   (C) then
   (D) these

6. I think I'll buy _____ one.

   (A) that
   (B) thin
   (C) these
   (D) a

7. _____ coffee isn't hot enough.

   (A) These
   (B) They
   (C) This
   (D) Those

8. I have to read all _____ articles before tomorrow.

   (A) this
   (B) that
   (C) there
   (D) these

9. _____ was a funny TV program.

   (A) Those
   (B) Their
   (C) That
   (D) These

10. _____ are Lily's glasses.

    (A) These
    (B) The
    (C) This
    (D) Thus

PREPOSITIONS OF TIME

Prepositions are used with time expressions.

At refers to specific hours:

   The movie begins at 8:00.
   I'll leave the office at noon.

On refers to specific days or dates:

   Let's meet for lunch on Tuesday.
   My birthday is on April 15th.
   We saw a parade on Independence Day.

In refers to months, seasons, and years:

   My birthday is in April.
   Gerald and Betty got married in 1998.

By means *on* or *before*:

   I'll finish this project by Friday.
   You must pay your bills by the end of the month.

From ... to refer to the duration of an activity:

I'll be in New York from Sunday to Wednesday.
I'm on vacation from July 15th to July 22nd.

Between ... and also refer to the duration of an activity.

That store is open between 8:30 and 6:30.
The beaches are usually crowded between June and August.

Choose the one word or phrase that best completes the sentence.

1. He'll arrive in London _____ September 20th.

   (A) on
   (B) in
   (C) from
   (D) at

2. We usually take our vacation _____ July.

   (A) between
   (B) in
   (C) with
   (D) at

3. James will be in his office _____ 10:30 and 2:00.

   (A) since
   (B) in
   (C) to
   (D) between

4. The restaurant opens _____ 5:30.

   (A) at
   (B) behind
   (C) during
   (D) on

5. I need to talk to you _____ Friday.

   (A) by
   (B) from
   (C) between
   (D) with

6. Susan will be out of town _____ December 21st to December 31st.

   (A) between
   (B) from
   (C) while
   (D) since

7. I want to find a new job _____ the end of the year.

   (A) on
   (B) beside
   (C) by
   (D) in

8. It rains a lot _____ the winter.

   (A) to
   (B) at
   (C) on
   (D) in

9. We're going to a concert _____ Saturday evening.

   (A) near
   (B) on
   (C) since
   (D) between

10. Julie graduated from high school _____ 1997.

   (A) to
   (B) while
   (C) in
   (D) at

PREPOSITIONS OF LOCATION

Prepositions show the location of things.

on	across from
in	near
between	

Sometimes there are two or more prepositions of location that have the same meaning.

over, above	in front of
under, below, beneath	behind, in back of
beside, next to, by	

Choose the one word or phrase that best completes the sentence.

1. There is a big garden _____ my house.

   (A) after
   (B) next
   (C) behind
   (D) between

2. Put your shoes _____ the bed.

   (A) under
   (B) over
   (C) between
   (D) to

3. Francine hung David's picture on the wall _____ her bed.

   (A) with
   (B) after
   (C) up
   (D) over

4. I will wait for you _____ the restaurant.

   (A) between
   (B) side
   (C) in front of
   (D) to

5. I keep all my pens _____ this drawer.

   (A) of
   (B) in
   (C) on
   (D) to

6. I'd like a seat _____ the window, please.

   (A) by
   (B) for
   (C) as
   (D) since

7. They're building a new hotel _____ the street from my office.

   (A) over
   (B) across
   (C) before
   (D) of

8. There's a huge garage _____ this building.

   (A) without
   (B) during
   (C) under
   (D) to

9. The bank is _____ the grocery store.

   (A) on
   (B) next to
   (C) for
   (D) from

10. You can use that telephone _____ the table.

    (A) of
    (B) between
    (C) on
    (D) for

Subjects and Verbs

All sentences and clauses in English must contain a subject and a verb.

The subject is a noun or nouns, or a pronoun or pronouns.

> <u>Dogs</u> make nice pets.
> <u>Julie and Dan</u> went shopping yesterday.
> <u>It</u> is raining right now.
> <u>You and I</u> are good friends.

The one exception is in the case of imperative sentences (orders or commands). In this case the subject, *you*, is understood but not mentioned.

> Open the window, please.
> Have a seat while you wait.

The verb usually comes after the subject. The verb shows the action or condition of the subject.

> You <u>look</u> nice today.
> The children <u>played</u> soccer last weekend.

Choose the one word or phrase that best completes the sentence.

1. Mark _____ at the party last night.

    (A) were happy
    (B) happy was
    (C) was happy
    (D) was he happy

2. _____ a lot in the mountains.

    (A) Snows it
    (B) Is snowing
    (C) It snows
    (D) Snowing is

3. Sarah and her husband _____ the movies last Saturday.

    (A) was going
    (B) went to
    (C) they went
    (D) went they to

4. Chicago _____ city in the Midwest.

    (A) is an important
    (B) an important is
    (C) important is
    (D) is it important

5. The price of oil _____ last month.

    (A) fell
    (B) it fell
    (C) fell it
    (D) felt

6. _____ important to have a good job.

    (A) Is it
    (B) It's
    (C) It
    (D) Is

7. _____ a good concert.

    (A) People enjoys
    (B) Enjoy them
    (C) People they enjoy
    (D) People enjoy

8. _____ us with the vocabulary exercises.

    (A) Our teacher helps
    (B) Always helps
    (C) Our teacher
    (D) Helps to

9. _____ a lot of food at Jim's house last weekend.

    (A) Ate we
    (B) We ate
    (C) Ate
    (D) We

10. Every morning _____ coffee with her breakfast.

    (A) Jane she drink
    (B) she drink
    (C) drinks
    (D) Jane drinks

REDUNDANT SUBJECTS

Every clause must have a subject, but it can have only one subject. It cannot have two subjects. This is a common confusion with relative clauses. A relative clause describes a noun in the main clause.

> The car, <u>which is red</u>, is parked in the garage.
> (relative clause)

The relative clause gives the information we need to identify the car. The pronoun *which* refers to the car and is the subject of the relative clause. You do not need two subjects in the clause.

> Incorrect: The car, which *it* is red, is parked in the garage.

A relative clause begins with a word we call a **relative pronoun**. Common relative pronouns are *who*, *which*, and *that*. Sometimes the relative pronoun refers to the subject of the clause, as in the example below. Do not add another subject to the clause.

> Correct: Most of the people <u>who came to my party</u> work at my office.
> Incorrect: Most of the people <u>who they came to my party</u> work at my office.

Sometimes the relative pronoun refers to the object of the clause.

> The car, <u>which John was driving last night</u>, is parked in the garage.

In this case, *John* is the subject of the clause. *Which* refers to the car and is the object of the clause.

Choose the one word or phrase that best completes the sentence.

1. The tree, _____ behind my house, gives a lot of shade.

   (A) which it grows
   (B) which grows
   (C) grows
   (D) it grows

2. The person _____ my hair usually does a very good job.

   (A) who he cuts
   (B) who cuts
   (C) cuts it
   (D) cuts

3. The dress _____ last night was very pretty.

   (A) that you wore
   (B) that wore
   (C) wore it
   (D) wore

4. All the classes _____ this semester are difficult.

   (A) that are taking
   (B) they are
   (C) are taking
   (D) that I am taking

5. Those keys _____ are yours.

   (A) are on the table
   (B) that are on the table
   (C) they are on the table
   (D) that they are on the table

6. The woman _____ at the meeting was very interesting.

   (A) spoke
   (B) who she spoke
   (C) who spoke
   (D) she spoke

7. The pizza _____ for lunch had too much cheese.

   (A) that we ate
   (B) it ate
   (C) ate
   (D) that ate we

8. The house _____ in the mountains was very expensive.

   (A) it is rented
   (B) that Robert rented
   (C) rented it
   (D) that it rented

9. A dictionary is a book _____ the meanings of words.

   (A) that explains
   (B) that it explains
   (C) explains
   (D) explains them

10. Susan is the woman _____ get my new job.

    (A) who she helped me
    (B) who helped me
    (C) who I helped her
    (D) she helped me

SUBJECT-VERB AGREEMENT

A singular noun takes a singular verb and a plural noun takes a plural verb. We call this subject-verb agreement.

Singular	Plural
My apartment has three rooms.	These apartments have big rooms.
My cousin lives in another city.	My cousins live in a beautiful apartment.
This street is very noisy.	The streets are quiet at night.

Be careful; sometimes the subject and verb are separated by a phrase or clause, but the subject and verb still must agree.

The article on page 16 explains that problem.
(subject)   (verb)

The articles in this book are useful for this class.
(subject)   (verb)

Most of the people who live in this building work downtown.
(subject)   (verb)

The movie we saw last night was very funny.
(subject)   (verb)

Sometimes the subject is a gerund. A gerund takes a singular verb.

Searching web sites is easier with a fast computer.
Working long hours is not good for your health.

Choose the one word or phrase that best completes the sentence.

1. Many people _____ this city every year.

   (A) visits
   (B) visit
   (C) is visiting
   (D) was visiting

2. Learning foreign languages _____ important.

   (A) is
   (B) are
   (C) have
   (D) are having

3. The music that they listen to _____ them to relax.

   (A) help
   (B) are helping
   (C) helps
   (D) helping

4. The articles that John has written _____ difficult to understand.

   (A) has been
   (B) was
   (C) are
   (D) is

5. Taking a trip to the mountains _____ more fun than going to the beach.

   (A) are
   (B) were
   (C) is
   (D) have been

6. The water in this swimming pool _____ too cold.

   (A) are feeling
   (B) feel
   (C) feels
   (D) was feeling

7. Exercising every day _____ good for your health.

   (A) are
   (B) be
   (C) were
   (D) is

8. Going to the movies last night _____ a lot of fun.

   (A) were
   (B) was
   (C) are
   (D) being

9. The clothes in those boxes _____ to my sister.

   (A) belong
   (B) was belonging
   (C) is belonging
   (D) belongs

10. Some children _____ too many toys.

   (A) has
   (B) has had
   (C) have
   (D) is having

PRESENT TENSE

There are several ways of expressing the present in English.

SIMPLE PRESENT

The simple present tense refers to facts or events that happen as a habit.

> Fact: The sun rises in the east.
> Habit: We clean the house every weekend.

Negative sentences in the simple present tense are formed with *don't* or *doesn't*.

> The sun doesn't rise in the west.
> We don't clean the house on weekdays.

Questions in the simple present tense are formed with *do* or *does*.

> Where do you work?
> When does he play soccer?

PRESENT PROGRESSIVE

The present progressive tense refers to actions that are happening now. To form the present progressive tense, use <u>am/is/are + verb+ing</u>.

> A: What are you doing?
> B: I'm looking up her phone number.

> The students are working on their research reports this week.

To form a negative sentence in the present progressive tense, use <u>am/is/are + not + verb+ing</u>.

> Mary isn't working today.

PRESENT PERFECT

To form the present perfect tense, use <u>have/has + the past participle</u> form of the verb.
    The present perfect tense can refer to uninterrupted actions that started in the past and continue to the present.

> Melissa has worked for this company since 1998.
> The Smiths have lived here for many years.

The present perfect tense can also refer to completed actions that happened in the past and may happen again in the future.

> We've seen three movies this month.
> She's been to Hong Kong several times.

The present perfect tense also refers to actions that happened at an unspecified time in the past.

> I've already seen that movie.

The present perfect tense can also mean that an action happened in the very recent past.

A: Have you finished that report?
B: Yes, I have.

To form a negative sentence in the present perfect tense, use <u>have/has + not/n't + the past participle</u> form of the verb.

John hasn't worked here for very long.

PRESENT PERFECT PROGRESSIVE

The present perfect progressive tense refers to actions that started in the past and continue to the present. To form the present perfect progressive tense, use <u>have/has + been + verb+ing</u>.

We've been working hard on this project since last week.
Bill has been selling cars for about five years.

To form a negative sentence in the present perfect progressive tense, use <u>have/has + not/n't + been + verb+ing</u>.

We haven't been waiting long.

If a verb can be used in the present progressive, it can also be used in the present perfect progressive. If a verb can be used only in the simple present, it cannot be used in the present perfect progressive.

Correct:	They're working.	They've been working.
Incorrect:	I'm wanting.	I've been wanting.

Choose the one word or phrase that best completes the sentence.

1. We always _____ a present to Elsa on her birthday.

   (A) are taking
   (B) taking
   (C) take
   (D) are taken

2. I _____ Michael for years.

   (A) have known
   (B) know
   (C) knowing
   (D) was known

3. Rita _____ class every day.

   (A) not to attend
   (B) doesn't attend
   (C) not attending
   (D) isn't attended

4. Kevin can't talk on the phone because he _____ dinner right now.

    (A) is eating
    (B) eats
    (C) has eaten
    (D) has been eating

5. We _____ since 5:00.

    (A) talk
    (B) are talking
    (C) talking
    (D) have been talking

6. I don't want to go outside today because it _____.

    (A) rain
    (B) rains
    (C) is raining
    (D) is rain

7. My parents _____ in Florida since 1999.

    (A) has lived
    (B) have lived
    (C) are living
    (D) live

8. Babies _____ when they are hungry.

    (A) cry
    (B) are crying
    (C) have been crying
    (D) cries

9. The store _____ two sales so far this year.

    (A) is having
    (B) has been having
    (C) has
    (D) has had

10. Mr. and Mrs. Wilson _____ some disputes with their neighbors.

    (A) having
    (B) have been having
    (C) have having
    (D) have been had

PAST TENSE

There are several ways of expressing the past in English.

SIMPLE PAST

The simple past tense refers to actions <u>that began and ended at a particular time in the past</u>.

> Howard called Marian last night.
> I found a new job two weeks ago.

Negative sentences in the simple past tense are formed with *didn't* and the base form of the verb.

> Max didn't come to class yesterday.

Questions in the simple past tense are formed with *did* and the base form of the verb.

> Where did you work?

PAST PROGRESSIVE

The past progressive tense is used to focus on the progress of an action in the past, not on its completion.

> I was eating dinner at 7:00 last night.

Often, the past progressive tense refers to an action in the past that was interrupted by another action.

> I was eating dinner when you called at 7:00 last night.

The past progressive tense also refers to two actions that were in progress at the same time in the past.

> Laura was watching TV while Rob was cooking dinner.

To form the past progressive tense, use <u>was/were + verb+ing</u>.

PAST PERFECT

The past perfect tense refers to an action that was *completed* before a time or before another action in the past.

> Bill had left work by 4:30.
> George had already eaten dinner when he got home.

To form the past perfect tense, use <u>had + the past participle</u> form of the verb.

PAST PERFECT PROGRESSIVE

The past perfect progressive tense refers to an action that was in progress before a time in the past or before another action in the past.

> By 10:30, we had been waiting for the bus for 45 minutes.
> We had been watching the news all morning when the phone rang.

To form the past perfect progressive tense, use <u>had + been + verb+ing</u>.

Choose the one word or phrase that best completes the sentence.

1. I _____ the house before you called.

   (A) leave
   (B) am leaving
   (C) had left
   (D) had been leaving

2. The Wagners _____ to Florida two years ago.

   (A) moved
   (B) had been moving
   (C) move
   (D) will move

3. We _____ to the baseball game when it started to rain.

   (A) are driving
   (B) drives
   (C) driven
   (D) were driving

4. Louise was listening to the radio while she _____ the house.

   (A) is cleaning
   (B) was cleaning
   (C) had cleaned
   (D) will clean

5. Paul and Linda _____ us to their party last weekend.

   (A) was inviting
   (B) invited
   (C) had been inviting
   (D) will invite

6. It _____ a lot last winter.

   (A) snows
   (B) has been snowing
   (C) snowed
   (D) snow

7. We _____ in the plane for hours when it finally took off.

   (A) had been sitting
   (B) have sat
   (C) will be sitting
   (D) will sit

8. Before the police arrived, the robbers _____ .

   (A) run
   (B) had run
   (C) have run
   (D) have been running

9. I _____ on the bus when I dropped my wallet.

   (A) am getting
   (B) get
   (C) have gotten
   (D) was getting

10. The telephone _____ ten times before Patsy finally answered it.

    (A) rings
    (B) ringing
    (C) had rung
    (D) is ringing

FUTURE TENSE

There are several ways to express future time in English.

SIMPLE FUTURE

The simple future with *will* refers to future plans, predictions, and willingness.

> We'll get together next week.
> John will be happy to see you tomorrow.
> I'll answer the phone.

To form the simple future tense, use <u>will + the base form of the verb</u>.
It is also common to use <u>am/is/are + going to + the base form</u> of the verb to refer to future plans and predictions.

> They are going to take the bus this afternoon.

FUTURE PROGRESSIVE

The future progressive tense refers to an action that will be in progress in the future. Often, this is an action that will be interrupted by another action.

> The children will be sleeping when Rita gets home tonight.

The future progressive also refers to an action that will be in progress in the future at the same time another action is taking place.

I will be enjoying my vacation while you're working at the office.

To form the future progressive tense, use <u>will + be + verb+ing</u>. It is also common to use <u>am/is/are + going to + be + verb+ing</u> to refer to a future progressive idea.

We are going to be painting the house while you are away.

FUTURE PERFECT

The future perfect tense refers to an action that will be completed before a time or before another action at a more distant point in the future.

I will have eaten dinner by 8:00.
The teacher will have started the lesson by the time you get to class.

To form the future perfect tense, use <u>will + have + the past participle</u> form of the verb.

FUTURE PERFECT PROGRESSIVE

The future perfect progressive tense refers to an action that will be in progress before a time or before another action in the future.

By next Friday, we will have been working on this report for two weeks.
By the time this course ends, I will have been studying English for ten months.

To form the future perfect progressive tense, use <u>will + have + been + verb+ing</u>.

THE PRESENT PROGRESSIVE

This verb form is very often used to indicate a planned action in the near future.

A: What are you doing tonight?
B: We're going to a hockey game. Want to come?

The students are working on their research papers next week.

THE SIMPLE PRESENT

This verb form can be used to refer to scheduled future events that take place just once or are repeated.

Ms. Kwan meets with the committee in Jakarta in two weeks.
Flight 897 leaves at 6:00 P.M. from Gate 29 tomorrow.

Choose the one word or phrase that best completes the sentence.

1. Barbara _____ that package to you tomorrow morning.

   (A) deliver
   (B) is going to deliver
   (C) are going to deliver
   (D) delivering

2. By next month, I _____ at this company for a year.

   (A) will work
   (B) will be working
   (C) will have been working
   (D) am going to work

3. By the time this movie is over, we _____ this entire bag of popcorn.

   (A) will have eaten
   (B) are eating
   (C) are going to be eating
   (D) will be eaten

4. We _____ soccer while you're swimming at the pool.

   (A) were playing
   (B) will have been playing
   (C) has been playing
   (D) are going to be playing

5. We _____ for you tomorrow when you arrive at the airport.

   (A) are waiting
   (B) will be waiting
   (C) wait
   (D) waited

6. The price of gasoline _____ up again next month.

   (A) will go
   (B) going
   (C) is going to
   (D) has gone

7. When we get to the party, everybody _____.

   (A) are dancing
   (B) will be dancing
   (C) has danced
   (D) dances

8. My schedule's perfect! I _____ in Rio de Janeiro just in time for Carnaval.

   (A) be arriving
   (B) will have arrived
   (C) arriving
   (D) arrive

9. I _____ five new books by the time my vacation is over.

   (A) will have read
   (B) be reading
   (C) have read
   (D) have been reading

10. Be careful. You _____ into delicate negotiations at the conference next week.

    (A) will have been entering
    (B) have entered
    (C) are entering
    (D) will have entered

STATIVE VERBS

Stative verbs describe a condition or a state rather than an action. Stative verbs may refer to:

feelings and desires: like, love, hate, fear, prefer, need, want
appearance: look, seem, appear
possession: have, own, belong
perception: see, hear, smell
ideas: think, believe, agree, know, understand

Stative verbs aren't usually used in progressive tenses.

Correct:	I understand a lot of English now.
Incorrect:	I am understanding a lot of English now.

Correct:	I saw some interesting art at the museum.
Incorrect:	I was seeing some interesting art at the museum.

Some verbs may have both a stative meaning and an action meaning. If they have an action meaning, they are used in progressive tenses.

I <u>have</u> a lot of money in my pocket. (stative—the money belongs to me)
They're <u>having</u> lunch with some visitors from out of town. (action—*have* means *eat* in this sentence)

You <u>look</u> tired today. (stative—your appearance is tired.)
I'm <u>looking</u> in the dictionary but I can't find that word. (action—it is something I am doing with my eyes)

They thought the price was too high. (stative—they believed the price was too high)
I was thinking about work when you called. (action—my mind was active)

Choose the one word or phrase that best completes the sentence.

1. Jack _____ cold weather.

    (A) dislike
    (B) was disliking
    (C) is disliking
    (D) dislikes

2. Carol and Sam really _____ the present we gave them.

    (A) love
    (B) was loving
    (C) loves
    (D) are loved

3. I need your advice because I _____ about buying a new car.

    (A) thinks
    (B) am thinking
    (C) thinking
    (D) think

4. I _____ it's time to leave now, don't you?

    (A) am thinking
    (B) think
    (C) was thinking
    (D) thought

5. My parents _____ to buy a new car this month.

    (A) is wanting
    (B) are wanting
    (C) want
    (D) wants

6. When I walked in the door, I _____ the telephone ring.

    (A) heard
    (B) hear
    (C) was hearing
    (D) am hearing

7. We _____ breakfast early this morning.

   (A) has
   (B) have been
   (C) having
   (D) are having

8. Please be quiet because I _____ to the radio right now.

   (A) listened
   (B) listen
   (C) am listening
   (D) was listening

9. While Harry was walking to work, he _____ a car accident

   (A) saw
   (B) was seeing
   (C) sees
   (D) is seen

10. We _____ a lot of interesting people when we lived in New York.

    (A) were knowing
    (B) knew
    (C) know
    (D) were known

GERUNDS AND INFINITIVES

Gerunds are formed by adding *–ing* to the base form of a verb: thinking, walking, studying.

Gerunds or gerund noun phrases can be used as the subject of a sentence:

> *Smoking* is bad for your health.
> *Learning languages* is fun.

Gerunds or gerund noun phrases are used after certain verbs such as *enjoy, finish, keep, mind,* and *practice* as the object of a sentence:

> Nigel enjoys bowling.
> Would you mind helping me with these statistics?

Gerunds follow prepositions:

> I am interested in working for your company.
> We talked about going to the beach.

Gerunds follow the main verb of a sentence:

> Carlos and Anna enjoy going to the movies.
> They finished painting the house last week.

Infinitives are formed by adding *to* to the base form of a verb: to think, to walk, to study. Infinitives follow adjectives:

It's important to get a good job.
It's easy to use a computer.

Infinitives, like gerunds, follow the main verb of a sentence:

Mario wants to go fishing tomorrow.
I need to call my mother tonight.

Some verbs can be followed only by gerunds, for example:

enjoy, finish, quit, consider, admit, discuss, avoid, practice, dislike, suggest

Some verbs can be followed only by infinitives, for example:

want, need, would like, choose, agree, plan, learn, expect, decide, seem, promise

Some verbs can be followed by either gerunds or infinitives, for example:

begin, continue, like, love, hate, prefer, start

Choose the one word or phrase that best completes the sentence.

1. Kim dislikes _____ to rock concerts because the music is too loud.

   (A) to go
   (B) goes
   (C) going
   (D) gone

2. I'm afraid of _____ alone at night.

   (A) to walk
   (B) walk
   (C) walked
   (D) walking

3. My parents would like _____ us next month.

   (A) to visit
   (B) visit
   (C) visits
   (D) will visit

4. _____ is fun when the weather's hot.

   (A) Swam
   (B) Swim
   (C) Swimming
   (D) Swims

5. We were so glad _____ you last week.

 (A) to see
 (B) saw
 (C) have seen
 (D) seen

6. John agreed _____ us at 8:00.

 (A) meets
 (B) to meet
 (C) meeting
 (D) met

7. My brother quit _____ five years ago.

 (A) smokes
 (B) smoke
 (C) smoked
 (D) smoking

8. You should learn _____ the piano.

 (A) to play
 (B) playing
 (C) will play
 (D) played

9. Sometimes Harry thinks about _____ to another city.

 (A) to move
 (B) moving
 (C) moves
 (D) move

10. My daughter will begin _____ Chinese next semester.

 (A) will study
 (B) to study
 (C) studies
 (D) study

VERBS PLUS PREPOSITIONS

Phrasal verbs are a combination of a verb and a preposition. They are very common in English. Be careful—the meaning of a phrasal verb might be very different from the meaning of a verb alone.

I <u>got</u> a present for my birthday. (Meaning: I received a present.)
I <u>got on</u> the bus. (Meaning: I entered the bus.)

Phrasal verbs are either separable or inseparable. The majority of them are separable. Separable phrasal verbs allow the object to be placed between the verb and the preposition or after the preposition.

> Mary called John up.
> Mary called up John.

If the object is a pronoun, it must be placed between the verb and preposition.

> Correct: Mary called him up.
> Incorrect: Mary called up him.

Some separable verbs:

> call back, call up, drop off, pick up, find out, give back, look up, hand in, help out, put away, put on, take off, turn on, turn off, think over

Inseparable verbs cannot be separated by the object. The object must be placed after the preposition, whether or not it is a pronoun.

> Correct: We will go over the homework in class.
>   We will go over it in class.
> Incorrect: We will go the homework over in class.

Some inseparable verbs:

> go after, run into, stick with, call on, come across, get on, get off, get over, go over, look after

Choose the one word or phrase that best completes the sentence.

1. I _____ at the mall last Saturday.

   (A) ran into some friends
   (B) ran them into
   (C) ran some friends into
   (D) ran some friends

2. Can you _____ with this report?

   (A) help out me
   (B) help me out
   (C) helping out me
   (D) help to me out

3. I have to _____ to John.

   (A) give back it
   (B) give back them
   (C) give back to this book
   (D) give back this book

4. Martha fell when she _____.

   (A) got the bus off
   (B) got off the bus
   (C) got her off
   (D) got off on the bus

5. I know this project is hard, but you should _____.

   (A) stick with it
   (B) stick the project with
   (C) stick it with
   (D) stick you with

6. I _____ and now I can't find them.

   (A) took off it
   (B) took off them
   (C) took my glasses off
   (D) my glasses took off

7. If you don't know a phone number, you can _____ in the directory.

   (A) look up it
   (B) look them up
   (C) look it up
   (D) look it

8. I can _____ while you're on vacation.

   (A) look them after
   (B) look after your cats
   (C) look your cats after
   (D) look it after

9. I _____ while reading this magazine.

   (A) came an idea across
   (B) came it across
   (C) came them across
   (D) came across an idea

10. After the children finish playing soccer, I will _____.

   (A) pick up them
   (B) pick it up
   (C) pick them up
   (D) pick him up

CONDITIONALS

In a conditional sentence, the *if* clause expresses the condition and the main clause expresses the result of the condition.

> I will go to the concert tonight if I have time.
>   main clause   *if* clause

Conditionals may be real or unreal. Real conditionals refer to things that are true or can be true. In a real conditional sentence, the *if* clause is always in the present tense. The main clause may be in the present tense or the future tense.

> present idea—I always take an umbrella if it rains.
> future idea—If the weather is nice next weekend, we will go on a picnic.

Unreal conditionals refer to things that are not true or cannot be true.

> I would buy a house if I had enough money.

This is unreal because it isn't true now. The truth is that I don't have enough money so I won't buy a house.

Unreal conditionals express present or past ideas. For a present unreal conditional, use a past tense verb in the *if* clause and *would + base form* of the verb in the main clause. *Could* or *might* can be used in place of *would*.

> If Mary lived in this city, I would see her every weekend.

This sentence is unreal because Mary doesn't really live in this city and I don't really see her every weekend.

In a present unreal conditional, when the main verb is *be*, always use *were*; never use *was*.

> Robert would enjoy this party if he were here.

Unreal conditionals about the past use the past perfect form of the verb in the *if* clause and *would + have + the past participle* form of the verb in the main clause. *Could* or *might* can be used in place of would.

> If you had come to the party last week, I would have danced with you.
> Mary might have gone to work yesterday if she hadn't been sick.

Choose the one word or phrase that best completes the sentence.

1. I'll help you with your homework if I _____ time tomorrow.

    (A) will have
    (B) have
    (C) would have
    (D) had

2. Tina and Doug always _____ a walk after dinner if the weather is nice.

   (A) took
   (B) would have taken
   (C) will have taken
   (D) take

3. If you had been more serious at your last job, you _____ that promotion.

   (A) will get
   (B) get
   (C) would have gotten
   (D) got

4. If that jacket _____ so expensive, I would buy it.

   (A) wasn't
   (B) weren't
   (C) isn't
   (D) won't be

5. Jack _____ so many accidents if he drove more carefully.

   (A) would have
   (B) wouldn't have
   (C) won't have
   (D) would have had

6. If you _____ me about your birthday last month, I would have sent you a card.

   (A) remind
   (B) would remind
   (C) will remind
   (D) had reminded

7. If we get to the restaurant early tonight, we _____ to wait for a table.

   (A) won't have
   (B) hadn't
   (C) don't have
   (D) wouldn't have

8. This apartment _____ perfect if the rooms were a little bit larger.

   (A) were
   (B) would be
   (C) will be
   (D) was

9. If you _____ a pet bird, you'll have to buy a cage, too.

   (A) buy
   (B) will buy
   (C) bought
   (D) had bought

10. If it _____ last weekend, we would have gone skiing.

   (A) snowed
   (B) would have snowed
   (C) had snowed
   (D) would snow

PASSIVE-ACTIVE MODES

Transitive verbs (verbs that can have objects) can be used in either the active voice or the passive voice.

In an active voice sentence, the subject performs the action. The subject is the focus of the sentence.

Subject	Active Verb	Object	
The office manager	*orders*	*new supplies*	every week.
The president	*gave*	*a speech*	last night.

In an active voice sentence, the subject is the *agent*, or performer, of the action. The object is the *receiver* of the action.

In a passive voice sentence, the subject is the receiver of the action. The focus is on the action. You may or may not mention the agent. Use the word *by* if you mention the agent.

Recipient	Passive Verb	Agent	
New supplies	*are ordered*		every week.
A speech	*was given*	*by the president*	last night.

Passive verbs are formed with the verb *to be* and the past participle of the verb.

present tense   Japanese *is spoken* here.
past tense   The reports *were written* last week.
future tense   The awards *will be presented* by the director.

Choose the one word or phrase that best completes the sentence.

1. Tropical fruits _____ by farmers in the lowland region.

   (A) are grown
   (B) grown
   (C) are growing
   (D) grow

2. Concert tickets _____ at the box office.

   (A) is selling
   (B) sold
   (C) are sold
   (D) is sold

3. Marilyn _____ her car to a friend because she couldn't drive.

   (A) were selling
   (B) sold
   (C) was sold
   (D) were sold

4. We _____ all the windows last weekend.

   (A) washed
   (B) were washed
   (C) was washing
   (D) wash

5. The new bridge _____ before the end of next month.

   (A) will be completed
   (B) will complete
   (C) is completed
   (D) completes

6. I _____ you a copy of the article tomorrow.

   (A) send
   (B) was sending
   (C) will send
   (D) will be sent

7. John always _____ his car in the lot by the school.

   (A) park
   (B) parks
   (C) is parked
   (D) was parked

8. Florida _____ by thousands of tourists every winter.

   (A) visited
   (B) visits
   (C) was visited
   (D) is visited

9. The electric lightbulb _____ by Thomas Edison.

   (A) invented
   (B) was invented
   (C) invents
   (D) is invented

10. I _____ your keys on the table by the bed last night.

    (A) saw
    (B) are seen
    (C) was seen
    (D) see

Adjectives and Adverbs

Adjectives describe nouns. They usually precede the noun.

> I live in a <u>quiet</u> <u>neighborhood</u>.
>   (adj)   (noun)

> We ate a <u>delicious</u> <u>meal</u> at that restaurant.
>   (adj)   (noun)

Adjectives follow the verb "to be" and certain other verbs called linking verbs, such as: look, seem, taste, feel, appear, sound.

> Susan is very creative.
> You look tired today.

Adjectives in English don't have a plural form.

> Correct: Those are beautiful flowers.
> Incorrect: Those are beautifuls flowers.

Adverbs give information about verbs. They often answer the question *How?* These adverbs are called *adverbs of manner*. They are usually formed by adding *–ly* to the end of an adjective. Adverbs usually follow the verb or the object.

> Please <u>talk</u> <u>quietly</u>.
>   (verb) (adverb)

> She <u>plays</u> the <u>piano</u> <u>beautifully</u>.
>   (verb)   (object) (adverb)

Adverbs also describe adjectives and other adverbs. They usually precede the adjective or adverb they describe.

That test was <u>surprisingly</u> <u>easy</u>.
  (adverb)   (adjective)

You answered the question <u>extremely</u> <u>well</u>.
  (adverb)   (adverb)

Choose the one word or phrase that best completes the sentence.

1. It's too _____ to work in here.

   (A) noisily
   (B) noisy
   (C) noise
   (D) noises

2. Your garden is _____ beautiful.

   (A) perfectly
   (B) perfect
   (C) perfected
   (D) perfection

3. We met several _____ people at the party.

   (A) interestingly
   (B) interest
   (C) interesting
   (D) interests

4. The weather is bad tonight so please drive _____.

   (A) careful
   (B) caring
   (C) cared
   (D) carefully

5. Steve ate his dinner _____.

   (A) quick
   (B) quickly
   (C) quicken
   (D) quickened

6. Elizabeth sounded _____ on the telephone last night.

   (A) happily
   (B) happening
   (C) happy
   (D) happens

7. Bill ordered two _____ pizzas.

   (A) large
   (B) largeness
   (C) largely
   (D) largest

8. The weather yesterday was extremely _____.

   (A) hotly
   (B) hot
   (C) heat
   (D) heater

9. These are very _____ chairs.

   (A) comfort
   (B) comfortably
   (C) comfortable
   (D) comforts

10. Please play that music _____.

    (A) softly
    (B) soften
    (C) soft
    (D) softens

ADJECTIVES—COMPARATIVE AND SUPERLATIVE

The comparative form of adjectives is used to compare two things.

> A car is fast. It's <u>faster</u> than a bicycle.
> Your house is beautiful. It's <u>more beautiful</u> than mine.

One-syllable adjectives and two-syllable adjectives that end with *–y* use *–er* in the comparative form.

> big—bigger, old—older, cold—colder, hard—harder, pretty—prettier, happy—happier, easy—easier

Most other two-syllable adjectives and adjectives of three or more syllables don't use *–er* in the comparative form. They use *more*.

> beautiful—more beautiful, comfortable—more comfortable, difficult—more difficult, interesting—more interesting

Be careful, *–er* and *more* are not used together.

> Correct: Today is hotter than yesterday.
> Incorrect: Today is more hotter than yesterday.

When two things are compared in one clause, the comparative adjective is followed by *than*.

My new car is bigger <u>than</u> my old car.

When one thing is compared to a group of three or more things, the superlative form of the adjective is used.

Mount Everest is <u>the highest</u> mountain in the world.
This is <u>the most expensive</u> computer in the store.

A superlative adjective is always preceded by *the*.

One-syllable adjectives and adjectives that end in *–y* use *–est* in the superlative form.

high—highest, old—oldest, long—longest, shiny—shiniest, easy—easiest

Most other two-syllable adjectives and adjectives of three or more syllables don't use *–est*. They use *most* in the superlative form.

expensive—the most expensive, delicious—the most delicious,
boring—the most boring

Be careful, *–est* and *most* are not used together.

Correct: The Nile is the longest river in the world.
Incorrect: The Nile is the most longest river in the world.

Some two-syllable adjectives can be used with either *–er* or *more* in the comparative form, and with either *–est* or *most* in the superlative form.

handsome   handsomer—more handsome   the handsomest—the most handsome
narrow   narrower—more narrow   the narrowest—the most narrow

Some more examples are *common, simple,* and *polite*.

Choose the one word or phrase that best completes the sentence.

1. My grandmother is _____ person in my family.

    (A) old
    (B) older
    (C) the oldest
    (D) oldest

2. Chris is _____ than his brother.

    (A) shorter
    (B) short
    (C) shortest
    (D) the shortest

3. We always travel by train because it is _____ than a bus.

   (A) comfortable
   (B) the comfortable
   (C) more comfortable
   (D) the most comfortable

4. I've tried all the desserts at this restaurant, but this one is _____ of them all.

   (A) delicious
   (B) the most delicious
   (C) most delicious
   (D) more delicious

5. I play checkers sometimes, but I think chess is _____.

   (A) an interesting
   (B) more interesting
   (C) more interesting than
   (D) interestingly

6. Biology is _____ of all my classes this semester.

   (A) the hardest
   (B) harder
   (C) hardly
   (D) harder than

7. Listening to music is _____ dancing.

   (A) relaxing than
   (B) the most relaxing
   (C) relaxing
   (D) more relaxing than

8. Today is _____ day we have had all week.

   (A) colder than
   (B) the coldest
   (C) colder
   (D) coldest

9. You should wear this dress because it's _____ that one.

   (A) elegant
   (B) the most elegant
   (C) more elegant than
   (D) the elegant

10. I like that sofa, but this one is _____.

   (A) cheaper
   (B) cheaper than
   (C) cheaply
   (D) cheapen

ADJECTIVES—DESCRIPTIVE PHRASES

Sometimes a phrase acts like an adjective. It describes a noun.

> The man <u>standing by the door</u> <u>comes</u> from China.
> (subject) (descriptive phrase) (verb)

Don't confuse words in the descriptive phrase with other words in the sentence. The main verb in this sentence is *comes*. *Standing* is not the main verb; it is part of the descriptive phrase. In this example, the descriptive phrase tells us which man comes from China.

There are several types of descriptive phrases:

- A **participle phrase** begins with a gerund or a past participle.

  > The boy <u>watching TV</u> is my son.
  > The car <u>parked outside</u> belongs to my neighbor.

- An **infinitive phrase** begins with an infinitive.

  > The last person <u>to get home</u> should turn out the lights.

- A **prepositional phrase** begins with a preposition.

  > The food <u>at that restaurant</u> is delicious.

Choose the one word or phrase that best completes the sentence.

1. The plant _____ the window needs water.

   (A) by the time
   (B) by
   (C) is by
   (D) is

2. The people _____ next door aren't very friendly.

   (A) are living
   (B) live
   (C) living
   (D) is living

3. Most of the programs _____ on TV aren't very interesting.

   (A) show
   (B) shows
   (C) shown
   (D) are showing

4. Kathleen was the only student _____ the test.

   (A) fails
   (B) is failing
   (C) failed
   (D) to fail

5. The people _____ this office are very helpful.

   (A) in
   (B) work
   (C) are working
   (D) work in

6. Neil Armstrong was the first person _____ on the moon.

   (A) has walked
   (B) to walk
   (C) walks
   (D) walks to

7. I want to buy the house _____ the end of the street.

   (A) to be
   (B) is
   (C) is at
   (D) at

8. The fruit _____ in this area is really delicious.

   (A) grows
   (B) grown
   (C) is growing
   (D) grow

9. That girl _____ in the corner looks lonely.

   (A) is sitting
   (B) sat
   (C) sitting
   (D) sits

10. Ivan was the last person _____ at the party.

   (A) to arrive
   (B) arrived
   (C) arrives
   (D) was arriving

ADVERBS—DATE, TIME, SEQUENCE

Certain adverbs describe when things happen. You must pay attention to grammar as well as to the meaning of the adverb.

These phrases must be followed by a complete clause:

By the time (before)

By the time the rain stopped, everyone had gone home.

As soon as (immediately after)

As soon as class is over, we'll go to the movies.

These words are followed by either a clause or a gerund:

While (at the same time)

Marina saw a bad accident while she was driving to work.
Sam cut his finger while preparing dinner.

When (after or while)

I'll cook dinner when I get home.
When we visited New York, we went to a lot of museums.
You should be careful when crossing the street.

These words are followed either by a clause, a noun, or a gerund:

After

It started to rain after Bob got home.
Let's talk about it after the meeting.
I always feel sleepy after eating a big meal.

Before

Before you watch TV, you should finish your homework.
I usually exercise before work.
I always finish my homework before eating dinner.

Since (describes when something begins)

I've learned a lot since I started my new job.
I've been feeling sick since this morning.
Marco has been feeling depressed since losing his job.

Choose the one word or phrase that best completes the sentence.

1. I read the book _____ seeing the movie.

   (A) by the time
   (B) as soon as
   (C) before
   (D) behind

2. Jane fell asleep _____ she was watching TV.

   (A) before
   (B) again
   (C) while
   (D) soon

3. It's been snowing _____ last night.

   (A) as soon as
   (B) while
   (C) by the time
   (D) since

4. Feed the dog _____ you get home.

   (A) soon
   (B) as soon as
   (C) as soon
   (D) sooner than

5. Cindy usually gets up early and works for an hour _____ breakfast.

   (A) while
   (B) before
   (C) when
   (D) as soon as

6. I felt better _____ talking to you.

   (A) by the time
   (B) as soon
   (C) after
   (D) later

7. I spent a lot of money _____ I went to the grocery store.

   (A) when
   (B) on
   (C) by
   (D) from

8. John has seemed more relaxed _____ he moved to the country.

   (A) from
   (B) by
   (C) on
   (D) since

9. _____ Richard got home, he called Lisa.

   (A) While
   (B) As soon as
   (C) Time
   (D) By

10. Please wash the dishes _____ dinner.

   (A) as soon as
   (B) when
   (C) after
   (D) on

ADVERBS OF FREQUENCY

Adverbs of frequency refer to how often something happens. Some common adverbs of frequency are:

(100%)
always
usually
often, frequently
sometimes, occasionally
rarely, seldom
never
(0%)

Most adverbs of frequency are next to the verb. They usually precede the verb.

I always come to class on time.
Ms. Gomez sometimes works late.
Bob rarely eats dessert.

Adverbs of frequency follow the verb *to be*.

The teacher is never late for class.
I'm always hungry at noon.
It's usually cold in the winter.

Never, *seldom*, and *rarely* are negative words. These words are not used with *not*.

We never stay home on weekends. (correct)
We don't never go to the movies. (incorrect)

Some adverbs of frequency can be put at the beginning or the end of the sentence.

sometimes
usually
frequently
generally

> Sometimes Mrs. Gomez works late.
> Mrs. Gomez works late sometimes.

Some adverbs always belong at the end of the sentence or clause.

daily (every day)
weekly (every week)
monthly (every month)
yearly (every year)
annually (every year)

> John plays golf weekly.
> We pay our taxes annually.

Words such as *daily*, *weekly*, and *yearly* can be adjectives and adverbs.

As Adjectives	As Adverbs
the daily paper	He reads the paper daily.
weekly lesson plans	She writes lesson plans weekly.
yearly property taxes	They pay their property taxes yearly.

Choose the one word or phrase that best completes the sentence.

1. I take a vacation with my family _____ .

   (A) always
   (B) yearly
   (C) daily
   (D) never

2. Exercise is important for your health so you should exercise _____ .

   (A) daily
   (B) usually
   (C) annually
   (D) yearly

3. Tina doesn't like coffee so she _____ drinks it.

   (A) always
   (B) weekly
   (C) often
   (D) never

4. Jack is a busy man who _____ has time to relax.

   (A) always
   (B) daily
   (C) rarely
   (D) yearly

5. My children enjoy soccer, which they _____ play on weekends.

   (A) often
   (B) rarely
   (C) seldom
   (D) never

6. Our office has a meeting every Friday because it's important to meet _____ .

   (A) annually
   (B) weekly
   (C) monthly
   (D) daily

7. I like to read the newspaper, but I don't _____ have time to read it.

   (A) daily
   (B) never
   (C) usually
   (D) weekly

8. It's _____ cheaper to buy things on sale.

   (A) always
   (B) never
   (C) daily
   (D) monthly

9. Sarah is a lazy student who doesn't _____ do her homework.

   (A) daily
   (B) never
   (C) usually
   (D) monthly

10. Don't forget to pay your rent _____ .

   (A) monthly
   (B) never
   (C) usually
   (D) seldom

Conjunctions

Conjunctions connect ideas in a sentence. Pay attention to the use of each conjunction.

And connects similar ideas:

> John likes pizza and ice cream.
> Mary works downtown, and Tom does too.

And can be used with *both:*

> Both Tom and Mary enjoy swimming.

Similar ideas are also connected with *not only...but also:*

> He's not only good-looking, but he's also rich.

Two negative ideas are connected with *neither...nor,* or with *and...not either:*

> Neither Chris nor Martha went to the party.
> Chris didn't go to the party, and Martha didn't either.

But connects opposite ideas or contradictions:

> Cindy doesn't like pizza, but she loves ice cream.
> Bruce usually watches TV in the evening, but Lisa doesn't.
> It was raining, but I didn't take an umbrella.

Or refers to a choice:

> We can spend our vacation at the beach or in the mountains.

Or and *either* can be used together:

> We can have either pizza or chicken for dinner tonight.

So refers to a result:

> Sue needed more money, so she got a second job.

Choose the one word or phrase that best completes the sentence.

1. It was cold outside, _____ I put on an extra sweater.

   (A) but
   (B) so
   (C) or
   (D) either

2. Our new house has a beautiful living room _____ a very nice kitchen.

   (A) but
   (B) so
   (C) both
   (D) and

3. Jack is not only a talented pianist _____ a very good singer.

   (A) nor
   (B) but also
   (C) and
   (D) either

4. Should we schedule the meeting for the morning _____ the afternoon?

   (A) so
   (B) but
   (C) or
   (D) nor

5. _____ Gloria nor Hank can come for dinner tonight.

   (A) Neither
   (B) Either
   (C) Both
   (D) But also

6. Elizabeth learned Korean when she was a child, _____ she speaks it fluently.

   (A) but
   (B) or
   (C) nor
   (D) so

7. _____ Bangkok and Paris are interesting cities to visit.

   (A) Either
   (B) But
   (C) Both
   (D) Not

8. We can _____ go to a museum or take a walk in the park.

   (A) either
   (B) but
   (C) neither
   (D) so

9. Rick likes to stay out late, _____ Kate doesn't.

   (A) either
   (B) or
   (C) but also
   (D) but

10. Dogs are great pets, _____ cats are too.

   (A) nor
   (B) so
   (C) and
   (D) or

Parallel Structure

Words and phrases that are connected by a conjunction, such as **and**, **but**, **or**, must have the same grammatical form.

Conjunctions connect two or more words that are the same part of speech.

> I like <u>ice cream</u> but not <u>pizza</u>.
>   (noun)   (noun)

> The weather last weekend was <u>hot</u>, <u>muggy</u>, and <u>cloudy</u>.
>   (adj) (adj)   (adj)

Conjunctions connect two or more verbs that have the same grammatical form or verb tense.

> I don't enjoy <u>swimming</u>, <u>fishing</u>, or <u>hiking</u>.
>   (gerund) (gerund) (gerund)

> John <u>opened</u> the door and <u>ran</u> outside.
> (past tense verb)   (past tense verb)

In the case of two infinitives, the *to* for the second verb doesn't have to be repeated.

> We want to <u>get up</u> early and <u>take</u> a walk.
>   (infinitive verb)   (infinitive verb)

Choose the one word or phrase that best completes the sentence.

1. We enjoy swimming every summer and _____ every winter.

   (A) to ski
   (B) skiing
   (C) skis
   (D) skied

2. That train ride was uncomfortable but _____ .

   (A) cheap
   (B) cheaply
   (C) cheapens
   (D) cheapen

3. Do your work slowly and _____ .

   (A) care
   (B) careful
   (C) carefully
   (D) cared

4. The children went to the park and _____ .

   (A) fun
   (B) had fun
   (C) funny
   (D) to have fun

5. I never ride the bus or _____ .

   (A) slow
   (B) the subway
   (C) drove
   (D) taking the train

6. Last weekend Herbert did the laundry and _____ the house.

   (A) cleaning
   (B) will clean
   (C) always cleans
   (D) cleaned

7. After dinner, Susan usually reads a book but Sam _____ a nap.

   (A) took
   (B) has taken
   (C) taking
   (D) takes

8. I want to leave work early and _____ dinner downtown.

   (A) eat
   (B) ate
   (C) am eating
   (D) I am eating

9. That pizza was _____ and delicious.

    (A) hottest
    (B) heat
    (C) hot
    (D) heating

10. You can finish that project quickly and _____ .

    (A) easier
    (B) easily
    (C) easy
    (D) easiest

Cause and Effect

Some sentences describe a **cause** (reason) and an **effect** (result).

> Louise speaks French fluently because she grew up in France.
>   (effect)   (cause)

> Eduardo always sleeps in class, so he usually fails his tests.
>   (cause)   (effect)

Certain words introduce the **cause**.
Because, since, as, as long as are <u>followed by a clause</u> with a subject and a verb:

> We didn't go to the beach as the weather was bad.
> Joe got sick because he went outside without a coat.

Because of, due to, as a result of, on account of, from are <u>followed by a noun or a gerund</u>:

> We didn't go to the beach on account of the bad weather.
> Joe got sick from going outside without a coat.

Other words introduce the **effect**.
So, therefore, consequently are <u>followed by a clause</u> with a subject and a verb:

> Jane spent all her money, so she couldn't go to the movies.
> I didn't study; consequently, I didn't do well on the test.

Be aware that *because* and *so* cannot appear in the same sentence showing cause and effect:

Correct: Because they failed to meet the deadline, they didn't get the bonus.
                 They failed to meet the deadline, so they didn't get the bonus.

Incorrect: Because they failed to meet the deadline, so they didn't get the bonus.

Choose the one word or phrase that best completes the sentence.

1. Several trees fell down last night _____ the strong wind.

    (A) because
    (B) because of
    (C) since
    (D) so

2. I walked to work today _____ my car had broken down.

    (A) because of
    (B) from
    (C) because
    (D) due to

3. John forgot to bring an umbrella, _____ he got very wet.

    (A) so
    (B) because of
    (C) as long as
    (D) from

4. Karen didn't get much sleep last night, _____ she was very tired at work today.

    (A) since
    (B) due to
    (C) as a result of
    (D) so

5. Steve has a sore elbow _____ playing a lot of tennis.

    (A) as
    (B) because
    (C) so
    (D) from

6. We arrived late at the airport, _____ we missed our plane.

    (A) because of
    (B) as a result of
    (C) so
    (D) due to

7. _____ her hard work and leadership skills, Marian got a promotion.

    (A) Since
    (B) As
    (C) Due to
    (D) Because

8. Florida is a good place to live _____ the nice weather.

   (A) as long as
   (B) because of
   (C) so
   (D) since

9. I want to take a long vacation, _____ I'm saving all my money.

   (A) so
   (B) because of
   (C) due to
   (D) from

10. I think we should stay inside today _____ the weather is very cold and wet.

    (A) so
    (B) due to
    (C) as
    (D) as a result of

Prefixes

Prefixes are added to the beginning of root words. They change the meaning of the word.

Here are some examples:

Dis- means *not*

dislike—not like
dishonest—not honest
disappear—not appear

I really dislike the taste of coffee so I never drink it.

Un- also means *not*

uncomfortable—not comfortable
uninterested—not interested
unfriendly—not friendly

It's hard to get along with Jim because he is so unfriendly.

Multi- means *many*

multilingual—many languages
multifamily—many families
multicolored—many colors

A multifamily house has several apartments in it.

Out- means *more than*

outgrow—grow more than
outtalk—talk more than
outwork—work more than

Mary is a very talkative girl who can outtalk everyone I know.

Re- means *again*

reread—read again
refill—fill again
resend—send again

They didn't get your e-mail message so you will have to resend it.

Pre- means *before*

precook—cook before
prearrange—arrange before
prepackage—package before

Don't worry about making plans for your trip; everything is prearranged.

Choose the one word or phrase that best completes the sentence.

1. You did a terrible job on your homework so now you have to _____ it.

    (A) prearrange
    (B) refill
    (C) rewrite
    (D) prepackage

2. You need to _____ those vegetables before you add them to the soup.

    (A) disappear
    (B) dislike
    (C) prefabricate
    (D) precook

3. Pat and Richard are always fighting because they _____ about everything.

    (A) disagree
    (B) resend
    (C) refill
    (D) disappear

4. I can't sleep on this hard bed because it is too _____ .

   (A) unhappy
   (B) uncomfortable
   (C) uninteresting
   (D) unpaid

5. A cheetah is a very fast wildcat that can _____ most other animals.

   (A) outdate
   (B) outspend
   (C) outtalk
   (D) outrun

6. _____ your shoes before you take them off.

   (A) Untie
   (B) Disappear
   (C) Outrun
   (D) Prepay

7. That movie was so _____ that I fell asleep in the middle of it.

   (A) uncomfortable
   (B) dishonest
   (C) uninteresting
   (D) outgrown

8. Turn off your computer and _____ it.

   (A) dislike
   (B) restart
   (C) disobey
   (D) regain

9. Our school is _____ because we have students from many countries.

   (A) unavailable
   (B) multistoried
   (C) uninteresting
   (D) multicultural

10. That program we saw on TV last night was _____ .

   (A) outtalked
   (B) prerecorded
   (C) outgrown
   (D) precooked

Part V: Reading Comprehension— Vocabulary Building Activities

In this section, you will learn words that could be used in any part of the TOEIC Bridge test. Studying the words here will also prepare you for the vocabulary used in Part V and in other parts of the TOEIC Bridge test.

VOCABULARY FOCUS

- Dining out
- School
- Housing
- Shopping
- Health

DINING OUT

WORDS IN CONTEXT

Directions: Use one of the words in the box to complete each sentence.

---

meal   mild   recommend   spicy   fried

---

1. If you don't know what to order, the waiter can _____ something to you.

2. I don't like food that is too _____ because it burns my mouth.

3. Some people prefer food with a lot of flavor and don't like dishes that are too _____ .

4. Breakfast is the most important _____ of the day.

5. _____ food can make you gain weight.

---

slice   baked   fresh   specialty   vegetarians

---

6. Peter _____ the cake too long and it got burned.

7. Don't drink milk if it doesn't smell _____ .

8. Some people become _____ because they don't want to kill animals for food.

9. I would like a _____ of bread with some butter, please.

10. This restaurant is a good place for dessert because their _____ is cakes and pies.

| tasty | serving | prepare | decor | selection |

11. There are many different ways to _____ potatoes, but I prefer them fried.

12. Most of the dishes at this restaurant come with a _____ of vegetables on the side.

13. I can't decide what to order because this menu has such a big _____ .

14. The _____ in this restaurant is not very pretty; they need a different color for the walls and a better-looking rug.

15. Roberta didn't finish her soup because she didn't think it was very _____ .

WORD FAMILIES

Directions: Choose the correct form of the word to complete the sentence.

noun	bakery
verb	bake
adjective	baked

16. Some people like _____ fish, but others prefer to eat it fried.

17. The _____ across the street makes delicious bread.

18. It takes about one hour to _____ a cake.

noun	freshness
adjective	fresh
adverb	freshly

19. That fruit isn't _____ so don't eat it.

20. Try some of this _____ cooked soup.

21. The _____ of this bread makes it very tasty.

noun	specialty
verb	specializes
adjective	special

22. That chef _____ in Italian cooking.

23. His _____ is spaghetti.

24. He prepared a _____ meal for my birthday.

SCHOOL

WORDS IN CONTEXT

Directions: Use one of the words in the box to complete each sentence.

> semester   deadline   advanced   tuition   require

1. The _____ for turning in this assignment is next Monday.

2. Some teachers _____ their students to do a lot of homework.

3. Most students take three or four classes each _____ .

4. If you can't pay the _____ , you will have to borrow some money.

5. You have to study the beginning levels first before you take an _____ level course.

> submit   accept   payment   permission   individual

6. Ask the teacher for _____ to leave the class early.

7. Some teachers let students turn in their assignments late, but others never _____ late work.

8. If a student doesn't understand the class work, he should ask the teacher for _____ help.

9. This course costs $500, and you must make your _____ before the first day of class.

10. If you don't _____ the assignment on time, you will get a lower grade.

| instructor | schedule | absent | attendance | registration |

11. I learned a lot in that class because the _____ explained everything so clearly.

12. If you are _____ from class too many times, you will fail.

13. To sign up for a class, fill out the _____ form at the back of the class catalog.

14. This school has a good _____ for working people because many classes are offered in the evenings and on weekends.

15. If you don't miss any classes, you will get a certificate for perfect _____.

WORD FAMILIES

Directions: Choose the correct form of the word to complete the sentence.

noun	payment
verb	pay
adjective	payable

16. The textbook costs $65 and it is _____ by cash or check.

17. Make your _____ for this class at the registration office.

18. You have to _____ for the class before the semester begins.

noun	permission
verb	permit
adjective	permissible

19. It is not _____ to talk to your classmates during a test.

20. Our teacher does not _____ us to arrive late.

21. You need the instructor's _____ to take this class.

noun	requirement
verb	require
adjective	required

22. A grade of A or B on all the tests is a _____ for passing this course.

23. This is a _____ course for every student in the school.

24. The teachers _____ all the students to arrive on time.

HOUSING

WORDS IN CONTEXT

Directions: Use one of the words in the box to complete each sentence.

> convenient   available   beautify   vacant   location

1. This is a _____ place for me to live because it is very close to my job.

2. That apartment is _____ now, but after we clean and paint it we will try to rent it to someone.

3. We would like to _____ the area in front of the building by planting a garden there.

4. People look for a house in a good _____ that is near stores and buses.

5. I need an apartment that will be _____ for rent soon because I have to move in just two weeks.

> application   tenant   landlords   occupied   owner

6. Most _____ ask people to pay the first two months' rent ahead of time.

7. A good _____ pays the rent on time every month.

8. Some people prefer to rent a house or apartment because they don't want the responsibilities of being a home _____.

9. There is an empty apartment on the first floor, but all of the rest of the apartments in this building are _____.

10. People who want to rent an apartment are usually asked to fill out an _____.

| residents | neighbor | property | current | rental |

11. The place where we live now is a _____ house but we want to buy our own house soon.

12. All the _____ of this building have a key to the front door.

13. This is a good time to buy _____ because prices are low now.

14. Our _____ across the street is very unfriendly and never speaks to us.

15. Our _____ apartment is very small so we are looking for a larger one.

WORD FAMILIES

Directions: Choose the correct form of the word to complete the sentence.

noun	convenience
adjective	convenient
adverb	conveniently

16. My new house is _____ located just one block from the bus stop.

17. This neighborhood is not very _____ because it is far from my job.

18. I chose this neighborhood for its _____.

noun	neighbor
noun	neighborhood
adjective	neighborly

19. I prefer to live in a quiet _____.

20. I like living in this building because the people here are very _____.

21. The _____ will take care of our cat when we take our vacation.

noun	resident
verb	reside
adjective	residential

22. This is a _____ area, so there are no stores or other businesses nearby.

23. There is a new _____ in the apartment upstairs.

24. We _____ at our beach house during the summer.

SHOPPING

WORDS IN CONTEXT

Directions: Use one of the words in the box to complete each sentence.

> quantity   shipping   total   items   discount

1. When you buy things over the Internet, you usually have to pay the company for _____ the things to your house.

2. If you plan to buy more than a few _____, get a shopping cart when you enter the store.

3. Sometimes you can get things at a lower price if you buy a large _____.

4. Many people prefer to shop at _____ stores because they like the low prices.

5. Check the bill for mistakes and add up the _____ yourself before you pay.

> guarantee   satisfied   order   customers   cashier

6. Count your change carefully because the _____ might make a mistake.

7. My TV came with a one-year _____, so the company had to give me a new one when it broke.

8. Most stores have a complaint office for people who are not _____ with something they bought.

9. Stores often have special sales in order to attract more _____.

10. When you buy something from a catalog, you can send in your _____ by mail or you can make it by phone.

returns	check out	purchase	receipt	refund

11. Although some stores don't take _____ , most stores will let you bring something back if it doesn't fit or is the wrong color.

12. I _____ a lot of things at that store because I like the things that they sell.

13. If something that you buy is damaged, the store should give you a full _____ .

14. A _____ shows when you bought something and how much you paid for it.

15. Large stores have express _____ lanes so that people who are buying just a few things can pay more quickly.

WORD FAMILIES

Directions: Choose the correct form of the word to complete the sentence.

noun	receipt
verb	receive
adjective	receptive

16. Customers will _____ a 25% discount on everything they buy this week.

17. You need to show a _____ when returning an item to the store.

18. The store manager is a _____ man and will listen to any suggestions you have.

noun	refund
verb	refund
adjective	refundable

19. All purchases are fully _____ if returned to the store within 30 days.

20. If your new radio doesn't work, ask the store for a _____.

21. The store will _____ your money if you return the item soon.

noun	satisfaction
verb	satisfy
adjective	satisfied

22. If our service doesn't _____ you, please let the manager know.

23. We hope our customers feel _____ with the purchases they make at our store.

24. The _____ of our customers is important to us.

HEALTH

WORDS IN CONTEXT

Directions: Use one of the words in the box to complete each sentence.

pharmacist	cure	physical	nourishing	work out

1. Candy and potato chips are not examples of _____ food.

2. One good way to keep healthy is to _____ at a gym several times a week.

3. I have to pick up my medicine from the _____ this afternoon.

4. Miranda's doctor said she needs to get more _____ exercise because she is gaining too much weight.

5. Doctors still are not able to _____ the common cold.

prescription	fit	benefit	symptom	treatment

6. You cannot buy this medicine without a _____ from your doctor.

7. You can stay _____ by following a regular program of exercise.

8. A simple problem like a headache could be a _____ of a more serious disease.

9. Aspirin used to be the most common _____ for a headache, but now there are several other medicines that people commonly use.

10. Diet and exercise can _____ your health in many ways.

| emergency | illness | patients | research | scientific |

11. Edward is suffering from a serious _____ and will be in the hospital for several weeks.

12. If you think you have a medical _____, go to the hospital immediately.

13. Drug companies have to do a lot of _____ before they can put a new drug on the market.

14. The doctor's schedule is full this week and she cannot see any new _____.

15. Many people believe that chicken soup can cure a cold, but _____ studies have not been able to prove this.

WORD FAMILIES

Directions: Choose the correct form of the word to complete the sentence.

noun	nourishment
verb	nourish
adjective	nourishing

16. Fruits and vegetables provide a lot of _____.

17. Children need to eat a lot of _____ food.

18. Parents want to _____ their children with good, healthful food.

noun	science
adjective	scientific
adverb	scientifically

19. Medical _____ has made many advances in the last 50 years.

20. Because of _____ knowledge, we are now able to treat many kinds of sickness.

21. All new drugs have to be _____ tested.

noun	treatment
verb	treat
adjective	treatable

22. Although Jane's illness is quite serious, it is _____.

23. You can _____ almost any kind of pain with aspirin.

24. Do you know a good _____ for the common cold?

Part V: Reading Comprehension—Skill Building Activities

There are 20 questions in Part V of the TOEIC Bridge test. You will read a notice, an e-mail, an advertisement, a sign, or some type of reading material. You will have to answer one or more questions about the reading material.

Reading Material:

SECURITY NOTICE
Remove coats before proceeding to the gate.

Possible Question: What should you do?
(A) Proceed with caution.
(B) Put something over you before going out.
(C) Take off your overcoat before going ahead.
(D) Remove all tags from your clothes.

The best possible answer to the question, "What should you do?" is (C) Take off your overcoat before going ahead.

The TOEIC Bridge test uses the following types of reading materials:

- Advertisements
- Charts, Tables, and Graphs
- Forms
- Notices and Signs
- Passages and Articles
- Correspondence

ADVERTISEMENTS

Questions 1–3 refer to the following advertisement.

> **FOR RENT**
> **Sunny one-bedroom apartment**
> **in small, six-apartment building.**
> **$950/month.**
> **Convenient location—bus, stores,**
> **restaurants nearby.**
> **Available on the fifteenth of the month.**
> **For more information call 637-1220**
> **evenings and weekends.**

1. What is being rented?

    (A) One bedroom.
    (B) One apartment.
    (C) Six apartments.
    (D) $950.

2. When can a new tenant move in?

    (A) On the weekend.
    (B) On the fifteenth day of the month.
    (C) In fifteen days.
    (D) As soon as the rent is paid.

3. What does the ad tell us about the place for rent?

    (A) It is small.
    (B) It is cheaper than nearby apartments.
    (C) It is close to restaurants and stores.
    (D) It is available this weekend.

Questions <u>4–6</u> refer to the following advertisement.

Don't spend your lunch hour waiting in line.

Come to Joe's Hamburger Grill for a quick and tasty lunch.

Our menu features 25 different types of hamburgers served with:
- cheese
- sliced onions or tomatoes
- spicy sauces and more!

Your order is guaranteed to be on your table within five minutes or it's free!

Joe's is located on North Main Street in the heart of the downtown business district.

See you there!

---

4. What is being advertised?

    (A) A restaurant.
    (B) A butcher's shop.
    (C) A grocery store.
    (D) A food delivery service.

5. What does the advertisement tell us about Joe's hamburgers?

    (A) They are big.
    (B) They are served with salad.
    (C) The sauce costs extra.
    (D) There are 25 different kinds.

6. Who would most likely go to Joe's?

    (A) Vegetarians.
    (B) Office workers.
    (C) Tourists.
    (D) Heart patients.

Questions 7–9 refer to the following advertisement.

Vacation Time Inc.

Specializing in discount vacations.
We make all your reservations for you.
We guarantee:
✔ **the lowest fares on all major airline routes.**
✔ **the most economical hotel rates.**
✔ **the least expensive rental cars.**

Why pay more?
Call us today.

---

7. What kind of a business is Vacation Time Inc.?

    (A) A travel agency.
    (B) An airline.
    (C) A hotel.
    (D) A vacation resort.

8. Which is the one service NOT mentioned?

    (A) Airline reservations.
    (B) Hotel reservations.
    (C) Rental car reservation.
    (D) Cruise reservations.

9. What is the core of Vacation Time's business?

    (A) High-end luxury goods.
    (B) Travel bargains.
    (C) Limousine pickup.
    (D) Self-arranged tours.

Questions 10–12 refer to the following advertisement.

INSTITUTE OF INTERNATIONAL COMMUNICATION

Have you always wanted to speak a foreign language? Or two or three?

Now you can! We offer classes for adults in:

English • French • Spanish • Japanese • Chinese • Korean

All levels from beginning through advanced.

Register for summer classes now.

We have both day and evening schedules.

Call 564-0284 M–F 7 A.M.–9:30 P.M.

Or visit us at 6793 Independence Boulevard, Suite 1001.

---

10. What kind of business is the Institute of International Communication?

    (A) Language school.
    (B) Telephone company.
    (C) Computer training.
    (D) Translation service.

11. When is the Institute open?

    (A) Every day of the week.
    (B) In the evenings only.
    (C) Monday through Friday.
    (D) In the mornings only.

12. Who would probably not use the Institute's services?

    (A) Beginners.
    (B) Children.
    (C) Office workers.
    (D) Adults.

<u>Questions 13–14</u> refer to the following advertisement.

Happy Mart

The country's favorite discount store.
Don't pay more at other stores.

We offer you the best prices in:
- Clothing for the whole family
- Household items
- Camping and sports equipment
- Gardening supplies and more!

100% customer satisfaction guaranteed or your money back.

We're open 7 days a week. Visit us soon.

13. What kind of business is Happy Mart?

   (A) Sports store.
   (B) Department store.
   (C) Mail order store.
   (D) Gardening store.

14. What is something that you probably cannot buy at Happy Mart?

   (A) Dresses.
   (B) Soccer balls.
   (C) Brooms.
   (D) Groceries.

CHARTS, TABLES, AND GRAPHS

Questions 1–4 refer to the following table.

How We Stay Fit

	Work out at Gym	Walk or Run	Bicycle	Other
Age 21–30	25%	30%	35%	10%
Age 31–40	25%	35%	20%	20%
Age 41–50	20%	40%	15%	25%
Age 51+	40%	35%	15%	10%

1. What information does this table tell us?

   (A) How often people of different ages exercise.
   (B) Which age group exercises most.
   (C) Where people prefer to exercise.
   (D) Which kinds of exercise people of different ages prefer.

2. Which is the most popular form of exercise for people aged 31–40?

   (A) Working out at a gym.
   (B) Walking or running.
   (C) Bicycle riding.
   (D) Other.

3. For which age group is working out at a gym the most popular form of exercise?

   (A) Age 21–30.
   (B) Age 31–40.
   (C) Age 41–50.
   (D) Age 51+.

4. What can we infer from this table?

   (A) People aged 21–30 exercise more than people in other age groups.
   (B) Most people aged 31–40 belong to a gym or health club.
   (C) Many people aged 41–50 don't enjoy bicycle riding.
   (D) People aged 51+ don't exercise as much as they used to.

<u>Questions 5–8</u> refer to the following chart.

Recommendations for Adult Women 18–45
(Men 18–45, see page 16. Children under 18, see page 17)

Food Group	No. of Recommended Daily Servings
Dairy Products (Milk and Milk Products, Eggs)	3
Meat (Fish, Chicken, Beef)	2
Vegetables (Carrots, Tomatoes, Spinach)	5
Fruit (Oranges, Apples, Berries)	3
Grains (Bread, Cereal, Rice)	4

5. Who is this chart for?

   (A) Women aged 18–45.
   (B) Women who want to lose 18–45 pounds.
   (C) Women who have children.
   (D) Women who cook for their families.

6. According to this chart, what should women do every day?

   (A) Eat three servings of meat.
   (B) Eat cereal for breakfast.
   (C) Eat five servings of vegetables.
   (D) Eat more fruit than vegetables.

7. According to this chart, what should men do?

   (A) Eat the same food as women.
   (B) Read the information on page 16.
   (C) Serve the meals.
   (D) Eat more meat.

8. Which of the following is a dairy product?

   (A) Crackers.
   (B) Chicken.
   (C) Onions.
   (D) Cheese.

Questions 9–11 refer to the following chart.

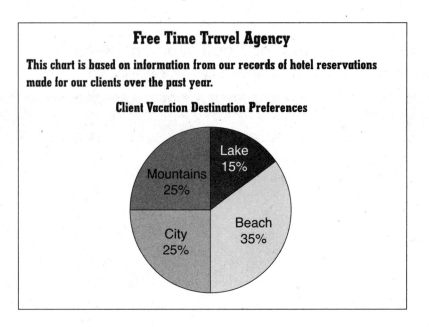

9. What information does this chart show us?

   (A) How much vacation time people spend in different places.
   (B) The places where the agency's clients prefer to spend their vacations.
   (C) How much money people spend in different vacation places.
   (D) The temperature at different vacation places.

10. Which vacation place is the most popular?

    (A) The beach.
    (B) The mountains.
    (C) The city.
    (D) The lake.

11. How did the agency get this information?

    (A) It called up hotels at the different vacation places.
    (B) It asked its clients.
    (C) It looked at its records.
    (D) It asked other travel agencies.

<u>Questions 12–14</u> refer to the following schedule.

Fall Semester—Art Department

Course Name	Instructor	Days	Times
Introduction to Art History	Smithson	M W	10:15–11:45
Art of the 20th Century	Jones	T Th	1:30–3:30
Beginning Painting	Smithson	T W Th	8:15–9:45
Advanced Painting*	Brown	M W	9:15–10:45
Beginning Drawing	Anderson	W F	9:30–11:00

Permission of instructor required before registering for this course.

12. What does this chart show?

    (A) A schedule of museum exhibits.
    (B) The instructors' office hour schedule.
    (C) A schedule of art classes.
    (D) A classroom schedule.

13. Who is the instructor for Beginning Drawing?

    (A) Smithson.
    (B) Jones.
    (C) Brown.
    (D) Anderson.

14. Which course requires permission from the instructor to register?

    (A) Introduction to Art History.
    (B) Art of the 20th Century.
    (C) Beginning Painting.
    (D) Advanced Painting.

Questions 15–17 refer to the following graph.

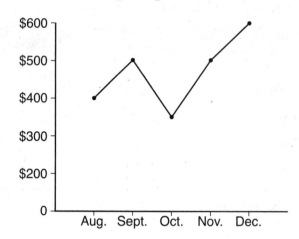

15. What does this graph show?

    (A) The changing cost of airline tickets.
    (B) The airline schedule.
    (C) The number of people traveling by plane.
    (D) The cost of airplane meals.

16. How much were airplane fares in October?

    (A) $300.
    (B) $350.
    (C) $400.
    (D) $450.

17. Which of the following statements is NOT true?

    (A) Fares were more expensive in September than in October.
    (B) Fares cost the same in September as in November.
    (C) Fares were the most expensive in December.
    (D) Fares cost the least in August.

FORMS

Questions 1–3 refer to the following form.

Smith & Sons Property Management Company
Residential Property Managers
Tenant Application

Name: *Edna S. Vincent*

Current Address: *705 Eastern Avenue, Greentown, NY*

Years at current address: *6 months*

Daytime phone: *347-0987*

Evening phone number: *347-9965*

Employer: *Griselli's Market*

Which apartment are you interested in? *1675 River Street, Apt. 4*

---

1. What is the business of Smith & Sons Company?

   (A) It rents out apartments.
   (B) It manages offices.
   (C) It rents commercial property.
   (D) It buys residential property.

2. What does Edna Vincent want to do?

   (A) She wants to paint her apartment.
   (B) She wants to work for Smith & Sons.
   (C) She wants to rent a new apartment.
   (D) She wants to get a new phone number.

3. What is 705 Eastern Avenue?

   (A) The place where Smith & Sons is located.
   (B) The place where Edna Vincent wants to live.
   (C) The place where Edna Vincent lives now.
   (D) The place where the application must be submitted.

Questions 4–6 refer to the following form.

Registration Form—Individual Music Instruction

Please return this form to:
Springfield University Music Department
PO Box 482
Springfield

Name _____

Address _____

Phone _____

Instrument _____

Check one: ☐ 30 min. ☐ 45 min. ☐ 1 hour

Preferred Days (check all that apply)
☐ Mon. ☐ Tues. ☐ Wed. ☐ Thurs. ☐ Fri. ☐ Sat.

I am interested in participating in the university orchestra ☐ yes ☐ no

The registration fee is $20. Please enclose a check with this form, made payable to Springfield University Music Department.

Tuition will be paid directly to the instructor at the first lesson.

---

4. What is the purpose of this form?

   (A) To apply for a job as a music instructor.
   (B) To apply to participate in the university orchestra.
   (C) To apply for individual music lessons.
   (D) To apply to rent a musical instrument.

5. How many days a week are music lessons available?

   (A) Three.
   (B) Four.
   (C) Five.
   (D) Six.

6. What will be paid to the instructor?

   (A) The money for music lessons.
   (B) The registration fee.
   (C) The cost of renting an instrument.
   (D) The orchestra membership fee.

<u>Questions 7–10</u> refer to the following form.

Howard's Mail Order Business Supply Company			
Item #	**Description**	**Quantity**	**Price**
715	Paper clips	100 boxes	$15.00
900	Photocopier paper	50 boxes	$300.00
346	Black felt-tipped pens	50 boxes	$75.00
012	Yellow pencils	75 boxes	$65.00
		Total	$455.00
		Tax	$20.00
		Shipping	
		Total due	$475.00

See table for shipping costs. Shipping is free on orders of $400 or more. Questions? Call Customer Service at 800-555-221

7. What is this form used for?

    (A) Ordering from a catalog.
    (B) Counting supplies on hand.
    (C) Planning a budget.
    (D) Writing a receipt.

8. What is the cost of photocopier paper?

    (A) $300 a box.
    (B) $50 a box.
    (C) $6.00 a box.
    (D) $9.00 a box.

9. Why is the cost of shipping not written on the form?

    (A) Because it isn't known.
    (B) Because the customer made a large order.
    (C) Because the items won't be shipped.
    (D) Because Customer Service will write it in.

10. Who probably filled out this form?

    (A) An office manager.
    (B) A teacher.
    (C) A student.
    (D) An artist.

Questions 11–14 refer to the following form.

Riverdale Restaurant

Your opinion is important to us. Please rate us in the following areas:

	excellent	good	fair	poor
Decor:	☐	☐	☒	☐
Speed of service:	☐	☐	☐	☒
Menu selection:	☐	☐	☒	☐

How was your meal?

	excellent	good	fair	poor
Soup or salad:	☐	☐	☒	☐
Entree:	☐	☐	☒	☐
Dessert:	☒	☐	☐	☐
Drink:	☐	☐	☐	☒

Comments: I had a very unpleasant meal. The service was terrible, and the menu selection isn't very interesting. The only part of the meal I enjoyed was the dessert. I recommend that you hire a new chef.

---

11. What is the purpose of this form?

    (A) To order food from a menu.
    (B) To give one's opinion of a restaurant.
    (C) To evaluate an employee's work.
    (D) To apply for a job at a restaurant.

12. Which part of the meal did this person like the least?

    (A) Soup or salad.
    (B) Entree.
    (C) Dessert.
    (D) Drink.

13. What is this person's opinion of the menu selection?

    (A) It is excellent.
    (B) It is good.
    (C) It is fair.
    (D) It is poor.

14. What is this person most likely to do in the future?

    (A) Apply for a job as a chef.
    (B) Order a different meal.
    (C) Eat at a different restaurant.
    (D) Invite his friends to the restaurant.

<u>Questions 15–18</u> refer to the following form.

```
┌─────────────────────────────────────────────────────────┐
│                   New Patient Form                       │
│                                                          │
│   Henry Richardson                                       │
│   NAME                                                   │
│   56 North Oak Street, Riverdale                         │
│   ADDRESS                                                │
│   28                                                     │
│   AGE                                                    │
│   When was your last physical exam?  3 years ago         │
│   How often do you exercise?  4 times a week             │
│   What symptoms do you currently have?                   │
│                                                          │
│   ☐ headache                                             │
│                                                          │
│   ☐ backache                                             │
│                                                          │
│   ☐ stomachache                                          │
│                                                          │
│   ☐ fatigue                                              │
│                                                          │
│   ☐ other                                                │
│                                                          │
│   (to be completed by nurse)                             │
│                                                          │
│   Height _____      Weight _____                     │
└─────────────────────────────────────────────────────────┘
```

15. What is the purpose of this form?

    (A) To give someone's physical description.
    (B) To elicit someone's health information.
    (C) To apply for a job.
    (D) To apply for a health club membership.

16. How often does Mr. Richardson exercise?

    (A) Three times a week.
    (B) Four times a week.
    (C) Five times a week.
    (D) He doesn't exercise.

17. What symptoms does Mr. Richardson have?

    (A) Headache.
    (B) Backache.
    (C) Stomachache.
    (D) None.

18. Who should complete this form?

    (A) The patient.
    (B) The nurse.
    (C) The doctor.
    (D) The receptionist.

NOTICES AND SIGNS

Questions 1–4 refer to the following notice.

Attention Students

This Friday, January 25, is the registration deadline for the spring semester.

Complete your registration form in the Administrative Office on the first floor between the hours of 8:30 A.M. and 6:30 P.M. Payment must be made at the time of registration, so bring your credit card, a money order, or cash with you. Personal checks will not be accepted. No late exceptions. Classes begin Monday, January 28.

---

1. Why is January 25th important?

   (A) It is the last day the Administrative Office will be open.
   (B) It is the last day to register for spring semester classes.
   (C) It is the first day of the spring semester.
   (D) It is the day all classwork must be submitted to the professor.

2. Where is the Administrative Office?

   (A) On the first floor.
   (B) On the second floor.
   (C) On the third floor.
   (D) On the fourth floor.

3. Which form of payment is NOT allowed?

   (A) Credit card.
   (B) Money order.
   (C) Cash.
   (D) Check.

4. What will probably happen if a student does not bring a form of payment to the Administrative Office by January 25th?

   (A) He or she will not be allowed to register.
   (B) He or she can pay on the first day of class.
   (C) He or she will receive a bill in the mail.
   (D) He or she will be charged extra.

<u>Questions 5–6</u> refer to the following notice.

Neighborhood Meeting

April 10, 7:30 P.M.
Community Recreation Center, Room 12

Whether you are a property owner or a renter, it's time to get involved in your neighborhood.
We will discuss:
- *Beautifying our neighborhood.*
- *Making our streets safe from crime.*
- *Organizing a neighborhood festival.*

All neighborhood residents are encouraged to attend.

---

5. What is the purpose of this notice?

   (A) To inform people of a meeting.
   (B) To notify neighbors of a crime.
   (C) To invite neighbors to use the recreation center.
   (D) To discuss the cost of owning property.

6. Who is this notice for?

   (A) Property owners only.
   (B) Renters only.
   (C) Everybody who lives in the neighborhood.
   (D) Employees of the recreation center.

Questions 7–9 refer to the following notice.

This evening's Flight 334 to Chicago is delayed due to dangerous weather conditions. Flight 334 is expected to depart tomorrow morning at 5:30 A.M. with a 7:45 A.M. arrival time in Chicago. Our gate agents will be glad to assist you with making hotel arrangements for this evening. The airline is not responsible for the hotel expenses. Any passengers wishing to make arrangements for a hotel room should speak with the gate agent on Concourse 2.

---

7. What is the purpose of this notice?

    (A) To give the Chicago weather report.
    (B) To notify travelers that the hotel is full.
    (C) To explain a schedule change.
    (D) To explain how to buy a ticket to Chicago.

8. When will Flight 334 arrive in Chicago?

    (A) This evening.
    (B) Tomorrow evening.
    (C) At 5:30 A.M.
    (D) At 7:45 A.M.

9. Who will pay for a hotel room?

    (A) The passengers.
    (B) The airline company.
    (C) The ticket agent.
    (D) The pilot.

Questions 10–12 refer to the following notice.

```
        This is an express checkout lane.

              Cash only.

   If you are purchasing more than 10 items or
 using a credit card, please go to another lane.
```

10. Where would you see this notice?

    (A) At a store.
    (B) At a restaurant.
    (C) At a train station.
    (D) On a highway.

11. What can you do at the express checkout lane?

    (A) Apply for a credit card.
    (B) Pay with cash.
    (C) Pay with a check.
    (D) Return items.

12. Who may use the express checkout lane?

    (A) Customers buying more than 10 items.
    (B) Anyone who is in a hurry.
    (C) Customers buying 10 items or fewer.
    (D) Anyone who is paying with a credit card.

Questions 13–14 refer to the following notice.

```
The doctors' office is closed for vacation until Monday, June 17.
   If you have a medical emergency, please go immediately
              to the West Side Clinic on State Street.
```

13. Why is the office closed?

    (A) It is the weekend.
    (B) The doctors had an emergency.
    (C) The office staff is on vacation.
    (D) The doctors are working at the clinic.

14. When will it be possible to see the doctors in their office?

    (A) On Monday.
    (B) Before Monday.
    (C) Until Monday.
    (D) On June 16.

PASSAGES AND ARTICLES

<u>Questions 1–4</u> refer to the following article.

Does chicken soup cure a cold? Scientific studies have not been able to show that this is true. Nevertheless, many people use it to treat their colds. Why is this? "Because it works," says Dr. Patty Wilson of New York. "My patients always say they feel better after treating their colds with a bowl of hot chicken soup. Scientific research may not show it, but my patients understand their own experience. And they know that chicken soup makes them feel better." Whether or not chicken soup really cures colds, it does have health benefits, especially when prepared with lots of vegetables. It is nourishing and it isn't fattening. It's also easy and inexpensive to make. Sick or healthy, chicken soup makes a delicious and healthful meal for anyone.

1. What is the purpose of this article?

   (A) To explain how to prepare chicken soup.
   (B) To discuss chicken soup as a treatment for colds.
   (C) To present scientific research about chicken soup.
   (D) To compare different treatments for colds.

2. According to Dr. Wilson, why do people treat colds with chicken soup?

   (A) Because it makes them feel better.
   (B) Because the doctor tells them to.
   (C) Because it has been proven by research.
   (D) Because it is inexpensive.

3. What is a benefit of eating chicken soup?

   (A) It cures colds.
   (B) It is the cheapest food available.
   (C) You can buy it anywhere.
   (D) It is nourishing.

4. What is the writer's opinion of chicken soup?

   (A) It is too expensive.
   (B) It is a good treatment for a cold.
   (C) It has too much salt.
   (D) Only sick people should eat it.

<u>Questions 5–7</u> refer to the following article.

If you are looking for an inexpensive place to enjoy a tasty meal, try the new Café Paris. The first thing you will notice is the interesting decor. Paintings of flowers on the walls and fresh flowers on every table make you feel like you are in a garden in Paris. The restaurant doesn't allow smoking so the air is garden-fresh. The specialty of the house is salads and they have a wide selection. Never have I tasted such delicious salads and I plan to return to the café several more times so that I can try them all. The soups are equally good, although the desserts could be better. But the coffee is delicious and makes a good ending to a pleasant and tasty meal at the Café Paris.

5. What is the purpose of this article?

    (A) To review a restaurant.
    (B) To describe Parisian food.
    (C) To discuss Parisian art.
    (D) To explain the writer's food preferences.

6. What is the writer's opinion of the Café Paris?

    (A) The walls need fresh paint.
    (B) The salads are very good.
    (C) The soups are better than the salads.
    (D) The desserts are too expensive.

7. Who would probably like to eat at Café Paris?

    (A) People who smoke.
    (B) People who like desserts.
    (C) People who don't like to spend a lot of money.
    (D) People who prefer meat.

Questions 8–11 refer to the following article.

Last night government officials announced an increase in fares on train service between all major cities in the country. "More and more people are riding the trains these days," said one official. "Trains are a popular form of transportation, but the cost of running them is going up. We need to increase the fares to cover these costs." No changes in train service were announced. Some government officials believe that the increase in train fares could cause more people to travel by bus. The new train fares go into effect at the end of next month.

---

8. What is the purpose of this article?

    (A) To report on the popularity of trains.
    (B) To report that train tickets will cost more.
    (C) To compare train travel with bus travel.
    (D) To explain the opinions of government officials.

9. When will train fares increase?

    (A) Next month.
    (B) In a few days.
    (C) Tonight.
    (D) At the end of this month.

10. Why will train fares increase?

    (A) Too many people ride the trains.
    (B) More train services will be offered.
    (C) The cost of running trains is increasing.
    (D) People prefer to take the bus.

11. Why might more people start traveling by bus?

    (A) Buses are faster.
    (B) Train tickets will become too expensive.
    (C) Bus service is better.
    (D) Trains don't go to many cities.

<u>Questions 12–13</u> refer to the following passage.

> Owning rental property is a good way to make some extra money, but it is important to manage your property well. The first thing to keep in mind is that you want to keep your property occupied. Every day that your rental apartment or house is vacant you lose money. This is why it is important to have a good advertising plan. Many landlords hire rental agents to help them find tenants. Others prefer to advertise and show the apartment or house themselves. Whichever way you choose, you want to find a tenant who is responsible and reliable.

12. Who is this passage for?

   (A) Landlords.
   (B) Tenants.
   (C) Rental agents.
   (D) Property managers.

13. According to this passage, when might a property owner lose money?

   (A) When he advertises.
   (B) When he hires a rental agent.
   (C) When his property is not occupied.
   (D) When he shows the property himself.

Questions 14–16 refer to the following article.

The Super Plus Department Store has started a new checkout system. Some checkout lanes now have computers instead of human cashiers. In each checkout lane, a computer reads the price on each item purchased and adds up the total. The customer then pays with a credit card or cash and the computer automatically prints a receipt. "Most customers like the new system," explained Rita Ortiz, the store manager. "It's much faster so people don't have to wait in line so long." Ms. Ortiz said the store owners are happy with the new system, too. Formerly, 10 cashiers at a time worked at the store. "That was 10 people we had to pay," said Ms. Ortiz. "Now we pay only two cashiers."

---

14. What is this article about?

    (A) A new store.
    (B) A new checkout system.
    (C) Credit cards.
    (D) Shopping malls.

15. Why do customers like the new system?

    (A) It's easy.
    (B) It's fast.
    (C) It's fun.
    (D) It's cheap.

16. Who might not like the new system?

    (A) The store owners.
    (B) The manager.
    (C) The cashiers.
    (D) The credit card company.

CORRESPONDENCE

Questions 1–3 refer to the following e-mail.

From: "Hughston, Muriel" <Muriel_Hughston@yahip.org>
Date: Mon Dec 1, 2010 4:12:35 PM US/Eastern
To: "Steve O'Hara" <s_ohara@verizon.net>,
Subject: Vacation highlights

Dear Steve,
I can't believe what a great time I am having here. I have a huge room with a beautiful view of the ocean. At first I had a different room without a view, but then I got lucky. Another guest cancelled his reservation, so I got his room.

It's wonderful to have some time off from work. I just relax on the sand all day. I know you don't like the beach, but I wish I could stay here forever. I've reserved a flight home next Sunday. I'm not looking forward to returning to work the next day, but I am looking forward to seeing you again.
Love,
Muriel

---

1. Where is Muriel now?

   (A) At work.
   (B) On an airplane.
   (C) At the beach.
   (D) At home.

2. Why does Muriel like her room?

   (A) It has a view of the ocean.
   (B) It isn't very big.
   (C) It is beautiful.
   (D) It isn't expensive.

3. What will Muriel do on Sunday?

   (A) She will return to work.
   (B) She will go to another hotel.
   (C) She will relax on the sand.
   (D) She will fly home.

Questions 4–6 refer to the following letter.

September 21, 2010

StyleSport Clothing Company
8672 Brooklyn Boulevard
West Windsor, VT 00034

To whom it may concern:

I am returning a shirt I ordered from your catalog last month. I would like a full refund for this item. When I received it, all the buttons were missing. When I spoke with your customer service representative on the phone yesterday, he informed me that I could not return the item because it was on sale. When I ordered the shirt, however, I did not expect to pay for one without buttons. I am not returning the shirt because of the color or size; I am returning it because it was damaged when I received it. This is the reason I would like my money back. I have been a satisfied customer in the past, and I know you will take care of this matter to my satisfaction.

Sincerely,

Roger Roberts

---

4. Why did Roger Roberts write this letter?

   (A) To complain about the customer service representative.
   (B) To ask for a refund.
   (C) To order a shirt.
   (D) To describe the type of shirt he likes.

5. Why doesn't Roger Roberts like the shirt?
   (A) Its buttons are too big.
   (B) It isn't a nice color.
   (C) It is too expensive.
   (D) It doesn't have any buttons.

6. What does Roger Roberts expect will happen?
   (A) He will get his money back.
   (B) The customer service representative will be fired.
   (C) His complaint will be ignored.
   (D) The company will send him a new shirt.

Questions 7–10 refer to the following letter.

Dear Agnes,

I'm so glad I came to Mexico for my vacation. The food here is quite tasty and there is fresh fruit everywhere. I have tried several of the local specialties. A lot of the food is too spicy for me, but they also serve some mild dishes. Some of the dishes are fried, which I don't like, but they also have other ways of preparing the food. I had a wonderful baked fish last night. And there is freshly baked bread every morning. You probably think that all I've done on this trip is eat. You're right! It's been cold and rainy most of the time, but I don't mind as long as I can enjoy a warm meal and a cup of coffee in a Mexican café. I hope you'll come here with me next year. You'll love it.

Love,

Hilda

7. Why did Hilda write this letter?

   (A) To tell Agnes about her vacation.
   (B) To tell Agnes about her favorite restaurant.
   (C) To explain to Agnes how to cook Mexican food.
   (D) To explain to Agnes what her favorite food is.

8. What kind of food does Hilda prefer?

   (A) Spicy.
   (B) Fried.
   (C) Baked.
   (D) Cold.

9. What does Hilda suggest to Agnes?

   (A) To go to a Mexican restaurant.
   (B) To visit Mexico next year.
   (C) To learn how to cook Mexican food.
   (D) To have a cup of coffee.

10. What does Hilda think of the weather?

   (A) She doesn't mind it.
   (B) It's very warm.
   (C) She loves it.
   (D) It should rain more.

Questions 11–13 refer to the following memo.

To: All staff members

From: Personnel Director

Date: January 2, 20___

Re: Company health benefits

All company employees are now allowed 12 days of sick leave a year. Remember, these days are to be used in case of illness and not as vacation days. In addition, starting next month, company employees can receive a 15% discount off all prescription medicine bought at the Center Pharmacy on Elm Street. Just show your company card to the pharmacist when ordering your medicine.

---

11. What is the purpose of this memo?

    (A) To explain where the Center Pharmacy is.
    (B) To announce new health benefits.
    (C) To explain the difference between sick leave and vacation days.
    (D) To discuss the cost of prescription medicine.

12. How many vacation days a year are company employees allowed?

    (A) 12 days.
    (B) 15 days.
    (C) One month.
    (D) It isn't mentioned.

13. What will happen starting next month?

    (A) All employees will get a vacation.
    (B) Employees will be able to get a discount on prescriptions.
    (C) Employees will be allowed 12 sick days a year.
    (D) All employees will be given a company card.

Questions 14–16 refer to the following memo.

To: All teachers
From: Wilma Harris, principal
Date: January 2, 20___
Re: Attendance Forms

It has come to my attention that many of you have been turning in your attendance forms late. Please remember that the deadline for submitting attendance forms is 3:30 P.M. on the last school day of every month. Also, you must call the parents of every child who is absent three or more times without an excuse.
Thank you.

---

14. Why did Wilma Harris write this memo?

    (A) Too many students have been absent from school.
    (B) Teachers have been submitting their attendance forms late.
    (C) Students haven't been paying attention in class.
    (D) Teachers have been arriving at school late.

15. How often must teachers turn in their attendance forms?

    (A) Every day.
    (B) Twice a month.
    (C) Once a month.
    (D) Once a year.

16. When should teachers call parents?

    (A) Every time a child is absent.
    (B) When a child doesn't have an attendance form.
    (C) When a child misses school three times.
    (D) Every time a child is late.

Mini-Test Answer Sheet
READING REVIEW

Part IV

51. (A) (B) (C) (D)
52. (A) (B) (C) (D)
53. (A) (B) (C) (D)
54. (A) (B) (C) (D)
55. (A) (B) (C) (D)
56. (A) (B) (C) (D)
57. (A) (B) (C) (D)
58. (A) (B) (C) (D)
59. (A) (B) (C) (D)
60. (A) (B) (C) (D)

61. (A) (B) (C) (D)
62. (A) (B) (C) (D)
63. (A) (B) (C) (D)
64. (A) (B) (C) (D)
65. (A) (B) (C) (D)
66. (A) (B) (C) (D)
67. (A) (B) (C) (D)
68. (A) (B) (C) (D)
69. (A) (B) (C) (D)
70. (A) (B) (C) (D)

71. (A) (B) (C) (D)
72. (A) (B) (C) (D)
73. (A) (B) (C) (D)
74. (A) (B) (C) (D)
75. (A) (B) (C) (D)
76. (A) (B) (C) (D)
77. (A) (B) (C) (D)
78. (A) (B) (C) (D)
79. (A) (B) (C) (D)
80. (A) (B) (C) (D)

Part V

81. (A) (B) (C) (D)
82. (A) (B) (C) (D)
83. (A) (B) (C) (D)
84. (A) (B) (C) (D)
85. (A) (B) (C) (D)
86. (A) (B) (C) (D)
87. (A) (B) (C) (D)

88. (A) (B) (C) (D)
89. (A) (B) (C) (D)
90. (A) (B) (C) (D)
91. (A) (B) (C) (D)
92. (A) (B) (C) (D)
93. (A) (B) (C) (D)
94. (A) (B) (C) (D)

95. (A) (B) (C) (D)
96. (A) (B) (C) (D)
97. (A) (B) (C) (D)
98. (A) (B) (C) (D)
99. (A) (B) (C) (D)
100. (A) (B) (C) (D)

Mini-Test for Reading Review— Parts IV and V

In this section of the test, you will have the chance to show how well you understand written English. There are TWO parts to this section, with special directions for each part. You should take no longer than 35 minutes to complete Parts IV and V of the test.

PART IV: INCOMPLETE SENTENCES

Directions: Questions 51–80 are incomplete sentences. Four words or phrases, marked (A), (B), (C), (D), are given beneath each sentence. You must choose the one word or phrase that best completes the sentence. Then, on your answer sheet, find the number of the question and mark your answer.

Example

He lives _____ Elm Street.
(A) in
(B) at
(C) on
(D) between

Sample Answer

Ⓐ Ⓑ Ⓒ Ⓓ

The sentence should read, "He lives on Elm Street." Therefore, you should choose answer (C).

Now begin work on the questions.

51. Sarah Smith is an _____ at the National University.

    (A) instruction
    (B) instructing
    (C) instructor
    (D) instructs

52. John doesn't have _____ money to buy a car.

    (A) many
    (B) very
    (C) enough
    (D) too

53. I _____ known your parents for many years.

    (A) did
    (B) have
    (C) will
    (D) would

54. Martha left the office _____ 1:30.

    (A) at
    (B) to
    (C) on
    (D) during

55. Our house will be _____ next summer.

    (A) painter
    (B) painting
    (C) painted
    (D) paint

56. You should call _____ tonight.

    (A) he
    (B) him
    (C) his
    (D) he'll

57. The cost of housing continues to
    _____ .

    (A) up
    (B) high
    (C) expensive
    (D) increase

58. _____ students must take the exam.

    (A) A
    (B) This
    (C) Every
    (D) All

59. It _____ a long time to learn to speak
    a foreign language.

    (A) makes
    (B) takes
    (C) goes
    (D) needs

60. The children _____ going to the
    beach.

    (A) amuse
    (B) fun
    (C) enjoy
    (D) nice

61. You need to study harder _____ you
    want to pass the test.

    (A) if
    (B) so
    (C) that
    (D) though

62. I have never seen a more _____ person
    than James.

    (A) study
    (B) studied
    (C) student
    (D) studious

63. I haven't read today's newspaper _____.

    (A) soon
    (B) yet
    (C) later
    (D) anymore

64. Martha was late for work this morning
    _____ she missed the bus.

    (A) even though
    (B) in spite of
    (C) consequently
    (D) because

65. We _____ the manager of the problem
    last night.

    (A) informed
    (B) information
    (C) inform
    (D) informer

66. They _____ us some very nice photo-
    graphs of their vacation.

    (A) looked
    (B) saw
    (C) showed
    (D) pictured

67. I want to thank you _____ all your
    help.

    (A) by
    (B) for
    (C) to
    (D) since

68. I _____ to them several times last
    week.

    (A) spoke
    (B) speak
    (C) spoken
    (D) speaking

69. _____ they'll call us tonight.

    (A) Maybe
    (B) Possible
    (C) Might
    (D) Soon

70. Robert fell off the ladder _____ he was painting the house.

    (A) still
    (B) while
    (C) so
    (D) during

71. This is not a good place to build a bridge because the river is very _____ .

    (A) size
    (B) much
    (C) fat
    (D) wide

72. What is the _____ number of chairs in this room?

    (A) every
    (B) all
    (C) more
    (D) total

73. It was a very _____ show and we laughed the whole evening.

    (A) entertainer
    (B) entertainment
    (C) entertaining
    (D) entertained

74. Please _____ off your shoes before you come inside.

    (A) get
    (B) put
    (C) take
    (D) give

75. We arrived _____ late to catch our plane.

    (A) too
    (B) much
    (C) a lot
    (D) enough

76. The meeting will be _____ at about 5:30.

    (A) finish
    (B) stop
    (C) end
    (D) over

77. The Wilsons bought _____ house five years ago.

    (A) they're
    (B) they
    (C) their
    (D) them

78. It wasn't easy to _____ this place.

    (A) find
    (B) found
    (C) finds
    (D) finding

79. Are _____ keys yours?

    (A) there
    (B) these
    (C) then
    (D) this

80. January is the _____ month of the year.

    (A) one
    (B) new
    (C) begin
    (D) first

PART V: READING COMPREHENSION

Directions: Questions 81–100 are based on a variety of reading materials (for example, notices, letters, forms, newspaper and magazine articles, and advertisements). You must choose the one best answer, (A), (B), (C), or (D), to each question. Then, on your answer sheet, find the number of the question and mark your answer. Answer all questions following a passage on the basis of what is **stated** or **implied** in that passage.

Read the following example.

Donut Shop Hours
Mon.–Fri.   8:30 A.M.–6:30 P.M.
Sat.   8:30 A.M.–8:30 P.M.
Closed Sun.

When is the Donut Shop open?   Sample Answer
(A) Monday through Friday.   (A) (B) (C) (D)
(B) Monday through Saturday.
(C) Every Sunday.
(D) Every day of the week.

The correct answer is (B).

Now begin work on the questions.

Questions 81–83 refer to the following notice.

The Star Company Guarantee.

If you are not satisfied with this product for any reason, return it to the address below. We will replace it free of charge. Or, call our Customer Service office at 800-428-1212 between the hours of 9 A.M. and 5 P.M., Monday through Friday.

The Star Company
1234 Oakdale Drive
Springfield, USA

81. What is the purpose of this notice?

   (A) To give the company's telephone number.
   (B) To tell how to repair a product.
   (C) To explain the job of the Customer Service office.
   (D) To explain the company's return policy.

82. What will happen when a customer returns a product?

   (A) The customer will be charged some money.
   (B) The customer will receive a letter.
   (C) The customer will be given a replacement.
   (D) The customer will get a phone call.

83. When can a customer call the Customer Service office?

   (A) At 8:00.
   (B) Before 9:00.
   (C) From 9:00 A.M. until 5:00 P.M.
   (D) Anytime.

Questions 84–85 refer to the following advertisement.

Jefferson's Department Store announces its

SEVEN DAY SALE!

All men's and women's summer shirts are two for the price of one (regular price $25 each).

Sale ends Saturday.

---

84. How much do two shirts cost?

   (A) $1.
   (B) $7.
   (C) $25.
   (D) $50.

85. How long will the sale last?

   (A) One day.
   (B) One weekend.
   (C) One week.
   (D) All summer.

Questions 86–87 refer to the following notice.

This parking garage is closed for repairs. You can park 24 hours a day in the garage on Second Avenue between 6 A.M. and 9 P.M. or in the lot at the bus station across the street 24 hours a day. This garage will reopen on the first of next month. We apologize for any inconvenience.

---

86. Why is the garage closed?

   (A) It is being fixed.
   (B) It is nighttime.
   (C) It is full.
   (D) It is for buses only.

87. What is suggested to the reader?

   (A) Park in the street.
   (B) Take the bus.
   (C) Park in another garage or lot.
   (D) Arrive earlier.

Questions 88–90 refer to the following memo.

To: Office Staff
From: Bill Jones, Director
Subject: Lunch Hour

All staff members are requested to eat their lunch in the employee lounge only. Please don't take food into the conference room and please don't eat at your desk. We want to keep the office clean. A dining table and chairs are available in the break room for your comfort. We also plan to buy a small refrigerator for the break room. You will be able to store food there. Thank you for your cooperation.

88. What is the purpose of this memo?

 (A) To invite staff members to a special lunch.
 (B) To announce a conference.
 (C) To discuss how the office is cleaned.
 (D) To explain to staff where they may eat.

89. Who is Bill Jones?

 (A) The director.
 (B) A meal planner.
 (C) An office cleaner.
 (D) A lunch server.

90. What are staff asked to do?

 (A) Eat at their desks.
 (B) Clean the table in the break room.
 (C) Keep food out of the conference room.
 (D) Buy their food at the store.

Questions 91–94 refer to the following graph.

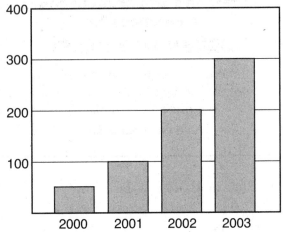

Number of students enrolled at the International Language Academy

91. How many students took classes at the Academy in 2003?

 (A) 50.
 (B) 100.
 (C) 200.
 (D) 300.

92. In which year did 100 students enroll at the Academy?

 (A) 2000.
 (B) 2001.
 (C) 2002.
 (D) 2003.

93. In which year did the smallest number of students enroll?

 (A) 2000.
 (B) 2001.
 (C) 2002.
 (D) 2003.

94. What does this graph tell us about the Academy?

 (A) The number of students is increasing.
 (B) It teaches many languages.
 (C) The classes are expensive.
 (D) The classes last several hours.

Questions 95–98 refer to the following bill.

```
Garden Restaurant
Table no. 12
No. of customers: 3

1 chicken sandwich        $6.25
2 hamburgers             $13.00
1 soda                    $1.50
1 juice                   $2.25
1 coffee                  $1.50
3 slices pie              $9.00
               Subtotal  $33.50
               tax        $1.70
               Total     $35.20
Please pay cashier.
```

Questions 99–100 refer to the following advertisement.

> *Piano Lessons*
> *for ages 5–15*
> *Experienced teacher*
> *Lessons in my home, conveniently*
> *located near subway and bus lines.*
> *Call Mrs. Suzuki*
> *783-4472*

95. How many people ordered food?

   (A) One.
   (B) Two.
   (C) Three.
   (D) Twelve.

96. What costs $2.25?

   (A) A cup of coffee.
   (B) A glass of juice.
   (C) A slice of pie.
   (D) A sandwich.

97. How much does one hamburger cost?

   (A) $1.50.
   (B) $6.25.
   (C) $6.50.
   (D) $13.00.

98. What are the customers asked to do?

   (A) Pay with cash.
   (B) Pay the waiter.
   (C) Leave a tip.
   (D) Give their money to the cashier.

99. Where will the piano lessons take place?

   (A) At the teacher's home.
   (B) At the student's home.
   (C) At the bus station.
   (D) At a school.

100. Who are the lessons for?

   (A) Adults only.
   (B) Experienced students only.
   (C) Children only.
   (D) Everybody.

Stop! This is the end of the test. If you finish before time is called, you may go back to Parts IV and V and check your work.

TOEIC Bridge Model Tests

CHAPTER 4

WHAT TO LOOK FOR IN THIS CHAPTER

- TOEIC Bridge Model Tests 1 and 2 with Answer Sheets

Model Test 1
ANSWER SHEET

Listening Comprehension

PART I: PHOTOGRAPHS

1. Ⓐ Ⓑ Ⓒ Ⓓ   5. Ⓐ Ⓑ Ⓒ Ⓓ   9. Ⓐ Ⓑ Ⓒ Ⓓ   13. Ⓐ Ⓑ Ⓒ Ⓓ
2. Ⓐ Ⓑ Ⓒ Ⓓ   6. Ⓐ Ⓑ Ⓒ Ⓓ   10. Ⓐ Ⓑ Ⓒ Ⓓ   14. Ⓐ Ⓑ Ⓒ Ⓓ
3. Ⓐ Ⓑ Ⓒ Ⓓ   7. Ⓐ Ⓑ Ⓒ Ⓓ   11. Ⓐ Ⓑ Ⓒ Ⓓ   15. Ⓐ Ⓑ Ⓒ Ⓓ
4. Ⓐ Ⓑ Ⓒ Ⓓ   8. Ⓐ Ⓑ Ⓒ Ⓓ   12. Ⓐ Ⓑ Ⓒ Ⓓ

PART II: QUESTION-RESPONSE

16. Ⓐ Ⓑ Ⓒ Ⓓ   21. Ⓐ Ⓑ Ⓒ Ⓓ   26. Ⓐ Ⓑ Ⓒ Ⓓ   31. Ⓐ Ⓑ Ⓒ Ⓓ
17. Ⓐ Ⓑ Ⓒ Ⓓ   22. Ⓐ Ⓑ Ⓒ Ⓓ   27. Ⓐ Ⓑ Ⓒ Ⓓ   32. Ⓐ Ⓑ Ⓒ Ⓓ
18. Ⓐ Ⓑ Ⓒ Ⓓ   23. Ⓐ Ⓑ Ⓒ Ⓓ   28. Ⓐ Ⓑ Ⓒ Ⓓ   33. Ⓐ Ⓑ Ⓒ Ⓓ
19. Ⓐ Ⓑ Ⓒ Ⓓ   24. Ⓐ Ⓑ Ⓒ Ⓓ   29. Ⓐ Ⓑ Ⓒ Ⓓ   34. Ⓐ Ⓑ Ⓒ Ⓓ
20. Ⓐ Ⓑ Ⓒ Ⓓ   25. Ⓐ Ⓑ Ⓒ Ⓓ   30. Ⓐ Ⓑ Ⓒ Ⓓ   35. Ⓐ Ⓑ Ⓒ Ⓓ

PART III: SHORT CONVERSATIONS AND SHORT TALKS

36. Ⓐ Ⓑ Ⓒ Ⓓ   40. Ⓐ Ⓑ Ⓒ Ⓓ   44. Ⓐ Ⓑ Ⓒ Ⓓ   48. Ⓐ Ⓑ Ⓒ Ⓓ
37. Ⓐ Ⓑ Ⓒ Ⓓ   41. Ⓐ Ⓑ Ⓒ Ⓓ   45. Ⓐ Ⓑ Ⓒ Ⓓ   49. Ⓐ Ⓑ Ⓒ Ⓓ
38. Ⓐ Ⓑ Ⓒ Ⓓ   42. Ⓐ Ⓑ Ⓒ Ⓓ   46. Ⓐ Ⓑ Ⓒ Ⓓ   50. Ⓐ Ⓑ Ⓒ Ⓓ
39. Ⓐ Ⓑ Ⓒ Ⓓ   43. Ⓐ Ⓑ Ⓒ Ⓓ   47. Ⓐ Ⓑ Ⓒ Ⓓ

Reading Comprehension

PART IV: INCOMPLETE SENTENCES

51. Ⓐ Ⓑ Ⓒ Ⓓ   59. Ⓐ Ⓑ Ⓒ Ⓓ   67. Ⓐ Ⓑ Ⓒ Ⓓ   75. Ⓐ Ⓑ Ⓒ Ⓓ
52. Ⓐ Ⓑ Ⓒ Ⓓ   60. Ⓐ Ⓑ Ⓒ Ⓓ   68. Ⓐ Ⓑ Ⓒ Ⓓ   76. Ⓐ Ⓑ Ⓒ Ⓓ
53. Ⓐ Ⓑ Ⓒ Ⓓ   61. Ⓐ Ⓑ Ⓒ Ⓓ   69. Ⓐ Ⓑ Ⓒ Ⓓ   77. Ⓐ Ⓑ Ⓒ Ⓓ
54. Ⓐ Ⓑ Ⓒ Ⓓ   62. Ⓐ Ⓑ Ⓒ Ⓓ   70. Ⓐ Ⓑ Ⓒ Ⓓ   78. Ⓐ Ⓑ Ⓒ Ⓓ
55. Ⓐ Ⓑ Ⓒ Ⓓ   63. Ⓐ Ⓑ Ⓒ Ⓓ   71. Ⓐ Ⓑ Ⓒ Ⓓ   79. Ⓐ Ⓑ Ⓒ Ⓓ
56. Ⓐ Ⓑ Ⓒ Ⓓ   64. Ⓐ Ⓑ Ⓒ Ⓓ   72. Ⓐ Ⓑ Ⓒ Ⓓ   80. Ⓐ Ⓑ Ⓒ Ⓓ
57. Ⓐ Ⓑ Ⓒ Ⓓ   65. Ⓐ Ⓑ Ⓒ Ⓓ   73. Ⓐ Ⓑ Ⓒ Ⓓ
58. Ⓐ Ⓑ Ⓒ Ⓓ   66. Ⓐ Ⓑ Ⓒ Ⓓ   74. Ⓐ Ⓑ Ⓒ Ⓓ

PART V: READING COMPREHENSION

81. Ⓐ Ⓑ Ⓒ Ⓓ   86. Ⓐ Ⓑ Ⓒ Ⓓ   91. Ⓐ Ⓑ Ⓒ Ⓓ   96. Ⓐ Ⓑ Ⓒ Ⓓ
82. Ⓐ Ⓑ Ⓒ Ⓓ   87. Ⓐ Ⓑ Ⓒ Ⓓ   92. Ⓐ Ⓑ Ⓒ Ⓓ   97. Ⓐ Ⓑ Ⓒ Ⓓ
83. Ⓐ Ⓑ Ⓒ Ⓓ   88. Ⓐ Ⓑ Ⓒ Ⓓ   93. Ⓐ Ⓑ Ⓒ Ⓓ   98. Ⓐ Ⓑ Ⓒ Ⓓ
84. Ⓐ Ⓑ Ⓒ Ⓓ   89. Ⓐ Ⓑ Ⓒ Ⓓ   94. Ⓐ Ⓑ Ⓒ Ⓓ   99. Ⓐ Ⓑ Ⓒ Ⓓ
85. Ⓐ Ⓑ Ⓒ Ⓓ   90. Ⓐ Ⓑ Ⓒ Ⓓ   95. Ⓐ Ⓑ Ⓒ Ⓓ   100. Ⓐ Ⓑ Ⓒ Ⓓ

TOEIC Bridge Model Test 1

LISTENING COMPREHENSION

In this section of the test, you will have the chance to show how well you understand spoken English. There are three parts to this section, with special directions for each part.

PART I: PHOTOGRAPHS

Directions: For each question, you will see a picture in your test book and you will hear four short statements. The statements will be spoken just one time. They will not be printed in your test book, so you must listen carefully.

When you hear the four statements, look at the picture in your test book and choose the statement that best describes what you see in the picture. Then, on your answer sheet, find the number of the question and mark your answer. Look at the sample below.

Now listen to the four statements.

Sample Answer

Ⓐ Ⓑ Ⓒ Ⓓ

Statement (B), "The boys are reading," best describes what you see in the picture. Therefore, you should choose answer (B).

1.

2.

3.

4.

5.

6.

7.

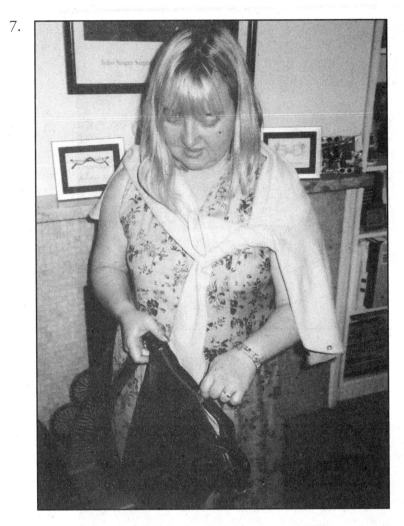

8.

9.

10.

11.

12.

Model Test 1

13.

14.

15.

PART II: QUESTION-RESPONSE

 Directions: In this part of the test, you will hear a question or statement spoken in English, followed by three responses, also spoken in English. The question or statement and the responses will be spoken just one time. They will not be printed in your test book, so you must listen carefully. Choose the best response to each question.

[Narrator]   Now listen to a sample question.

[Narrator]   You will hear:
[Woman B]   Excuse me, where is the bus stop?

[Narrator]   You will also hear:
[Man A]   (A) It's across the street.
          (B) It's underneath.
          (C) It arrives in 10 minutes.

[Narrator]   The best response to the question *Where is the bus stop?* is Choice (A), *It's across the street.* Therefore, you should choose answer (A).

16. Mark your answer on your answer sheet.

17. Mark your answer on your answer sheet.

18. Mark your answer on your answer sheet.

19. Mark your answer on your answer sheet.

20. Mark your answer on your answer sheet.

21. Mark your answer on your answer sheet.

22. Mark your answer on your answer sheet.

23. Mark your answer on your answer sheet.

24. Mark your answer on your answer sheet.

25. Mark your answer on your answer sheet.

26. Mark your answer on your answer sheet.

27. Mark your answer on your answer sheet.

28. Mark your answer on your answer sheet.

29. Mark your answer on your answer sheet.

30. Mark your answer on your answer sheet.

31. Mark your answer on your answer sheet.

32. Mark your answer on your answer sheet.

33. Mark your answer on your answer sheet.

34. Mark your answer on your answer sheet.

35. Mark your answer on your answer sheet.

PART III: SHORT CONVERSATIONS AND SHORT TALKS

Directions: In this part of the test, you will hear 15 short conversations or short talks only once, so you must listen carefully.

In your test book, you will read a question about each conversation or talk. The question will be followed by four short answers. Choose the best answer to each question and mark it on your answer sheet.

36. What is the woman doing?

    (A) Cleaning her house.
    (B) Helping the man with his math.
    (C) Completing her schoolwork.
    (D) Finishing her housework.

37. Where are the speakers?

    (A) In a restaurant.
    (B) In a bookstore.
    (C) In a clothing store.
    (D) In a train.

38. What does the woman want to buy?

    (A) Meat.
    (B) Eggs.
    (C) Vegetables.
    (D) Fruit.

39. What will Sam probably do?

    (A) See a doctor.
    (B) Talk to a lawyer.
    (C) Have lunch.
    (D) Go to the tennis courts.

40. When does the woman want to finish?

    (A) In three weeks.
    (B) By the end of the week.
    (C) By the end of the day.
    (D) At the beginning of the week.

41. Who is the speaker introducing?

    (A) A neighbor.
    (B) A famous actor.
    (C) A painter.
    (D) A writer.

42. Why does the man ask for help?

    (A) He wants his pants repaired.
    (B) He needs something bigger.
    (C) The pants are too big.
    (D) He fell down.

43. Where are the speakers?

    (A) At a furniture store.
    (B) At a photography store.
    (C) At school.
    (D) At a movie theater.

44. What is wrong with the man?

    (A) He is busy on Tuesday.
    (B) He doesn't like doctors.
    (C) He doesn't feel well.
    (D) He is overweight.

45. Who are the men?

    (A) Farmers.
    (B) Grocery store owners.
    (C) Police officers.
    (D) Weather reporters.

46. What is the talk about?

    (A) Last year's projects.
    (B) The students' writing assignments.
    (C) An exam on Friday.
    (D) The students' poor grades.

47. Who is speaking?

    (A) A weather forecaster.
    (B) A lifeguard.
    (C) A nurse.
    (D) A baker.

48. Who is the man talking with?

    (A) A gate agent.
    (B) A passenger.
    (C) A travel agent.
    (D) A pilot.

49. What time does the show begin?

    (A) At 10:00 A.M.
    (B) At 2:30 P.M.
    (C) At 5:00 P.M.
    (D) At 7:00 P.M.

50. Where does this announcement take place?

    (A) At a bus terminal.
    (B) At a police station.
    (C) At an airport.
    (D) At a public park.

STOP

This is the end of the Listening Comprehension portion of the test. Turn to Part IV in your test book.

READING COMPREHENSION

In this section of the test, you will have the chance to show how well you understand written English. There are TWO parts to this section, with special directions for each part.

YOU WILL HAVE 35 MINUTES TO COMPLETE PARTS IV AND V OF THE TEST.

PART IV: INCOMPLETE SENTENCES

Directions: Questions 51–80 are incomplete sentences. Four words or phrases, marked (A), (B), (C), (D), are given beneath each sentence. You must choose the one word or phrase that best completes the sentence. Then, on your answer sheet, find the number of the question and mark your answer.

Example   Sample Answer

    This soup doesn't _____ good.   Ⓐ Ⓑ Ⓒ Ⓓ
    (A) tasteful
    (B) tasty
    (C) taste
    (D) tasted

The sentence should read, "This soup doesn't taste good." Therefore, you should choose answer (C).

Now begin work on the questions.

51. A pound _____ meat is equal to 2.2 kilos.

    (A) of
    (B) with
    (C) for
    (D) on

52. Her mother's brother _____ coming to visit in August.

    (A) are
    (B) were
    (C) will
    (D) is

53. Eat three servings of fruits and vegetables _____ day.

    (A) every
    (B) no
    (C) only
    (D) several

54. The weather is expected to be hot and _____.

    (A) cold
    (B) wind
    (C) rain
    (D) sunny

55. _____ plane will arrive in 45 minutes.

    (A) These
    (B) The
    (C) Then
    (D) Those

56. Chin _____ the violin in the school band.

    (A) play
    (B) playing
    (C) plays
    (D) player

57. We _____ need $25.

    (A) yet
    (B) still
    (C) ever
    (D) while

58. Jack was _____ in December.

    (A) bear
    (B) bore
    (C) born
    (D) bearing

59. The concert begins _____ 7:00.

    (A) on
    (B) in
    (C) for
    (D) at

60. They met each other _____ the shopping center.

    (A) on
    (B) between
    (C) in front of
    (D) through

61. Biology is a common subject for students _____ want to study medicine.

    (A) whose
    (B) who
    (C) when
    (D) where

62. I'll start my new job _____ Monday.

    (A) in
    (B) on
    (C) at
    (D) for

63. She _____ two sisters and one brother.

    (A) have
    (B) has had
    (C) has
    (D) have had

64. We _____ both pesos and dollars.

    (A) acceptable
    (B) accept
    (C) acceptance
    (D) accepts

65. _____ world's best tennis players play at Wimbledon.

    (A) A
    (B) That
    (C) An
    (D) The

66. There is an apartment for rent on the corner of High Street _____ Park Blvd.

    (A) still
    (B) and
    (C) or
    (D) but

67. The new video game will _____ on sale on Friday, May 15.

    (A) went
    (B) gone
    (C) goes
    (D) go

68. The guitar player started playing when she was _____ years old.

    (A) fourth
    (B) quarter
    (C) four
    (D) three quarters

69. _____ members will travel by train.

    (A) All
    (B) Every
    (C) Each
    (D) Half

70. Carol went to _____ agency that prepared her resume.

    (A) a
    (B) an
    (C) and
    (D) am

71. The actress thanked _____ family and friends for supporting her career.

    (A) their
    (B) his
    (C) her
    (D) its

72. They left for the office an _____ ago.

    (A) minute
    (B) second
    (C) hour
    (D) year

73. The restaurant _____ take out service.

    (A) offering
    (B) offers
    (C) are offered
    (D) offer

74. The table and chairs _____ too big for the room.

    (A) be
    (B) are
    (C) been
    (D) is

75. It hasn't stopped raining _____ three weeks.

    (A) for
    (B) with
    (C) on
    (D) under

76. The piano _____ broke her finger and couldn't play.

    (A) play
    (B) playing
    (C) player
    (D) played

77. There were five girls and _____ boys in her family.

    (A) not
    (B) none
    (C) never
    (D) no

78. The publisher translated _____ book into 10 languages.

    (A) the
    (B) it
    (C) an
    (D) any

79. Only doctors and nurses can _____ this door.

    (A) using
    (B) used
    (C) use
    (D) to use

80. Nan ordered 100 copies _____ the magazine.

    (A) with
    (B) of
    (C) at
    (D) in

PART V: READING COMPREHENSION

Model Test 1

Directions: Questions 81–100 are based on a variety of reading materials (for example, notices, letters, forms, newspaper and magazine articles, and advertisements). You must choose the one best answer, (A), (B), (C), or (D), to each question. Then, on your answer sheet, find the number of the question and mark your answer. Answer all questions following a passage on the basis of what is **stated** or **implied** in that passage.

Read the following example.

Notice of Schedule Change:

The departure time for the morning bus to
Riverdale has been changed from 10:15 to 10:45.
Arrival in Riverdale is scheduled for 1:30.
The one-way fare is still $10.00.

What time will the bus leave for Riverdale?
(A) 10:15
(B) 10:45
(C) 10:00
(D) 1:30

Sample Answer

Ⓐ Ⓑ Ⓒ Ⓓ

The notice says that the new departure time is 10:45. Therefore, you should choose answer (B).

Now begin work on the questions.

Question 81 refers to the following advertisement.

Clearance Sale!

Saturday and Sunday only!
10:00 A.M.–9:00 P.M.
All women's clothing and shoes
are on sale.

81. Which statement is true about the clothing?

(A) It will be very costly.
(B) It will be free.
(C) It will be less expensive.
(D) It will be the same price.

Question 82 refers to the following sign.

Please, do not feed the animals!
Come watch our zookeepers feed
the animals.
Zebras and Horses: 2:00
Lions and Tigers: 3:00
Elephants and Rhinoceroses: 4:00

82. Which animals will eat last?

(A) Horses.
(B) Elephants.
(C) Lions.
(D) Zebras.

Question 83 refers to the following advertisement.

Opening Night!

Call now for tickets to see
Broadway's new show:

The Way Under

Seats are limited. Call 877-545-2323

83. What do we know about *The Way Under*?

(A) It is just closing.
(B) It has few seats available.
(C) It is an old show.
(D) It received bad reviews.

Question 84 refers to the following sign.

Notice!

Due to high winds and surf, Point Dune
Beach is closed. Listen to radio station
KCCR (88.5) for more information.

84. Why is the beach closed?

(A) It is too hot.
(B) There are sharks.
(C) The waves are dangerous
(D) They are recording a radio program.

Question 85 refers to the following sign.

NO TRESPASSING!
Private property.
Do not enter.

85. What should readers do?

(A) Go inside.
(B) Buy the land.
(C) Call the owner.
(D) Stay outside.

Question 86 refers to the following form.

Please complete the form and return by June 18.

Date of your last visit: _____

Name of your Doctor: _____

Birth date:

_____

Weight: _____

Height: _____

86. Who will fill out the form?

(A) A nurse.
(B) The doctor.
(C) A patient.
(D) An accountant.

Question 87 refers to the following newspaper article.

The new amusement park opened on
June 1. It took five years to finish the park.
Over 1,000 people stood in line on opening day to experience the new rides and
games. The park is open daily from 9–6.

87. What happened on June 1?

(A) The park closed at 9.
(B) Construction was started.
(C) A new game was released.
(D) A park opened.

Question 88 refers to the following advertisement.

1-888-532-1222!

Call now to try <u>Today's Music</u>.

This is a free offer. If you don't want to continue the subscription, you can cancel anytime.

88. What is being advertised?

(A) A concert.
(B) A new CD.
(C) A magazine.
(D) An instrument.

Question 89 refers to the following memo.

Our office will be closed on Friday, June 1.
We are sorry for any inconvenience.
We will reopen on Monday at 9:00 A.M.

89. What is true about the office?

(A) It is new.
(B) It is usually open on Friday.
(C) It is out of business.
(D) It will be closed on Monday.

Question 90 refers to the following announcement.

The customer service desk is open from 10–6, Monday through Saturday. It is located on the 3rd floor.

90. Where can customers receive help?

(A) Outside.
(B) From 10–6.
(C) On the third level.
(D) On Sunday.

Question 91 refers to the following graph.

Housing prices (January-June)

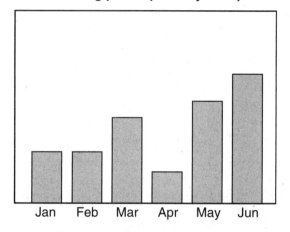

91. What does the graph show?

(A) Prices were higher in January.
(B) Prices were the lowest in April.
(C) Prices stayed the same.
(D) Prices decreased in May.

Question 92 refers to the following advertisement.

Super Grocery Store Special
This week only
Sugar: $1.00 a pound
$4.50 for 5 pounds
Store open from 6:00 A.M. to 8:30 P.M. daily.

92. How much will shoppers pay for five pounds of sugar?

(A) $4.50
(B) $5.00
(C) $1.00
(D) $8.30

Question 93 refers to the following advertisement.

> **Sign up now to visit the world's highest waterfall!**
> **Angel Falls in Venezuela is 979 meters high.**

93. What is Angel Falls?

    (A) A tourist site.
    (B) A tall mountain.
    (C) A beach.
    (D) A wide lake.

Question 94 refers to the following announcement.

> *Don't miss the concert at the beach!*
> *Every Thursday night from 8–11, listen to*
> *a different band. Concerts will run from*
> *June to August.*

94. When will the concerts begin?

    (A) At the beach.
    (B) In June.
    (C) At 11:00.
    (D) In August.

Question 95 refers to the following chart.

Meat Consumption in the United States

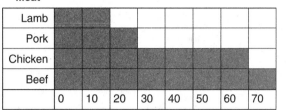

Pounds per person per year

95. What is the least popular meat?

    (A) Lamb.
    (B) Pork.
    (C) Chicken.
    (D) Beef.

Question 96 refers to the following advertisement.

> **Earn 1,000 bonus miles every time you buy**
> **a round-trip ticket at flyfast.com!**

96. What type of transportation is advertised?

    (A) Ships.
    (B) Cars.
    (C) Trains.
    (D) Planes.

Model Test 1

Question 97 refers to the following schedule.

		Steve's Weekly Schedule		
Monday	Tuesday	Wednesday	Thursday	Friday
soccer 3–4	piano 7–7:30	soccer 3–4	soccer 3–4	swim lessons 4–5

97. How many times a week does Steve practice sports?

   (A) Once.
   (B) Four times.
   (C) Twice.
   (D) Three times.

Question 98 refers to the following directory.

Ultramore Travel
365 West 52nd Street
New York, New York

Reception	888-455-3666
Fax Number	888-455-3888
General Manager	888-455-3699
Vice President, Operations	888-455-3677

98. At which number could you find the receptionist?

   (A) At 888-455-3677.
   (B) At 888-455-3888.
   (C) At 888-455-3666.
   (D) At 888-455-3699.

Question 99 refers to the following invitation.

You are invited to a reception in honor of our local Senator.
6–8 P.M.
April 22
55 Long Beach Avenue
Please RSVP by April 10.

99. When should people respond to the invitation?

   (A) On April 22.
   (B) At 6 P.M.
   (C) By April 10.
   (D) By 8 P.M.

Question 100 refers to the following notice.

There will be a meeting of all residents next Wednesday. We will discuss the problems with trash collection and plans for a new recreation area. Please come.

100. Who should go to the meeting?

   (A) Everyone who lives there.
   (B) Only people who use the recreation section.
   (C) People without trash.
   (D) People who collect things.

STOP

This is the end of the Reading portion of the test.

Answer Key for
MODEL TEST 1

Listening Comprehension

PART I

1. A	4. C	7. D	10. C	13. D
2. D	5. B	8. A	11. A	14. C
3. B	6. A	9. C	12. B	15. A

PART II

16. A	20. B	24. B	28. C	32. A
17. B	21. B	25. B	29. A	33. C
18. A	22. C	26. A	30. C	34. B
19. C	23. A	27. A	31. B	35. B

PART III

36. C	39. D	42. C	45. A	48. C
37. B	40. B	43. D	46. B	49. A
38. C	41. D	44. C	47. A	50. C

Reading Comprehension

PART IV

51. A	57. B	63. C	69. A	75. A
52. D	58. C	64. B	70. B	76. C
53. A	59. D	65. D	71. C	77. D
54. D	60. C	66. B	72. C	78. A
55. B	61. B	67. D	73. B	79. C
56. C	62. B	68. C	74. B	80. B

PART V

81. C	85. D	89. B	93. A	97. B
82. B	86. C	90. C	94. B	98. C
83. B	87. D	91. B	95. A	99. C
84. C	88. C	92. A	96. D	100. A

Correct Responses = _____

EXPLANATORY ANSWERS FOR TOEIC BRIDGE MODEL TEST 1

Listening Comprehension

PART I: PHOTOGRAPHS

1. **(A)** A family is eating a meal, probably breakfast. The other choices do not identify the action. Choice (B) uses the associated word *dishes*. Choice (C) uses the word *waiting* associated with *waiter*. Choice (D) uses the associated word *food*.

2. **(D)** The two-lane country road curves to the right. None of the other choices describe the location. Choice (A) uses the associated word *highway*. Choice (B) uses the associated words *cars, park,* and *street*. Choice (C) uses the associated word *ground*.

3. **(B)** A nurse is sitting at her desk and talking on the phone. The other choices do not identify the action. Choice (A) tries to confuse by using the similar-sounding words *taking* for *talking* and *loan* for *phone*. Choice (C) uses the similar-sounding words *walking* for *talking* and *alone* for *phone*. Choice (D) uses the similar-sounding word *shawl* for *call*.

4. **(C)** Two students wearing caps and in uniform are carrying their bags through the street. The other choices do not identify the people. Choice (A) repeats words seen in the photo: *wearing a cap*. Choice (B) repeats words seen in the photo: *carrying his briefcase* (bag). Choice (D) repeats the word *bag*.

5. **(B)** There are four buses parked on the left side of the lot and one bus parked near them. The other choices do not identify the location. Choice (A) is not true; there is only one car in the lot. Choices (C) and (D) cannot be seen. There are no passengers or motorcycles in the picture.

6. **(A)** The man with the hard hat at work is a construction worker or road repair person repairing a city street. The other choices do not identify the person.

7. **(D)** The woman is pulling the zipper of her purse to open it. The other choices do not match the action. Choice (A) repeats the word seen in the photo: *sweater*. Choice (B) repeats the word seen in the photo: *picture*. Choice (C) tries to confuse by using the word *closing* rather than *opening*.

8. **(A)** This is a parking lot for motorcycles or scooters. The other choices do not match the photo. Choice (B) tries to confuse using the similar-sounding word *bicycles* for *motorcycles*. Choice (C) tries to confuse by repeating the word *motor* but, there are no parts. Choice (D) tries to confuse by using the similar-sounding word *skewers* for *scooters*.

9. **(C)** A couple is standing in front of a display case in the food department of a large department store. The other choices do not identify the action or the location. Choice (A) identifies the location, but not the action. Choice (B) uses words related to *food* such as *cooking* and *dinner*. Choice (D) identifies the action *choosing*, but they are shopping for food not shopping for a *car*.

10. **(C)** A plane is on the runway, taxiing to take off. The other choices do not identify the location or the action. Choice (A) uses the similar-sounding word *taxi* for the verb *to taxi*, which is what planes do on runways. Choice (B) uses the similar-sounding word *train* for *plane*. Choice (D) misidentifies the form of transportation and the location.

11. **(A)** The man is pointing his finger toward something in the distance; he might be giving directions. The other choices do not identify the action. Choice (B) uses the word *house*, which is found in the photo. Choice (C) uses the word *street*, which one would expect to find in front of a house. Choice (D) uses the associated word *map* with the idea that he is giving directions.

12. **(B)** A woman, probably a secretary or administrative assistant, is putting a document into a file folder in the file cabinet. The other choices do not identify the person. Choice (A) tries to confuse by using the word *newspaper*. Choice (C) repeats the words *cabinet* and *drawer*. Choice (D) uses the similar-sounding word *mile* for *file*.

13. **(D)** The ship, a large freighter or tanker, is on a river. The other choices do not identify the thing or the location. Choice (A) uses the similar-sound word *sheep* for *ship*. Choices (B) and (C) misidentify the type of ship and the location.

14. **(C)** The man (a carpenter) with a nail and a hammer is getting ready to hammer a nail in the wall. The other choices do not identify the action. Choice (A) repeats the word *wall*. Choice (B) tries to confuse by using the similar-sound word *hammock* for *hammer*. Choice (D) uses the similar-sounding word *hall* for *wall*.

15. **(A)** The computer and notebook are on the desk. Choice (B) uses the similar-sounding word *commuter* for *computer*. Choice (C) misidentifies the location of the notebook. Choice (D) is the opposite of what the photo shows.

PART II: QUESTION-RESPONSE

16. **(A)** *Tomorrow, after 3:00* answers *When?* Choice (B) would answer *How much?* Choice (C) confuses the similar-sounding words *ready* and *red*.

17. **(B)** *OK, thank you* is a polite response to the information offered about the train. Choices (A) and (C) confuse the similar-sounding words *plane* and *rain* with *train*.

18. **(A)** *What message?* is a possible response indicating that the listener did not hear the message in question. Choice (B) confuses the similar-sounding words *here* and *hear*. Choice (C) repeats the word *hear* out of context.

19. **(C)** *We always play with five* answers *How many players?* Choice (A) repeats the word *teams*. Choice (B) associates *game* with *players* and *teams*.

20. **(B)** *It's Helen* gives the listener's first name. Choice (A) confuses *surname* with *first name*. Choice (C) associates *second* with *first*.

21. **(B)** *Sure, here you are* is a correct response to a request. Choice (A) repeats the word *pass* out of context. Choice (C) confuses the similar-sounding words *fault* and *salt*.

22. **(C)** *OK. What channel is it on?* is a correct response to a request to turn on a TV program. Choice (A) repeats the word *minutes*. Choice (B) confuses the similar-sounding words *shoes* and *news*.

23. **(A)** *At least 45* answers *How many are going?* Choice (B) associates *bus* with *trip* and would be an answer to *How are they going?* Choice (C) associates *stop* and *Indonesia* with trip and would be an answer to *Where are they going?*

24. **(B)** *No, I don't like their music* explains why the listener hasn't heard the new CD. Choice (A) associates *louder* with *heard*. Choice (C) confuses the similar-sounding words *hand* and *band*.

25. **(B)** *Sorry, I can't* is a correct response to an invitation to lunch. Choice (A) associates *eat salad* with *have lunch*. Choice (C) associates *hungry* with *have lunch*.

26. **(A)** *Didn't I show it to you?* is a correct response to a request to see something. Choice (B) confuses the similar-sounding words *sea* and *see*. Choice (C) associates *arrive* with *ticket*.

27. **(A)** *We'll be late* is a correct response to a suggestion to hurry. Choice (B) confuses the similar-sounding words *most* and *almost*. Choice (C) confuses the similar-sounding words *worry* and *hurry*.

28. **(C)** *1.55 dollars* tells the exchange rate. Choice (A) confuses the similar-sounding words *change* and *exchange*. Choice (B) associates *exchange* with *counter* (where one would go in a store to exchange a purchase).

29. **(A)** *Sure, we have 20 minutes* answers *Will we get there on time?* Choice (B) confuses the similar-sounding words *ate* and *eight*. Choice (C) uses *show* out of context.

30. **(C)** *50–35* answers *What's the score of the game?* Choice (A) answers *What time is the game?* Choice (B) answers *What kind of game?*

31. **(B)** *Just water* is a correct response to an offer of something to drink. Choice (A) confuses the similar-sounding words *sink* and *think*. Choice (C) repeats the word *like* out of context.

32. **(A)** *Julie and John* answers the question *Who?* Choice (B) associates *cook* with *dinner*. Choice (C) answers the question *Whose?*, confusing it with *who's*.

33. **(C)** *Thanks* is a correct response to a compliment. Choice (A) associates *ugly* with *beautiful*. Choice (B) associates *this* with *that*.

34. **(B)** The woman says she has to go to the post office and the man offers *I'll go with you*. Choice (A) repeats the word *office*. Choice (C) confuses the similar-sounding words *packing* and *package*.

35. **(B)** *Is Sarah there?* is a correct response when someone answers the telephone. Choice (A) confuses the similar-sounding words *yellow* and *hello*, and *jacket* and *Jack*. Choice (C) confuses the similar-sounding words *back* and *Jack*.

PART III: SHORT CONVERSATIONS AND SHORT TALKS

36. **(C)** Choice (C) is correct because *school work* and *homework* have the same meaning. Choice (A) associates *house* with *home* in the word *homework*. Choice (B) is incorrect because the woman is the one who wants help, not the man. Choice (D) confuses *housework* with *homework*.

37. **(B)** The speakers mention different types of books—mystery story, cookbook, novel—so they are in a bookstore. Choice (A) associates *restaurant* with *cook*. Choice (C) is not mentioned. Choice (D) associates *train* with *aisle*.

38. **(C)** The woman is asking about potatoes, which are vegetables. Choices (A) and (D) are things that can be bought by the pound. Choice (B) associates *eggs* with *dozen* and *white*.

39. **(D)** Sam says *I'll meet you at the court*. Choice (A) confuses *sick*, which is a reason one might visit a doctor, with *six*, the time at which the friends will meet. Choice (B) confuses the meaning of the word *court*—a place where a lawyer works, or a place where tennis is played. Choice (C) associates *lunch* with *dinner*.

40. **(B)** The woman says she wants to finish the work *by Friday*. Choice (A) is the amount of time they are allowed for finishing the project. Choice (C) repeats the word *day*. Choice (D) is not mentioned.

41. **(D)** The speaker is introducing an *author*. Choice (A) is not mentioned. Choices (B) and (C) are what the author writes about.

42. **(C)** He asks for smaller pants and says that the ones he has are large. Choice (A) is not mentioned. Choice (B) is incorrect because he asks for something smaller. Choice (D) repeats the word *fell (falling)* out of context.

43. **(D)** They are going inside a theater to see a film. Choice (A) associates *furniture* with *seat*. Choice (B) associates *film* with *photography*. Choice (C) is not mentioned.

44. **(C)** The man has a bad fever and needs to see a doctor. Choice (A) is incorrect because it is the doctor, not the man, who is busy and Tuesday is mentioned as the first day the doctor will be free. Choice (B) is incorrect because the man obviously wouldn't try to make a doctor's appointment if he didn't like doctors. Choice (D) confuses the similar-sounding words *overweight* and *wait*.

45. **(A)** The men are farmers because they are discussing growing corn and wheat. Choice (B) associates *grocery stores* with *wheat* and *corn*. Choice (C) is not mentioned. Choice (D) repeats the word *weather*.

46. **(B)** The woman is explaining the essays the students will have to write. Choice (A) is incorrect because the talk is about *this year*, not *last year*. Choice (C) is incorrect because Friday is mentioned as the day essays are due, not as an exam day. Choice (D) repeats the word *grades*.

47. **(A)** The man is giving information about the weather. Choice (B) associates *lifeguard* with *beach*. Choices (C) and (D) associate *nurse* and *baker* with temperature.

48. **(C)** The woman is most likely a travel agent as she works for a company called World Travel and has information about flights to Paris. Choices (A), (B), and (D) are associated with airplane travel, but they are incorrect because people don't usually ask gate agents, passengers, or pilots for information about different flights.

49. **(A)** is the time the doors open. Choice (B) is actually the model number of the car that is mentioned. Choices (C) and (D) are actually ticket prices.

50. **(C)** We know this is an airport because the words *airport* and *flight* are mentioned. Choice (A) repeats the word *terminal*. Choice (B) associates *security* with *police*. Choice (D) repeats the word *park* out of context.

Reading Comprehension

PART IV: INCOMPLETE SENTENCES

51. **(A)** *Of* is the correct preposition to use with a quantity word. Choices (B), (C), and (D) cannot be used correctly in this situation.

52. **(D)** The singular subject requires a third-person singular verb form. Choices (A) and (B) can only be used with plural subjects. Choice (C) needs to be followed by the base form of the verb, not the *-ing* form.

53. **(A)** *Every* is the only choice that gives meaning to this sentence. Choices (B) and (C) cannot be used before the word *day*. Choice (D), *several*, requires a plural noun.

54. **(D)** It is logical that weather will be both hot and sunny. Choice (A) is incorrect because it is impossible for the weather to be hot and cold at the same time. Choices (B) and (C) are incorrect because they are nouns, but an adjective is needed here.

55. **(B)** The subject of a sentence can be preceded by an article. (A) and (D) are incorrect because they must precede plural, not singular, nouns. (C) is incorrect because *Then* cannot be used in this position in a sentence.

56. **(C)** is the correct verb form to follow a singular subject. Choice (A) needs a plural subject. Choice (B) is missing a form of the verb *to be* to make a progressive tense. Choice (D) is a noun, but a verb is needed here.

57. **(B)** *Still* has the correct meaning and can be placed in this position in the sentence. Choices (A) and (C) are usually used in negative sentences or questions. Choice (D) is usually used to begin a new clause.

58. **(C)** This is a passive voice sentence so it needs the past participle form of the verb. Choices (A), (B), and (D) are all forms of the verb *bear*, but are not the past participle form.

59. **(D)** *At* is the correct preposition to use when mentioning a time of day. Choices (A), (B), and (C) are not the correct use of the preposition.

60. **(C)** *In front of the shopping center* is a possible place to meet. Choice (A) would mean *on top of the shopping center*, which is not likely. Choice (B) is incorrect because two places have to be mentioned when using *between*. Choice (D) cannot be used with the verb *meet*.

61. **(B)** *Who* is the correct relative pronoun to use when referring to people (*students*). Choice (A) refers to a possessive noun. Choice (C) refers to time. Choice (D) refers to a place.

62. **(B)** *On* is the correct preposition to use with a day of the week. Choices (A), (C), and (D) cannot be correctly used in this situation.

63. **(C)** *Has* is the correct form of the verb to use with the third-person singular subject *She*. Choice (A) requires a plural subject. Choice (B) is the wrong verb tense for this situation. Choice (D) requires a plural subject and is also the wrong verb tense.

64. **(B)** A verb is needed to follow the subject. Choice (A) is an adjective. Choice (C) is a noun. Choice (D) is a verb but does not agree with the subject, *We*.

65. **(D)** This is a definite subject so it requires a definite article. Choices (A), (B), and (C) are not definite articles.

66. **(B)** *And* correctly connects the two places mentioned, telling the location of the apartment. Choice (A) is an adverb and cannot be correctly used in this position. Choices (C) and (D) do not have the correct meaning for this sentence.

67. **(D)** The modal verb *will* is always followed by the base form of a verb. Choices (A), (B), and (C) do not give the correct verb form.

68. **(C)** A cardinal number is required here. Choice (A) is an ordinal number. Choices (B) and (D) are fractions.

69. **(A)** *All* precedes a plural noun. Choices (B) and (C) precede singular nouns. Choice (D) must be followed by *the* or *of the* and then the plural noun.

70. **(B)** The indefinite article *an* precedes a noun that begins with a vowel sound. Choice (A) must precede a noun that begins with a consonant sound. Choices (C) and (D) look similar to the correct answer but are actually completely different words.

71. **(C)** Both *actress* and *her* refer to a *woman*. Choice (A) refers to several people. Choice (B) refers to a man. Choice (D) refers to a thing.

72. **(C)** *Hour* begins with a vowel sound because the *h* is silent, so it correctly follows the article *an*. Choices (A), (B), and (D) each begin with a consonant sound and so must follow *a*, not *an*.

73. **(B)** The third-person singular form of the verb follows the singular subject. Choice (A) is missing *is* to make the present progressive tense. Choices (C) and (D) require plural subjects.

74. **(B)** This is the correct present tense form of the verb to follow the plural subject. Choice (A) is the base form. Choice (C) is the past participle form. Choice (D) is present tense but needs a singular subject.

75. **(A)** *For* is the correct preposition to use when mentioning a quantity of time. Choices (B), (C), and (D) cannot be correctly used in this situation.

76. **(C)** This is the subject of the sentence so a noun is needed. Choices (A), (B), and (D) are verb forms.

77. **(D)** *No* makes the noun, *boys*, negative. Choice (A) makes a verb negative. Choice (B) is a pronoun. Choice (C) is an adverb.

78. **(A)** The article *the* precedes a noun. Choice (B) is a pronoun. Choice (C) is an article but must precede a noun that begins with a vowel sound. Choice (D) is a verb.

79. **(C)** The modal verb *can* must be followed by the base form of a verb. Choices (A), (B), and (D) are not base form.

80. **(B)** *Of* is the correct preposition to use with a quantity word. Choices (A), (C), and (D) cannot be used correctly in this situation.

PART V: READING COMPREHENSION

81. **(C)** When something is *on sale*, it is sold at a lower price. For the same reason, choices (A), (B), and (D) cannot be correct.

82. **(B)** The zookeepers will feed the elephants at 4:00. The animals in choices (A), (C), and (D) will eat at 2:00 or 3:00.

83. **(B)** *Limited* means that there is a small number. Choices (A) and (C) are incorrect because the show is just opening. Choice (D) is not mentioned.

84. **(C)** *High winds and surf* means that it is windy and the waves are very big. Choices (A) and (B) are not mentioned. Choice (D) confuses *listen to the radio* with *recording a radio program*.

85. **(D)** *No trespassing* and *do not enter* both mean that people should stay outside. Choice (A) is the opposite of the correct answer. Choices (B) and (C) are not mentioned.

86. **(C)** This form is for a person who is visiting the doctor, therefore, a patient. Choices (A) and (B) are incorrect because this is information the patient must give, not the doctor or nurse. Choice (D) is incorrect because a doctor would not ask an accountant for this type of information.

87. **(D)** The first sentence tells us that the park opened on June 1. Choice (A) is incorrect because the park closes at 6, not 9. Choice (B) is incorrect because the park opened on June 1 so we know that construction started long before then. Choice (C) associates *amusement* with *game*.

88. **(C)** A *subscription* is an order to receive a magazine or newspaper. Choices (A), (B), and (D) associate *concert*, *CD*, and *instrument* with *music*.

89. **(B)** If the office were not usually open on Friday, there would be no reason to write this notice. Choice (A) is not mentioned. Choices (C) and (D) are incorrect because the notice states that the office will reopen on Monday.

90. **(C)** The *third level* is the same as the *3rd floor*. Choice (A) cannot be correct because the service desk is inside on the 3rd floor. Choice (B) answers the question *when*. Choice (D) answers the question *when* and is the one day that the service desk is closed.

91. **(B)** The line graph shows a dip in prices in April. Choice (A) is not true. Prices in January were not as high as February, March, May, or June. Choice (C) is not true. Prices were always different. Choice (D) is not true. There was an increase in May.

92. **(A)** The ad states that 5 pounds of sugar costs $4.50. Choice (B) is five times the cost of one pound of sugar. Choice (C) is the price of one pound of sugar. Choice (D) is actually the time the store closes.

93. **(A)** The ad tells us that Angel Falls is a place that people like to visit. Choices (B), (C), and (D) are incorrect because Angel Falls is a high waterfall, not a mountain, beach, or lake.

94. **(B)** *The concerts will run from June to August* means that they will begin in June and end in August. Choice (A) answers the question *where*. Choice (C) tells the hour when the concerts end. Choice (D) tells the month when the concerts end.

95. **(A)** The title, *Meat consumption*, means that the graph shows how much meat people eat. The smallest part of the bar graph is labeled *lamb*, so lamb is the meat that people eat the least. Choices (B), (C), and (D) mention meat that is more popular than lamb.

96. **(D)** Since airplanes fly, a web site called *flyfast.com* must be about airplanes. Choices (A), (B), and (C) mention forms of transportation that are not related to *fly*.

97. **(B)** Steve practices soccer three times a week and swimming once a week. Choice (A) is the number of times he has piano lessons. Choice (C) is not mentioned. Choice (D) is the number of times he plays soccer only.

98. **(C)** The receptionist works at the reception desk. Choices (A), (B), and (D) are phone numbers for other people or purposes.

99. **(C)** *RSVP* means respond to an invitation. Choice (A) is the date of the reception. Choices (B) and (D) are the hours of the reception.

100. **(A)** *All residents* means *everyone who lives there*. Choice (B) mentions the recreation area, but the meeting is not only about this topic. Choice (C) mentions trash, but since the meeting will discuss trash, it is not for people who don't have trash. Choice (D) uses the word *collect* out of context.

Model Test 2
ANSWER SHEET

Listening Comprehension

PART I: PHOTOGRAPHS

1. Ⓐ Ⓑ Ⓒ Ⓓ 5. Ⓐ Ⓑ Ⓒ Ⓓ 9. Ⓐ Ⓑ Ⓒ Ⓓ 13. Ⓐ Ⓑ Ⓒ Ⓓ
2. Ⓐ Ⓑ Ⓒ Ⓓ 6. Ⓐ Ⓑ Ⓒ Ⓓ 10. Ⓐ Ⓑ Ⓒ Ⓓ 14. Ⓐ Ⓑ Ⓒ Ⓓ
3. Ⓐ Ⓑ Ⓒ Ⓓ 7. Ⓐ Ⓑ Ⓒ Ⓓ 11. Ⓐ Ⓑ Ⓒ Ⓓ 15. Ⓐ Ⓑ Ⓒ Ⓓ
4. Ⓐ Ⓑ Ⓒ Ⓓ 8. Ⓐ Ⓑ Ⓒ Ⓓ 12. Ⓐ Ⓑ Ⓒ Ⓓ

PART II: QUESTION-RESPONSE

16. Ⓐ Ⓑ Ⓒ Ⓓ 21. Ⓐ Ⓑ Ⓒ Ⓓ 26. Ⓐ Ⓑ Ⓒ Ⓓ 31. Ⓐ Ⓑ Ⓒ Ⓓ
17. Ⓐ Ⓑ Ⓒ Ⓓ 22. Ⓐ Ⓑ Ⓒ Ⓓ 27. Ⓐ Ⓑ Ⓒ Ⓓ 32. Ⓐ Ⓑ Ⓒ Ⓓ
18. Ⓐ Ⓑ Ⓒ Ⓓ 23. Ⓐ Ⓑ Ⓒ Ⓓ 28. Ⓐ Ⓑ Ⓒ Ⓓ 33. Ⓐ Ⓑ Ⓒ Ⓓ
19. Ⓐ Ⓑ Ⓒ Ⓓ 24. Ⓐ Ⓑ Ⓒ Ⓓ 29. Ⓐ Ⓑ Ⓒ Ⓓ 34. Ⓐ Ⓑ Ⓒ Ⓓ
20. Ⓐ Ⓑ Ⓒ Ⓓ 25. Ⓐ Ⓑ Ⓒ Ⓓ 30. Ⓐ Ⓑ Ⓒ Ⓓ 35. Ⓐ Ⓑ Ⓒ Ⓓ

PART III: SHORT CONVERSATIONS AND SHORT TALKS

36. Ⓐ Ⓑ Ⓒ Ⓓ 40. Ⓐ Ⓑ Ⓒ Ⓓ 44. Ⓐ Ⓑ Ⓒ Ⓓ 48. Ⓐ Ⓑ Ⓒ Ⓓ
37. Ⓐ Ⓑ Ⓒ Ⓓ 41. Ⓐ Ⓑ Ⓒ Ⓓ 45. Ⓐ Ⓑ Ⓒ Ⓓ 49. Ⓐ Ⓑ Ⓒ Ⓓ
38. Ⓐ Ⓑ Ⓒ Ⓓ 42. Ⓐ Ⓑ Ⓒ Ⓓ 46. Ⓐ Ⓑ Ⓒ Ⓓ 50. Ⓐ Ⓑ Ⓒ Ⓓ
39. Ⓐ Ⓑ Ⓒ Ⓓ 43. Ⓐ Ⓑ Ⓒ Ⓓ 47. Ⓐ Ⓑ Ⓒ Ⓓ

Reading Comprehension

PART IV: INCOMPLETE SENTENCES

51. Ⓐ Ⓑ Ⓒ Ⓓ 59. Ⓐ Ⓑ Ⓒ Ⓓ 67. Ⓐ Ⓑ Ⓒ Ⓓ 75. Ⓐ Ⓑ Ⓒ Ⓓ
52. Ⓐ Ⓑ Ⓒ Ⓓ 60. Ⓐ Ⓑ Ⓒ Ⓓ 68. Ⓐ Ⓑ Ⓒ Ⓓ 76. Ⓐ Ⓑ Ⓒ Ⓓ
53. Ⓐ Ⓑ Ⓒ Ⓓ 61. Ⓐ Ⓑ Ⓒ Ⓓ 69. Ⓐ Ⓑ Ⓒ Ⓓ 77. Ⓐ Ⓑ Ⓒ Ⓓ
54. Ⓐ Ⓑ Ⓒ Ⓓ 62. Ⓐ Ⓑ Ⓒ Ⓓ 70. Ⓐ Ⓑ Ⓒ Ⓓ 78. Ⓐ Ⓑ Ⓒ Ⓓ
55. Ⓐ Ⓑ Ⓒ Ⓓ 63. Ⓐ Ⓑ Ⓒ Ⓓ 71. Ⓐ Ⓑ Ⓒ Ⓓ 79. Ⓐ Ⓑ Ⓒ Ⓓ
56. Ⓐ Ⓑ Ⓒ Ⓓ 64. Ⓐ Ⓑ Ⓒ Ⓓ 72. Ⓐ Ⓑ Ⓒ Ⓓ 80. Ⓐ Ⓑ Ⓒ Ⓓ
57. Ⓐ Ⓑ Ⓒ Ⓓ 65. Ⓐ Ⓑ Ⓒ Ⓓ 73. Ⓐ Ⓑ Ⓒ Ⓓ
58. Ⓐ Ⓑ Ⓒ Ⓓ 66. Ⓐ Ⓑ Ⓒ Ⓓ 74. Ⓐ Ⓑ Ⓒ Ⓓ

PART V: READING COMPREHENSION

81. Ⓐ Ⓑ Ⓒ Ⓓ 86. Ⓐ Ⓑ Ⓒ Ⓓ 91. Ⓐ Ⓑ Ⓒ Ⓓ 96. Ⓐ Ⓑ Ⓒ Ⓓ
82. Ⓐ Ⓑ Ⓒ Ⓓ 87. Ⓐ Ⓑ Ⓒ Ⓓ 92. Ⓐ Ⓑ Ⓒ Ⓓ 97. Ⓐ Ⓑ Ⓒ Ⓓ
83. Ⓐ Ⓑ Ⓒ Ⓓ 88. Ⓐ Ⓑ Ⓒ Ⓓ 93. Ⓐ Ⓑ Ⓒ Ⓓ 98. Ⓐ Ⓑ Ⓒ Ⓓ
84. Ⓐ Ⓑ Ⓒ Ⓓ 89. Ⓐ Ⓑ Ⓒ Ⓓ 94. Ⓐ Ⓑ Ⓒ Ⓓ 99. Ⓐ Ⓑ Ⓒ Ⓓ
85. Ⓐ Ⓑ Ⓒ Ⓓ 90. Ⓐ Ⓑ Ⓒ Ⓓ 95. Ⓐ Ⓑ Ⓒ Ⓓ 100. Ⓐ Ⓑ Ⓒ Ⓓ

TOEIC Bridge Model Test 2

LISTENING COMPREHENSION

In this section of the test, you will have the chance to show how well you understand spoken English. There are three parts to this section, with special directions for each part.

PART I: PHOTOGRAPHS

Directions: For each question, you will see a picture in your test book and you will hear four short statements. The statements will be spoken just one time. They will not be printed in your test book, so you must listen carefully.

When you hear the four statements, look at the picture in your test book and choose the statement that best describes what you see in the picture. Then, on your answer sheet, find the number of the question and mark your answer. Look at the sample below.

Now listen to the four statements.

Sample Answer

Ⓐ Ⓑ © Ⓓ

Statement (B), "The boys are reading," best describes what you see in the picture. Therefore, you should choose answer (B).

1.

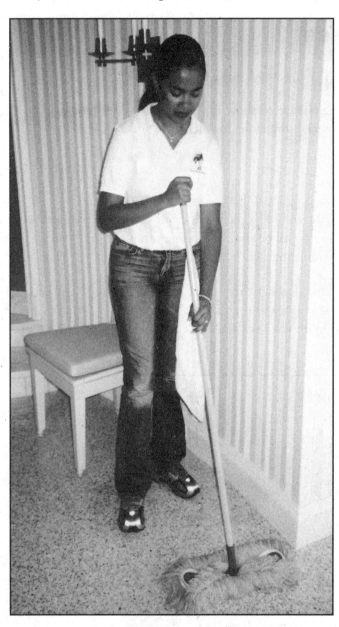

2.

3.

4.

5.

6.

7.

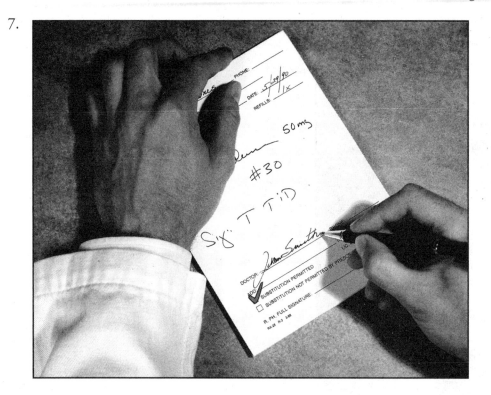

8.

9.

10.

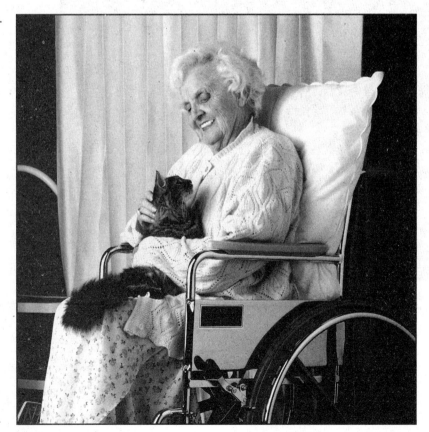

11.

12.

13.

14.

15.

PART II: QUESTION-RESPONSE

> **CD 2 Track 9**
>
> **Directions:** In this part of the test, you will hear a question or statement spoken in English, followed by three responses, also spoken in English. The question or statement and the responses will be spoken just one time. They will not be printed in your test book, so you must listen carefully. Choose the best response to each question.
>
> | [Narrator] | Now listen to a sample question. |
> |---|---|
> | [Narrator] | You will hear: |
> | [Woman B] | Excuse me, where is the bus stop? |
> | [Narrator] | You will also hear: |
> | [Man A] | (A) It's across the street. |
> | | (B) It's underneath. |
> | | (C) It arrives in 10 minutes. |
> | [Narrator] | The best response to the question *Where is the bus stop?* is Choice (A), *It's across the street.* Therefore, you should choose answer (A). |

16. Mark your answer on your answer sheet.

17. Mark your answer on your answer sheet.

18. Mark your answer on your answer sheet.

19. Mark your answer on your answer sheet.

20. Mark your answer on your answer sheet.

21. Mark your answer on your answer sheet.

22. Mark your answer on your answer sheet.

23. Mark your answer on your answer sheet.

24. Mark your answer on your answer sheet.

25. Mark your answer on your answer sheet.

26. Mark your answer on your answer sheet.

27. Mark your answer on your answer sheet.

28. Mark your answer on your answer sheet.

29. Mark your answer on your answer sheet.

30. Mark your answer on your answer sheet.

31. Mark your answer on your answer sheet.

32. Mark your answer on your answer sheet.

33. Mark your answer on your answer sheet.

34. Mark your answer on your answer sheet.

35. Mark your answer on your answer sheet.

Model Test 2

PART III: SHORT CONVERSATIONS AND SHORT TALKS

Directions: In this part of the test, you will hear 15 short conversations or short talks only once, so you must listen carefully.

In your test book, you will read a question about each conversation or talk. The question will be followed by four short answers. Choose the best answer to each question and mark it on your answer sheet.

36. What does the woman tell the man?

    (A) The library's hours.
    (B) Directions to the library.
    (C) A way to the corner store.
    (D) The name of a bookstore.

37. What will you hear next?

    (A) A talk show for teens.
    (B) More music.
    (C) Sports results.
    (D) Soccer and basketball advertisements.

38. Who should respond?

    (A) People who like to travel.
    (B) People who like music.
    (C) People who are weak.
    (D) People who are busy.

39. What is the weather forecast?

    (A) Snow in the southwest.
    (B) Temperatures below 70.
    (C) A nice day.
    (D) A windless day.

40. Who is speaking?

    (A) A passenger.
    (B) A tour guide.
    (C) A train conductor.
    (D) A hotel clerk.

41. What is the man's occupation?

    (A) He is a doctor.
    (B) He is a waiter.
    (C) He is a pharmacist.
    (D) He is a weather reporter.

42. What does Jenny Lau have to do?

    (A) Leave Manila.
    (B) Read a report.
    (C) Pay a fine.
    (D) Get on the plane.

43. What will the man probably do next?

    (A) Buy a new wallet.
    (B) Write a check.
    (C) Look for the wallet.
    (D) Clean the table.

44. Who are the speakers?

    (A) Chef and customer.
    (B) Husband and wife.
    (C) Employer and employee.
    (D) Teacher and student.

45. What does the announcer say?

    (A) The men are safe.
    (B) The search continues.
    (C) One climber was lost.
    (D) A mountain village was found.

46. What will the woman talk about?

    (A) International economy.
    (B) Japanese banks.
    (C) Inviting Japanese friends.
    (D) Speaking Japanese.

47. Why are they unhappy?

    (A) The prizes cost a lot of money.
    (B) Cars are very expensive.
    (C) They think the car is too big.
    (D) They don't like shopping.

48. What are the speakers discussing?

    (A) The quality of the water.
    (B) Where to buy cups.
    (C) The size of a cup.
    (D) How to make coffee.

49. What will the man do?

    (A) Meet the woman at the airport.
    (B) Change reservations.
    (C) Say good-bye.
    (D) Take the woman to the airport.

50. Who will be interested in the announcement?

    (A) Construction workers.
    (B) Unemployed mechanics.
    (C) Home buyers.
    (D) House painters.

This is the end of the Listening Comprehension portion of the test. Turn to Part IV in your test book.

READING COMPREHENSION

In this section of the test, you will have the chance to show how well you understand written English. There are TWO parts to this section, with special directions for each part.

YOU WILL HAVE 35 MINUTES TO COMPLETE PARTS IV AND V OF THE TEST.

PART IV: INCOMPLETE SENTENCES

Directions: Questions 51–80 are incomplete sentences. Four words or phrases, marked (A), (B), (C), (D), are given beneath each sentence. You must choose the one word or phrase that best completes the sentence. Then, on your answer sheet, find the number of the question and mark your answer.

Example   Sample Answer

This soup doesn't _____ good.   Ⓐ Ⓑ Ⓒ Ⓓ
(A) tasteful
(B) tasty
(C) taste
(D) tasted

The sentence should read, "This soup doesn't taste good." Therefore, you should choose answer (C).

Now begin work on the questions.

51. Can you _____ the telephone?

    (A) answered
    (B) answering
    (C) to answer
    (D) answer

52. Star Market is giving away a _____ trip to Hawaii.

    (A) free
    (B) freedom
    (C) frees
    (D) freely

53. She hasn't arrived _____ .

    (A) only
    (B) yet
    (C) still
    (D) soon

54. The _____ practice three times a week.

    (A) play
    (B) players
    (C) playing
    (D) played

55. They studied in California _____ six months.

    (A) on
    (B) at
    (C) for
    (D) with

56. An ounce is smaller _____ a pound.

    (A) these
    (B) than
    (C) that
    (D) the

57. School will _____ in three weeks.

    (A) done
    (B) completion
    (C) over
    (D) finish

58. Let's meet on the corner _____ Gate Street and Charles Way.

    (A) of
    (B) for
    (C) over
    (D) from

59. The restaurant is _____ for its desserts.

    (A) knowing
    (B) knew
    (C) known
    (D) knowledge

60. Cynthia and Paula helped Luciana _____ into a new apartment.

    (A) change
    (B) ready
    (C) move
    (D) prepare

61. Her cousin comes to visit _____ August.

    (A) always
    (B) every
    (C) never
    (D) almost

62. Professor Ngyuen gives _____ lectures.

    (A) interest
    (B) interesting
    (C) interested
    (D) interests

63. Juan _____ the dog in the park every day at 5:30.

    (A) motions
    (B) moves
    (C) walks
    (D) goes

64. You will sleep very _____ in this hotel.

    (A) comfortable
    (B) comfort
    (C) comforter
    (D) comfortably

65. Tax is added to the _____ price.

    (A) finish
    (B) final
    (C) end
    (D) stop

66. Charlie wrote _____ own name on all the books in the room.

    (A) his
    (B) its
    (C) their
    (D) our

67. They _____ delicious meals at this restaurant.

    (A) service
    (B) serve
    (C) serving
    (D) server

68. You may return this computer _____ within 14 days.

    (A) print
    (B) printed
    (C) printer
    (D) printing

69. Brenda is _____ her mother.

(A) as tall as
(B) taller
(C) the tallest
(D) tall

70. I can buy a new car now _____ I have enough money.

(A) but
(B) because
(C) before
(D) between

71. Write your name _____ this paper.

(A) at
(B) on
(C) over
(D) between

72. Melody _____ reads three or more books a week.

(A) yet
(B) ever
(C) often
(D) until

73. The _____ train to the airport leaves in seven minutes.

(A) next
(B) after
(C) soon
(D) near

74. You can swim, fish, _____ camp at the park.

(A) but
(B) neither
(C) and
(D) either

75. This _____ holds three liters.

(A) contains
(B) containing
(C) contain
(D) container

76. Please put those boxes _____ the bed.

(A) down
(B) under
(C) low
(D) fall

77. Tom mailed _____ application to the State University.

(A) he
(B) he's
(C) him
(D) his

78. _____ plants need water and sunlight.

(A) A
(B) This
(C) The
(D) An

79. The houses across the street _____ very expensive.

(A) are
(B) was
(C) is
(D) be

80. That is the same woman _____ we saw in the park.

(A) who
(B) whose
(C) which
(D) where

PART V: READING COMPREHENSION

Directions: Questions 81–100 are based on a variety of reading materials (for example, notices, letters, forms, newspaper and magazine articles, and advertisements). You must choose the one best answer, (A), (B), (C), or (D), to each question. Then, on your answer sheet, find the number of the question and mark your answer. Answer all questions following a passage on the basis of what is **stated** or **implied** in that passage.

Read the following example.

Notice of Schedule Change:
The departure time for the morning bus to
Riverdale has been changed from 10:15 to 10:45.
Arrival in Riverdale is scheduled for 1:30.
The one-way fare is still $10.00.

What time will the bus leave for Riverdale?
(A) 10:15
(B) 10:45
(C) 10:00
(D) 1:30

Sample Answer

(A) (B) (C) (D)

The notice says that the new departure time is 10:45. Therefore, you should choose answer (B).

Now begin work on the questions.

Questions 81–82 refer to the following announcement.

Sign up for a summer class now!
Registration begins June 1, Classes begin June 25.

Classes offered in the following subjects:
Art
History
Languages
Economics

81. What class is not offered?

(A) Swimming.
(B) Languages.
(C) History.
(D) Art.

82. When will classes start?

(A) On June 1.
(B) On June 25.
(C) In July.
(D) Between June 1 and June 25.

Questions 83–84 refer to the following form.

```
GIFT CERTIFICATE: CORNER BOOKS AND MUSIC
Amount:        $25
To:            Kim Young
From:          Sunhee Young
Message:       Happy Birthday!
Date:          November 12, 2010

This certificate is good for ONE YEAR from the date above.
```

83. Why did Kim receive this gift certificate?

    (A) She got a new job at a bookstore.
    (B) She graduated.
    (C) It's a holiday.
    (D) It's her birthday.

84. How long can Kim use the gift certificate?

    (A) Until November 12, 2011.
    (B) For two months.
    (C) Until November 12, 2010.
    (D) For 25 days.

Questions 85–86 refer to the following form.

Use this Suggestion Form to help us improve our service.
Suggestion:

Why don't you offer special children's meals that are smaller and cheaper? Offer food that kids like, such as hamburgers and peanut butter sandwiches.

Send to: Happy King, Inc.
16 San Carlos Avenue
Concord, CA 94500

85. What kind of business is Happy King?

    (A) A toy store.
    (B) A restaurant.
    (C) A children's clothing store.
    (D) A grocery store.

86. How will the company receive the information?

    (A) By telephone.
    (B) In person.
    (C) By fax.
    (D) By mail.

Model Test 2

Questions 87–90 refer to the following schedule.

Carol's Schedule

Tuesday

8:00	Doctor's appointment
10:00	Meeting with architects
12:00	Lunch with Mom at *The Border Grill*
3:00	Conference call with New York office
4:30	Coffee with John—remind him about planning meeting tomorrow.

---

87. What will Carol do before meeting with the architects?

    (A) Meet with her staff.
    (B) Eat a meal at a restaurant.
    (C) Talk on the telephone.
    (D) Visit the doctor.

88. Where will Carol have lunch?

    (A) At the *Border Grill*.
    (B) Near her doctor's office.
    (C) In New York.
    (D) At her mother's house.

89. When is the planning meeting?

    (A) At 4:30.
    (B) On Wednesday.
    (C) At 10:00.
    (D) On Thursday.

90. Who will probably attend the planning meeting?

    (A) The doctor.
    (B) Carol's mom.
    (C) John.
    (D) The architects.

Questions 91–92 refer to the following notice.

**We will close Sanjay's Restaurant in Antioch
during the month of May for repairs.
Visit our other location on
Hilltop Avenue in Richmond.
Join us on July 1 for the GRAND REOPENING.**

---

91. Why is this sign posted?

    (A) To show a new menu.
    (B) To announce that one restaurant will be closed.
    (C) To advertise a new supermarket.
    (D) To sell a business.

92. What will happen on July 1?

    (A) Sanjay's restaurant will be closed.
    (B) Repairs will begin.
    (C) The restaurant in Antioch will open again.
    (D) The restaurant in Richmond will close for repairs.

Questions 93–95 refer to the following article.

> Police discovered a 6-year-old girl at a train station yesterday. She was lost for 48 hours. Her parents told police that she was playing at a park close to her house. When she didn't come home for dinner, her mother looked for her in the park. Then she called neighbors, friends, and, finally, the police. The police found the girl, Talia Newhouse, sleeping on a bench at the train station near her house.

93. Who did the police find?

   (A) Some friends.
   (B) The father.
   (C) The mother's neighbor.
   (D) Talia Newhouse.

94. Where was the person found?

   (A) At the park.
   (B) At a neighbor's house.
   (C) At a train station.
   (D) At the police station.

95. What did the mother do?

   (A) She took a walk in the park.
   (B) She called the police.
   (C) She went to the train station.
   (D) She waited in her house.

Questions 96–98 refer to the following notice.

> **Buy your tickets now for the season. Prices range from $10–$110 per game. There are games twice every day from Friday through Sunday. The afternoon starting time is at 2:00 P.M. and the night starting time is at 7:00 P.M.**

96. What is the notice about?

   (A) A movie theater.
   (B) An airline schedule.
   (C) Tickets for a sports event.
   (D) The weekly TV schedule.

97. How much does a ticket cost?

   (A) Less than $10.
   (B) Between $10 and $110.
   (C) More than $110.
   (D) Between $2 and $7.

98. When can you see a game?

   (A) On Fridays and Sundays only.
   (B) On Monday through Thursday.
   (C) On Fridays, Saturdays, and Sundays.
   (D) Every day of the week.

Questions 99–100 refer to the following graph.

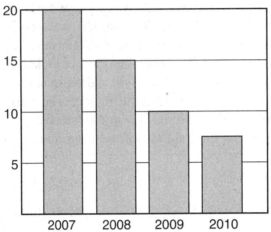

99. What does this graph show?

    (A) The number of koala bears born in different years.
    (B) The number of people who visit koala bears at the zoo.
    (C) The cost of baby koala bears.
    (D) The number of wild koala bears caught every year.

100. What is true about the number of koala bears?

    (A) The number stays the same.
    (B) The number is increasing.
    (C) The number is decreasing.
    (D) The number goes up and down.

STOP

This is the end of the Reading portion of the test.

Answer Key for
MODEL TEST 2

Listening Comprehension

PART I

1. B	4. C	7. B	10. C	13. B
2. A	5. A	8. A	11. C	14. D
3. D	6. C	9. D	12. A	15. B

PART II

16. C	20. A	24. C	28. C	32. A
17. A	21. A	25. A	29. B	33. A
18. B	22. B	26. C	30. A	34. C
19. B	23. A	27. B	31. B	35. C

PART III

36. B	39. C	42. D	45. A	48. D
37. C	40. B	43. C	46. B	49. A
38. B	41. A	44. B	47. B	50. C

Reading Comprehension

PART IV

51. D	57. D	63. C	69. A	75. D
52. A	58. A	64. D	70. B	76. B
53. B	59. C	65. B	71. B	77. D
54. B	60. C	66. A	72. C	78. C
55. C	61. B	67. B	73. A	79. A
56. B	62. B	68. C	74. C	80. A

PART V

81. A	85. B	89. B	93. D	97. B
82. B	86. D	90. C	94. C	98. C
83. D	87. D	91. B	95. B	99. A
84. A	88. A	92. C	96. C	100. C

Correct Responses = _____

EXPLANATORY ANSWERS FOR TOEIC BRIDGE MODEL TEST 2

Listening Comprehension

PART I: PHOTOGRAPHS

1. **(B)** The woman, a housekeeper, is running a mop over a floor to clean it. The other choices do not identify the action. Choices (A), (C), and (D) use words associated with housework: *washing, dusting,* and *wiping.*

2. **(A)** A passenger ship (either a cruise ship or a ferry) is on the water, at sea. The other choices do not identify the photo or the location. Choice (B) uses the similar-sounding word *sheep* for *ship* and *me* for *sea.* Choice (C) uses words associated with sea, *sailor* and *shore.* Choice (D) uses a word that sounds like sailor, *tailor,* and uses the word associated with sea, *water.*

3. **(D)** A man (a father or grandfather or uncle) is carrying a baby on his back. The other choices do not identify the person or the action. Choice (A) repeats the word *baby.* Choice (B) uses words associated with family: *father, son.* Choice (C) also uses words associated with family: *mother, baby.*

4. **(C)** A firefighter is aiming the water at a blaze. A lot of smoke is coming from a house on fire. The other choices do not identify the person or the action. Choice (A) uses a word associated with *water: washing.* Choice (B) repeats the word *home* and *house.* Choice (D) repeats the word *watering.*

5. **(A)** A woman is walking on the platform alongside a stopped underground train. There is a sign above her head. The other choices do not identify the action. Choice (B) repeats the word *platform.* Choice (C) uses a word associated with transportation, *bus.* Choice (D) repeats the word *sign.*

6. **(C)** A doctor is signing his name on a prescription form. The other choices do not identify the occupation or action. Choice (A) uses similar words: *pharmacist, label, prescription.* Choice (B) uses words associated with illness: *patient, medication.* Choice (D) repeats the word *name.*

7. **(B)** A couple is sitting on a park bench. She is reading a newspaper; he is wearing a cap and watching something in the distance. The other choices do not identify the action. Choice (A) uses the word *news,* which sounds like *newspaper.* Choice (C) uses the word *paper,* which sounds like *newspaper.* Choice (D) uses the word *nap,* which sounds like *cap.*

8. **(A)** A Boeing 747 is on the taxiway preparing to take off. The other choices do not identify the photo or the action. Choice (B) uses the similar-sounding word *taxi.* Choice (C) uses a phrase associated with acceleration for take off: *speed up.* Choice (D) repeats the word *runway.*

9. **(D)** A young person wearing a chef's hat is putting decorations on a cake. Choice (A) correctly identifies the location but not the person or the action. Choice (B) associates *dessert* with *cake.* Choice (C) correctly identifies an object in the picture, *tray,* but not the person or the action.

10. **(C)** A woman in a wheelchair is petting her cat. The other choices do not identify the photo or the action. Choice (A) uses the similar-sounding word *rat* for *cat.* Choice (B) misidentifies the pet. Choice (D) repeats the word *sweater* that the woman is wearing not *knitting.*

11. **(C)** There is a blackboard, a globe, several children, and one adult, so this must be a teacher and students in a classroom. Choice (A) is incorrect because it is the boy, not the girl, who is writing in a notebook. Choice (B) is incorrect because the children are already sitting down. Choice (D) is incorrect because it is the girl, not the boy, who has a microscope.

12. **(A)** Two people are skiing down a snow-covered mountain. The other choices do not identify the action. Choice (B) misidentifies the sport. Choice (C) repeats the word *snow*. Choice (D) uses the sport *water skiing*, which sounds like *snow skiing*.

13. **(B)** A crowd of pedestrians is walking on the street. Since many carry briefcases they are probably office workers. The other choices do not identify the photo or the action. Choice (A) repeats words seen in the photo: *men* and *street*. Choice (C) uses the word *peas*, which has a similar sound to *persons* or *people*. Choice (D) uses the associated word *workers*.

14. **(D)** A man is using a marker to make notes on a large chart on a board. The other choices do not match the action. Choice (A) repeats the word *chart*. Choice (B) refers to the *letters* written at the top of the board. Choice (C) uses the word *waiting*, which sounds like *writing*, and *bed*, which sounds like *board*.

15. **(B)** A woman is standing at the end of the lawn watching birds fly around. The other choices do not match the photo. Choice (A) tries to confuse by using the word *feeding*, which is associated with bird watching. Choice (C) uses another word associated with birds, *cage*. Choice (D) misidentifies the action. She is not *sitting* on the lawn.

PART II: QUESTION-RESPONSE

16. **(C)** The woman says that she will get off at the next train stop. Choice (A) associates *ride* and *car* with *train*. Choice (B) confuses the similar-sounding words *sit* and *city*.

17. **(A)** *Isn't it horrible?* is a possible reaction after hearing some bad news. Choice (B) confuses the similar-sounding words *here* and *hear*. Choice (C) associates *old* with *news*.

18. **(B)** *It's Mrs. Clark now* names the supervisor. Choices (A) and (C) answer *Who?* by using people's names, but they do not answer the complete question *Who is your supervisor?*

19. **(B)** This answer gives the location of the movie theater. Choice (A) confuses the similar-sounding words *moved* and *movie*. Choice (C) associates *actor* with *movie*.

20. **(A)** *How was the food?* is a proper response to a comment about a restaurant. Choice (B) confuses the similar-sounding words *rest* and *restaurant*. Choice (C) repeats the word *Italian* out of context.

21. **(A)** *I left it in the car* is a possible thing to do with a jacket. Choice (B) associates *coat* with *jacket*. Choice (C) associates *clothes* with *jacket*.

22. **(B)** This choice answers the question *How much?* Choices (A) and (C) associate *bus* and *plane* with *tickets*.

23. **(A)** This choice gives the name of the dentist. Choice (B) answers the question *Where?* Choice (C) answers the question *How?*

24. **(C)** This is a proper response to a request for a favor. Choice (A) confuses the similar-sounding words *flavor* and *favor*. Choice (B) repeats the word *can* out of context.

25. **(A)** *Let's go* is a possible answer to the question *Are you ready?* Choices (B) and (C) confuse the similar-sounding words *read*, *Freddy*, and *ready*.

26. **(C)** *I hope you win!* is a possible response to a comment about an election. Choice (A) confuses the similar-sounding words *selection* and *election*. Choice (B) associates *homework* with *school*.

27. **(B)** *Take an umbrella* is an appropriate response to a question about rain. Choices (A) and (C) confuse the similar-sounding words *train*, *plane*, and *rain*.

28. **(C)** *At University Hospital* answers the question *Where?* Choice (A) answers *Who?* and Choice (B) answers *When?*

29. **(B)** *I would like to open a checking account* is something one might say when calling a bank. Choice (A) confuses the similar-sounding words *customs* and *customer*. Choice (C) confuses the similar-sounding words *serve* and *service*.

30. **(A)** *It's 30 minutes late* tells that the flight is not on time. Choice (B) associates *plane* with *flight*. Choice (C) confuses the similar-sounding words *light* and *flight*.

31. **(B)** *So did we* tells that the man also went to the concert. Choice (A) associates *late* with *night*. Choice (C) associates *singing* with *concert*.

32. **(A)** *I leave in two weeks* answers the question *When?* Choice (B) answers *How long?* Choice (C) answers *Where?*

33. **(A)** *He has a cat* answers the question about the brother's pet. Choice (B) associates *sister* with *brother*. Choice (C) associates *animals* with *pet*.

34. **(C)** *I don't have a bike* is a possible response to an invitation to take a bicycle ride. Choice (A) associates *race* with *bicycle*. Choice (B) repeats the word *ride* out of context.

35. **(C)** *In room 401* answers the question *Where?* Choice (A) associates *budget* with *meeting*. Choice (B) answers the question *When?*

PART III: SHORT CONVERSATIONS AND SHORT TALKS

36. **(B)** The woman tells the location of the library, *just around the corner*. Choice (A) is incorrect because the woman doesn't say anything about the library's hours. Choice (C) repeats the word *corner* out of context. Choice (D) associates *book* with *library*.

37. **(C)** *Scores* means the same as *sports results*. Choice (A) confuses the similar-sounding words *teens* and *teams*. Choice (B) is not mentioned. Choice (D) repeats *soccer* and *basketball*, but the talk mentions nothing about advertisements.

38. **(B)** People who like music would probably enjoy doing volunteer work at an opera house. Choice (A) is not mentioned. Choice (C) confuses the similar-sounding words *weak* and *week*. Choice (D) mentions the opposite of what the man asked for—people who have extra free time.

39. **(C)** The talk predicts a beautiful and sunny day. Choice (A) repeats the word *southwest*, but the talk mentioned nothing about snow. Choice (B) mentions the opposite of the information in the talk—temperatures above 70. Choice (D) also mentions the opposite of the correct information—light winds.

40. **(B)** The tour guide is trying to get his customers ready for the city tour. Choice (A) associates *passenger* with *bus*. Choice (C) associates *train* with *leaving*. Choice (D) associates *hotel clerk* with *luggage*.

41. **(A)** The man is helping a person who feels sick, and he recommends medicine. Choice (B) confuses the similar-sounding words *waiter* and *water*. Choice (C) associates *pharmacist* with *aspirin*. Choice (D) associates *weather* with *cold*.

42. **(D)** *Board the plane* means *get on the plane*. Choice (A) is incorrect because Jenny Lau is going to Manila so she can't be leaving it. Choice (B) uses the word *report* out of context. Choice (C) confuses the similar-sounding words *fine* and *nine*.

43. **(C)** *Check* can mean *look for*. Choice (A) is not mentioned. Choice (B) uses the word *check* out of context. Choice (D) repeats the word *table*.

44. **(B)** The husband and wife are discussing eating dinner together and taking care of their children. Choice (A) associates *chef* with *dinner*. Choice (C) associates *employer and employee* with *work*. Choice (D) associates *teacher and student* with *school*.

45. **(A)** The men are safe and healthy. Choice (B) is the opposite of the information given in the talk—the search is over. Choice (C) associates *lost* with *found*. Choice (D) confuses *a mountain village was found* with *mountain climbers were found*.

46. **(B)** The woman says she will focus on Japanese banks. Choice (A) repeats the word *economy*. Choice (C) repeats the word *inviting*. Choice (D) repeats the word *speak*.

47. **(B)** Prices are high. Choice (A) confuses the similar-sounding words *prizes* and *prices*. Choice (C) is not mentioned. Choice (D) repeats the word *shopping*.

48. **(D)** They are discussing how much water and coffee to use to make coffee. Choice (A) repeats the word *water*. Choices (B) and (C) repeat the word *cup*.

49. **(A)** The man says *I'll see you tomorrow at the airport*. Choice (B) repeats *change reservations*. Choice (C) is not mentioned. Choice (D) is the opposite of the correct answer.

50. **(C)** Home buyers are interested in buying new houses. Choice (A) associates *construction workers* with *new houses*. Choice (B) associates *mechanics* with *garages*. Choice (D) associates *house painters* with *new houses*.

Reading Comprehension

PART IV: INCOMPLETE SENTENCES

51. **(D)** The modal verb *can* is followed by the base form of a verb. Choices (A), (B), and (C) are other verb forms.

52. **(A)** An adjective in this position describes the noun *trip*. Choice (B) is a noun. Choice (C) is a verb. Choice (D) is an adverb.

53. **(B)** *Yet* is used in negative sentences and can be placed at the end of the sentence. It is commonly used with the present perfect tense. Choices (A) and (C) cannot be placed at the end of a sentence. Choice (D) is not usually used with the present perfect tense.

54. **(B)** A noun is needed to complete the subject of the sentence. Choices (A), (C), and (D) are all verb forms.

55. **(C)** *For* is the correct preposition to use with a quantity of time. Choices (A), (B), and (D) cannot be correctly used in this sentence.

56. **(B)** *Than* is the correct word to use with a comparative adjective. Choices (A), (C), and (D) are not comparative words.

57. **(D)** All the choices have similar meanings, but the base form of a verb is needed to follow the modal verb *will*. Choice (A) is a past participle form. Choice (B) is a noun. Choice (C) is an adjective.

58. **(A)** *Of* is the correct preposition to follow *corner*. Choices (B), (C), and (D) cannot be correctly used in this sentence.

59. **(C)** An adjective in this position describes the subject, *restaurant.* Choice (A) is a gerund. Choice (B) is a past tense verb. Choice (D) is a noun.

60. **(C)** *Move* means to go live in a new home. Choices (A) and (D) do not have this meaning. Choice (B) is an adjective, but a verb is needed here.

61. **(B)** *Every* goes before a noun. Choices (A), (C), and (D) are adverbs and are usually placed before a verb.

62. **(B)** An *interesting* lecture is one that makes the listeners feel interested. Choices (A) and (D) cannot be used as adjectives. Choice (C) can be used as an adjective, but to describe the listeners, not the lecture.

63. **(C)** *Walk the dog* means *take the dog for a walk.* Choices (A), (B), and (D) cannot be used with this meaning.

64. **(D)** An adverb is needed to describe the verb *sleep.* Choice (A) is an adjective. Choice (B) can be used as a verb or a noun, but not as an adverb. Choice (C) is a noun.

65. **(B)** All the choices have similar meanings, but an adjective is needed to describe the noun *price.* Choice (A) is a verb. Choices (C) and (D) can be used as verbs or nouns.

66. **(A)** *His* is a possesive adjective that refers to a man, in this case, *Charlie.* Choice (B) refers to a thing. Choice (C) refers to several people. Choice (D) refers to *you and I.*

67. **(B)** A simple present tense verb is needed to follow the subject of the sentence. Choice (A) is a noun. Choice (C) is a gerund or a noun. Choice (D) is a noun.

68. **(C)** A noun is needed to complete the object of the sentence. Choices (A), (B), and (D) are different verb forms.

69. **(A)** *As tall as* is a complete and correct comparative form. Choice (B) is missing the word *than.* Choice (C) is a superlative, not a comparative, adjective. Choice (D) is not a comparative form.

70. **(B)** *Because* introduces a reason. Choice (A) introduces a contradiction or unexpected idea. Choices (C) and (D) indicate time or place.

71. **(B)** *On* is the correct preposition to indicate the place to write your name. Choices (A), (C), and (D) cannot be correctly used in this sentence.

72. **(C)** *Often* is an adverb of frequency that is usually placed before the verb. Choices (A) and (B) are usually used in negative sentences or questions. Choice (D) usually introduces a time phrase or clause.

73. **(A)** An adjective is needed to describe the noun *train.* Choices (B) and (C) are adverbs. Choice (D) does not have the correct meaning.

74. **(C)** *And* is used to complete a list. Choice (A) introduces a contradiction or opposite idea. Choices (B) and (D) indicate a choice.

75. **(D)** A noun is needed to complete the subject of the sentence. Choices (A), (B), and (C) are different verb forms.

76. **(B)** A preposition is needed to indicate location. Choices (A), (C), and (D) are not prepositions.

77. **(D)** A possessive adjective in this position tells who owns the application. Choice (A) is a subject pronoun. Choice (B) is a contraction of a pronoun and a verb. Choice (C) is an object pronoun.

78. **(C)** *The* is the only one of these choices that can precede a plural noun. Choices (A), (B), and (D) can only precede singular nouns.

79. **(A)** The subject, *houses*, is plural and takes a plural verb. Choices (B), (C), and (D) cannot be used with a plural subject.

80. **(A)** *Who* refers to a person (*woman*). Choice (B) refers to a possessive noun. Choice (C) refers to a thing. Choice (D) refers to a place.

PART V: READING COMPREHENSION

81. **(A)** Swimming is the one choice not mentioned in the announcement. Choices (B), (C), and (D) are all mentioned.

82. **(B)** shows the correct date. Choice (A) is the date that registration begins. Choice (C) is not mentioned. Choice (D) gives the dates for both registration and the beginning of classes.

83. **(D)** The message on the certificate is *Happy Birthday* so we can assume that it is a birthday gift. Choice (A) mentions the bookstore, where the gift certificate was sold. Choices (B) and (C) are not mentioned.

84. **(A)** The certificate is good for one year, so Kim can use it until November, 2011. Choice (B) is not mentioned. Choice (C) is the date the certificate was sold. The number in Choice (D) is actually the cost of the gift certificate.

85. **(B)** The suggestion is about meals so the business must be a restaurant. Choices (A) and (C) relate *toy store* and *children's clothing store* to *children*. Choice (D) relates *grocery store* to *hamburgers* and *peanut butter*.

86. **(D)** The writer is asked to send the form to a street address. Choices (A), (B), and (C) are not mentioned.

87. **(D)** Carol's doctor's appointment is at 8:00 and her meeting with the architects is at 10:00. Choice (A) is not mentioned. Choices (B) and (C) are incorrect because she will both eat at a restaurant and talk on the telephone after the meeting with the architects.

88. **(A)** *The Border Grill* is the name of the restaurant where Carol will eat lunch with her mother. Choice (B) is incorrect because her visit to the doctor is much earlier in the day. Choice (C) is incorrect because New York is mentioned only as the place where she will telephone. Choice (D) is incorrect because Carol's mother is mentioned, but her house is not.

89. **(B)** Today is Tuesday and the planning meeting is tomorrow, Wednesday. Choice (A) is the time Carol will talk to John about the meeting. Choice (C) is the time Carol will have a meeting with the architects. Choice (D) is not mentioned.

90. **(C)** Carol will remind John to attend the planning meeting. Choices (A), (B), and (D) mention people Carol will meet with at other times.

91. **(B)** The notice states *We will close Sanjay's Restaurant.* Choice (A) associates *menu* with *restaurant*. Choice (C) is not mentioned. Choice (D) associates *business* with *restaurant*.

92. **(C)** The grand reopening is on July 1. Choice (A) is the opposite of the correct answer. Choice (B) is incorrect because the notice states that the repairs will begin in May. Choice (D) is mentioned but it is not the restaurant that will close.

93. **(D)** Talia Newhouse is the name of the lost girl. Choices (A), (B), and (C) are mentioned, but are not the people who were lost.

94. **(C)** She was found at a train station near her house. Choice (A) is the place where she was playing before she got lost. Choices (B) and (D) refer to people who were mentioned in the article.

95. **(B)** This is the last thing the mother did. Choices (A), (C), and (D) repeat places mentioned in the article.

96. **(C)** The notice mentions *games*, which are sports events. Choices (A) and (B) mention things that require tickets, but people don't normally watch games at these places. Choice (D) is incorrect because people usually don't buy tickets to watch TV.

97. **(B)** This means the same as *prices range from $10–$110*. Choice (A) is incorrect because $10 is the lowest price available. Choice (C) is incorrect because $110 is the highest price available. Choice (D) confuses the price with the times the games start.

98. **(C)** This means the same as *Friday through Sunday*. Choice (A) confuses *Friday and Sunday* with *Friday through Sunday*. Choice (B) mentions the days when you cannot see games. Choice (D) repeats *every day* out of context.

99. **(A)** *Birth* is the noun form of *born*. Choices (B), (C), and (D) are not mentioned.

100. **(C)** *Decreasing* means getting smaller. The graph shows that fewer koala bears are born every year; therefore, choices (A), (B), and (D) are not correct.

CHAPTER 5

Appendix A– Answer Keys and Answer Explanations

WHAT TO LOOK FOR IN THIS CHAPTER

- Answer Key for Listening Comprehension
- Answer Key for Mini-Test for Listening Comprehension Review—Parts I, II, and III
- Answer Key for Reading
- Answer Key for Mini-Test for Reading Review—Parts IV and V

ANSWER KEY FOR LISTENING COMPREHENSION
Part I: Vocabulary Building Activities

DIRECTIONS

1. drive	7. entrance	13. construction	19. direction
2. corner	8. shortcut	14. exit	20. direct
3. straight	9. behind	15. pass	21. directly
4. map	10. direct	16. continuation	22. driver
5. block	11. traffic light	17. continually	23. driveway
6. lane	12. Follow	18. Continue	24. drive

CLOTHING

1. scarf	7. bathing suit	13. boots	19. dress (noun)
2. shoes	8. wear	14. sew	20. dresser
3. pocket	9. rings	15. tight	21. dress (verb)
4. secondhand	10. expensive	16. comforter	22. tights
5. comfortable	11. button	17. comfort	23. tight
6. pants	12. socks	18. comfortable	24. tighten

NATURE

1. air	7. ocean	13. desert	19. pollutants
2. sunlight	8. natural	14. pollute	20. pollution
3. insects	9. biologists	15. season	21. pollute
4. plants	10. recycle	16. recycling	22. desert (noun)
5. environment	11. oxygen	17. recyclable	23. deserted
6. minerals	12. leaves	18. recycle	24. deserts (verb)

DAILY ROUTINES

1. brush	7. read	13. clean up	19. sleep
2. sleepy	8. ready	14. homework	20. asleep
3. education	9. bathe	15. bathroom	21. sleepy
4. kitchen	10. television	16. education	22. bather
5. dream	11. laundry	17. educate	23. bath
6. breakfast	12. take part in	18. educator	24. bathe

CULTURE

1. stories	7. tribe	13. prepare	19. festivities
2. festival	8. songs	14. tradition	20. festival
3. customs	9. costumes	15. folktales	21. festive
4. instruments	10. ancestors	16. believe	22. prepare
5. beliefs	11. fireworks	17. beliefs	23. preparatory
6. legend	12. ancient	18. believable	24. preparation

Part I: Photographs—Skill Building Activities

LOCATION

1. **(A)** The clues are the caravan and other trailers parked at the campsite. There are also tents. Choice (B) is incorrect because although there are cars, this is not a place (a lot) where cars are sold. Choice (C) tries to confuse you by using the word *park*, which is associated with camping, but it has a different meaning in Choice (C). Choice (D) tries to confuse you by repeating the word *tent*.

2. **(D)** People are playing volleyball in a swimming pool. The pool has a lot of people in it. The clues are the pool, the net, the ball in the air, the swimmers/players in the water. Choice (A) tries to confuse by repeating the word *net*. Choice (B) tries to confuse by using a word associated with swimming pools, *water*. Choice (C) uses the word *playing*, which is correct, but they are not playing pool (a table game with colored balls).

3. **(B)** A long, narrow road has trees along the side. The clues are the road and the trees. All of the choices use words similar to *road*: *street*, *path*, and *highway*. Choice (A) tries to confuse by repeating the word *wood*, but the road is not made of wood. Choice (C) does not describe the setting: the trees are *alongside* the road not *across* it. Choice (D) misidentifies the type of road. *Forest* is a word related to trees but there are rows of trees in the picture, not a forest.

4. **(C)** The passengers are waiting on a platform at the train station. The clues are the railroad tracks, the train coming into the station, the signboard giving the details of the arriving train. Choices (A), (B), and (D) try to confuse by using words that sound similar to train: *drain*, *plane*, *rain*.

5. **(A)** People on bikes are riding through a city. The clues are the people, the bikes, and the buildings. All of the choices use words common to bike riders: *cyclists*, *commuters*, and *bikers*. Choice (B) does not describe the location correctly. Choice (C) misidentifies the action and therefore the location. Choice (D) misidentifies the location of the bikers. They are on a city street, not a bridge.

LISTENING PRACTICE: LOCATION

1. **(A)** The boat is on the water. The clues are the boat crowded with passengers and water that could be a river, a lake, or a bay. Choices (B), (C), and (D) misidentify the type of boat and the location.

2. **(C)** People are eating at an outdoor café. The clues are the tables, customers, waiter, sun umbrellas, and landscape in the background. The other choices all use food-related words, but misidentify the action and the location.

3. **(D)** People are walking down a street closed to car traffic, but open to foot traffic. The clues are the street crowded with people but no cars. The other choices misidentify the location.

4. **(A)** The visitors are admiring the art hanging on the walls of the gallery. The clues are the pictures in the art gallery, the frames around the pictures, the art lovers in the gallery. All of the choices have words related to art: *paintings, frames, pictures*. They all misidentify the location of the art work.

5. **(D)** A Boeing 747 is in flight above the clouds. The clues are the plane, the sky, and the clouds. No land is visible. Choice (A) tries to confuse by using the similar-sounding word *fly*. Choice (B) uses a word associated with airplanes, *climb* as in *climbing to a higher altitude*. It also uses a weather related word, *fog*. Choice (C) tries to confuse by using a similar-sounding word, *crane*, a bird that also flies through the air.

PEOPLE

1. **(D)** The young man is probably a student. Clues: A young man is carrying a book bag on his back and is looking for books in a library, probably for homework. Choice (A) associates *reading* and *story* with *books*, but the person in the picture isn't reading a story. Choice (B) associates an occupation, *librarian*, with the location, *library*, and confuses the similar-sounding words *walking* (the young man is walking down the aisle) and *talking*. Choice (C) correctly identifies an object in the picture, *shelves*, and associates *bookseller* with *books*, but the person in the photo isn't painting anything.

2. **(C)** A man is putting food on the table for customers. Clues: He is wearing an apron, the setting is a restaurant. Choice (A) correctly identifies the customers, but does not describe what they are doing. Choice (B) uses words associated with a restaurant, but that do not identify the people in the photo. Choice (D) correctly identifies the diners, but does not describe what they are doing.

3. **(B)** Two musicians are playing a saxophone and a trumpet on a stage. Clues: musician instruments, lights, drum set in background, two musicians. Choice (A) uses a word associated with music, *composers*, but if these two men are composers, they are not taking a break. Choice (C) may be true, but you do not see the audience in this photograph. Choice (D) uses the word *players*, which is used with people who play musical instruments, but the phrase *hitting the ball* is used for players of sports.

4. **(A)** The woman is drawing the flower bed. Clues: artist, easel, art paper. Choice (B) uses words related to garden (*gardener, planting, flowers*) but that do not describe the person, her occupation, or her action. Choice (C) tries to confuse you by using the similar-sounding word *drawer* for *draw*, but does not correctly identify the person. Choice (D) uses words associated with the outdoors, but does not describe the person in the photo.

5. **(B)** Two people in a shoe store are looking at shoes. Clues: Shoes and boots on a shelf, a store-like setting. Choice (A) uses a word, *buyers*, that describes the people, but they are shopping for shoes, not shirts. Choice (C) correctly identifies an object in the picture, *boots*, put the people are not cowboys and they are not wearing the boots. Choice (D) correctly identifies the people, but not their action.

LISTENING PRACTICE: PEOPLE

1. **(A)** The man wearing protective gloves is using dentist tools to examine a woman's teeth. Clues: open mouth, white jacket, protective gloves, dentist tools. Choice (B) uses the related word *open* for open mouth, but does not describe the person. Choice (C) uses the related word *tools*, but does not describe the dentist. Choice (D) uses a word related to the medical profession, but this man is a dentist not a baby doctor.

2. **(C)** Two men on a golf course are getting ready to tee off or play a round of golf. Clues: fairway, golf clubs, posture. Choice (A) misidentifies the people and tries to confuse by using the word *course* in a different context. Choice (B) uses the word *players* as in *golf players*, but tries to confuse by using the word *tea* instead of *tee*. Choice (D) tries to confuse by using the similar-sounding word *gophers* (the rodents) for *golfers*.

3. **(D)** A young doctor is talking with an elderly patient. Clues: stethoscope, doctor's uniform, she's writing down information. Choice (A) correctly identifies the young woman's action, but not her occupation. Choice (B) confuses similar-sounding words *writing* and *riding*. Choice (C) correctly identifies one of the people in the picture but not her action—she is sitting, not lying down.

4. **(B)** The woman in the lab coat is probably a technician is a research laboratory. Clues: microscope, uniform. Choice (A) uses the associated word *laboratory*. Choice (C) uses the associated word *examining*. Choice (D) uses the associated word *checking*.

5. **(A)** The uniformed man standing in front of the helicopter is probably the pilot. Clues: uniform with epaulets, name tag above pocket, sunglasses. Choice (B) tries to confuse you by using the similar-sounding word *cop* (which is another term for police officer) for *helicopter*. Choice (C) uses words associated with airplanes: *flight attendant, boarding, plane*. Choice (D) tries to confuse by using words associated with machines, like *mechanic, repair*, and *engine*.

ACTION

1. **(A)** A woman and her child are washing their pet dog. Clues: dog, washtub, wet dog, towel. Choice (B) uses words associated with the photo: *woman, child, pet*. Choice (C) uses the related word *washing*. Choice (D) repeats the word *dog*.

2. **(D)** A teacher is pointing to a book in front of a young student. Clues: schoolroom, teacher, student, book. Choice (A) rightly says the woman is *pointing*, but not at her student. Choice (B) is not one of the actions seen in the photograph. Choice (C) repeats the word *book*.

3. **(A)** A couple at a weekend art show are admiring the sketches made by the artist sitting down. Clues: art on easels, couple, artist, woman posing. Choice (B) uses the associated word *art*. Choice (C) confuses the woman who is *posing* with the couple who is not. Choice (D) uses the associated word *drawing*.

4. **(C)** A woman is visiting the ophthalmologist and is having her eyes checked. Clues: eye examine machine, position of woman's face. Choice (A) uses the associated word *checking* and a similar-sounding word *pies* that sounds like *eyes*. Choice (B) uses the associated word *glasses*. Choice (D) repeats the word *right*, which is the eye being examined.

5. **(B)** A man is returning a file to a shelf. Clue: shelves full of files, one file being returned. Choice (A) repeats the word *file*, but does not identify the action. Choice (C) repeats the word *file*. Choice (D) repeats the word *shelves*.

LISTENING PRACTICE: ACTION

1. **(C)** The doctor is looking in the boy's throat. Clues: doctor's uniform, stethoscope, tongue depresser. Choice (A) uses the word *boy*, but the action does not match the photo. Choice (B) again uses the word *boy*, but the action and the person do not match the photo. Choice (D) uses the word *son*. The open mouth might suggest feeding, but the action does not match the photo.

2. **(A)** Four contestants are racing down lanes toward a finish line. Clues: running people, finish line, lanes drawn on the grass. Choice (B) uses the similar-sounding word *rubbing* for *running* and uses the associated word *foot*. Choice (C) repeats the word line. Choice (D) uses *time* to suggest the time it takes to run.

3. **(D)** The passengers are boarding the plane using the stairs. Clues: plane, line of passengers, people climbing up into the plane. Choice (A) tries to confuse by using the associated words *tourists*, and the similar-sounding word *train*. The passengers are *getting on* (boarding) not *getting off* (deplaning). Choice (B) uses the associated word *travelers*. They are climbing the *stairs*, not a *ladder*. Choice (C) uses the associated word *visitors* and the similar-sounding word *rain*.

4. **(B)** The woman is putting flowers in a vase. Clues: flowers, vase with water. Choice (A) uses the associated word *plants*. Choice (C) uses the similar sound word *flour* for *flower*. Choice (D) uses the associated word *garden*.

5. **(C)** A group of people are singing songs around a piano. Clues: five people, open mouths, staring at music on piano. Choice (A) uses the associated word *performing*, but there are more than two people (a *duet*) singing. Choice (B) uses a word often associated with piano, *playing*. Choice (D) uses the word *keyboard* that is associated with piano *keys*.

Part II: Question-Response—Vocabulary Building Activities

WEATHER

1. temperature	7. warm	13. expect	19. predict
2. melt	8. foggy	14. cool	20. predictable
3. freeze	9. humid	15. blizzard	21. prediction
4. thunder	10. breeze	16. cool (verb)	22. warm (adjective)
5. lightning	11. flood	17. coolness	23. warmth
6. predict	12. thermometer	18. cool (noun)	24. warm (verb)

FAMILY AND FRIENDS

1. introduce	7. spouse	13. related	19. inviting
2. uncle	8. niece	14. engaged	20. invite
3. invite	9. divorced	15. aunt	21. invitation
4. friendly	10. get together	16. marry	22. relationship
5. cousins	11. gets along	17. married	23. relatives
6. married	12. nephew	18. marriage	24. related

NEWS AND NEWSPAPERS

1. advertisements	9. subscribe	17. speech
2. deliver	10. headlines	18. speaker
3. article	11. report	19. advertise
4. announce	12. sections	20. Advertisers
5. magazine	13. international	21. advertisement
6. journalist	14. interviews	22. announcer
7. speech	15. comics	23. announcement
8. live	16. speak	24. announce

OFFICE

1. reply	9. in charge	17. supervisor
2. due	10. turn in	18. supervision
3. meeting	11. raise	19. assist
4. salary	12. assistant	20. assistant
5. supervisor	13. fire	21. assistance
6. hire	14. type	22. employ
7. employees	15. discuss	23. employer
8. earn	16. supervise	24. employees

TRAVEL

1. arrive	9. luggage	17. delayed
2. return	10. flight	18. delay (noun)
3. depart	11. first-class	19. reservation
4. passengers	12. delayed	20. reserve
5. round-trip	13. schedule	21. reserved
6. check in	14. transportation	22. transport
7. fares	15. subway	23. transportation
8. reserve	16. delay (verb)	24. transportable

Part II: Question-Response—Skill Building Activities

WORDS REPEATED

1. A	3. C	5. A	7. A	9. C
2. B	4. B	6. C	8. B	10. A

LISTENING PRACTICE: WORDS REPEATED

1. B	4. A	7. A	10. B	13. C
2. C	5. A	8. C	11. A	14. B
3. A	6. C	9. C	12. A	15. B

SIMILAR SOUNDS

1. A	3. A	5. C	7. A	9. A
2. C	4. B	6. B	8. B	10. B

LISTENING PRACTICE: SIMILAR SOUNDS

1. A	4. C	7. A	10. C	13. B
2. B	5. B	8. A	11. C	14. A
3. B	6. A	9. C	12. B	15. C

ASSOCIATED WORDS

1. B	3. C	5. A	7. C	9. B
2. B	4. B	6. B	8. A	10. A

LISTENING PRACTICE: ASSOCIATED WORDS

1. B	4. C	7. C	10. C	13. C
2. A	5. A	8. C	11. A	14. A
3. A	6. B	9. C	12. B	15. B

HOMONYMS

1. A	3. B	5. B	7. C	9. B
2. A	4. C	6. C	8. A	10. C

LISTENING PRACTICE: HOMONYMS

1. B	4. C	7. C	10. A	13. A
2. C	5. B	8. C	11. B	14. B
3. A	6. A	9. B	12. A	15. C

SAME SOUND AND SPELLING BUT DIFFERENT MEANING

1. C	3. B	5. B	7. B	9. B
2. A	4. C	6. C	8. A	10. A

LISTENING PRACTICE: SAME SOUND AND SPELLING BUT DIFFERENT MEANING

1. B	4. A	7. A	10. C	13. C
2. A	5. C	8. A	11. A	14. B
3. B	6. C	9. C	12. B	15. A

OPPOSITES

1. B	3. C	5. B	7. C	9. A
2. A	4. B	6. A	8. B	10. C

LISTENING PRACTICE: OPPOSITES

1. C	4. A	7. B	10. A	13. B
2. B	5. C	8. A	11. B	14. C
3. B	6. A	9. B	12. A	15. B

WORD ORDER

1. C	3. C	5. B	7. B	9. C
2. A	4. A	6. B	8. A	10. A

LISTENING PRACTICE: WORD ORDER

1. B	4. C	7. A	10. A	13. A
2. A	5. B	8. B	11. C	14. A
3. B	6. C	9. C	12. B	15. B

MORE LISTENING PRACTICE

1. A	4. A	7. C	10. C	13. A
2. B	5. A	8. A	11. B	14. A
3. C	6. C	9. C	12. B	15. C

Part III: Short Conversations and Short Talks—Vocabulary Building Activities

DATES AND TIME

1. hours	9. sunset	17. time (verb)
2. early	10. evening	18. timer
3. watch	11. later	19. weekly
4. clock	12. midnight	20. weekend
5. afternoon	13. seconds	21. week
6. minutes	14. week	22. seconds (noun)
7. month	15. calendar	23. secondary
8. time	16. time (noun)	24. second (adjective)

MEASUREMENT AND NUMBERS

1. million	9. add	17. measurement
2. few	10. ruler	18. measure
3. measure	11. Multiply	19. addition
4. Subtract	12. annual	20. add
5. plenty	13. Mathematics	21. additional
6. feet	14. kilometers	22. multiplication
7. triple	15. amount	23. multiple
8. dozen	16. measurable	24. multiply

MONEY

1. Count	9. tax	17. freedom
2. spend	10. earn	18. free
3. free	11. bank	19. taxable
4. lend	12. cheap	20. tax (verb)
5. borrow	13. currency	21. tax (noun)
6. expensive	14. check	22. bankrupt
7. wallet	15. poor	23. banker
8. coin	16. freely	24. bank

ACTIVITIES

1. games	9. sport	17. camper
2. hobby	10. family	18. camp (verb)
3. join	11. club	19. exciting
4. camp	12. kite	20. excitement
5. groups	13. rink	21. excite
6. teamwork	14. competition	22. competitive
7. park	15. outdoor	23. compete
8. exciting	16. camp (noun)	24. competition

FEELINGS AND EMOTIONS

1. angry	9. upset	17. depression
2. kind	10. embarrassed	18. depress
3. depressed	11. scared	19. argue
4. tears	12. frown	20. argument
5. frustrating	13. kiss	21. argumentative
6. cry	14. argue	22. scare
7. cheer up	15. love	23. scared
8. smile	16. depressed	24. scary

Part III: Short Conversations and Short Talks—Skill Building Activities

WORDS REPEATED

1. C	3. B	5. C	7. D	9. C
2. B	4. D	6. B	8. A	10. B

SIMILAR SOUNDS

1. C	3. C	5. B	7. C	9. D
2. B	4. A	6. D	8. B	10. D

ASSOCIATED WORDS

1. A	3. B	5. C	7. B	9. C
2. D	4. C	6. A	8. D	10. B

HOMONYMS

1. B	3. A	5. D	7. C	9. B
2. A	4. C	6. B	8. A	10. D

SAME SOUND AND SPELLING BUT DIFFERENT MEANING

1. D	3. A	5. D	7. D	9. C
2. C	4. B	6. A	8. B	10. A

OPPOSITES

1. C	3. A	5. D	7. B	9. C
2. B	4. A	6. A	8. C	10. B

INTONATION

1. C	3. B	5. C	7. B	9. A
2. D	4. A	6. D	8. D	10. B

ANSWER KEY FOR MINI-TEST FOR LISTENING COMPREHENSION REVIEW—PARTS I, II, AND III

Part I

1. **(B)** A large truck is traveling down the road. The other choices do not identify the photo. Choice (A) uses the associated word for a form of transportation, *car*. Choice (C) tries to confuse by using the similar-sounding word *duck* for *truck*. Choice (D) also uses an associated word for a form of transportation, *bus*.

2. **(C)** The sign says that the road is closed (not open) to traffic. Choice (A) repeats the word *closed*. Choice (B) tries to confuse by using the similar-sounding word *clothes* for *close* and by repeating the word *street*. Choice (D) uses the similar-sounding word *rodeo* for *road* and repeats the word *closed*.

3. **(B)** The man is putting gas in the tank of his car. He is filling his car with gas. The other choices do not match the action. Choice (A) tries to confuse by using the similar-sounding words *red oil* for *petrol* and *cart* for *car*. Choice (C) repeats the word *van*, which is a type of car. Choice (D) uses the associated word for a form of transportation, *bus*.

4. **(D)** The man in a uniform is behind the counter of a pharmacy or drugstore. He is holding a bottle of pills in his left hand. He is probably a pharmacist explaining medication to a customer. The other choices do not identify the person or the action. Choice (A) uses words associated with illness: *patient* and *medicine*. Choice (B) uses the similar-sounding words *pillow* for *pill* and *rug* for *drug*. Choice (C) tries to confuse by using the similar-sounding words *farmer* for *pharmacist* and *till* for *pill* or for *fill a prescription*.

5. **(A)** A father and his child are fishing in a small lake. The other choices do not identify the action or the location. Choice (B) uses words associated with water: *swimming* and *river*. Choice (C) uses a word associated with water: *beach*. Choice (D) uses a word associated with water: *boat*.

6. **(C)** The engines (locomotives) of two fast trains are in a train station. The other choices do not identify the form of transportation or the location. Choice (A) uses the similar-sounding word *trays are in* for *train*. Choice (B) uses the similar-sounding word *planes* for *trains*. Choice (D) uses another form of transportation, *taxis*, and uses a word associated with trains: *tracks*.

7. **(B)** There are two students sharing a desk. They are holding pens in their hands and are writing on paper or in their notebooks spread out on the desk. The other choices do not identify the photo or the location. Choice (A) uses the associated word *books*. Choice (C) misidentifies the location of the *pens*; the students are holding them. Choice (D) misidentifies the location of the *papers*; they are on the desk.

8. **(A)** A man is crossing a street. He is not using the crosswalk marked by lines. The other choices do not identify the action. Choice (B) uses the word *driving* associated with a person in a business district. Choice (C) uses the associated word *building*. Choice (D) repeats the word *line* seen in the lines in the crosswalk.

9. **(D)** The pilot of a plane is sitting in the cockpit. He is surrounded by the dials and gauges that are part of the controls of the plane. The other choices do not identify the occupation of the person. Choice (A) uses the associated word *watch*. Choice (B) uses the associated words *observe* and *dials*. Choice (C) uses the associated word *watching*.

10. **(C)** Dishes displaying the menu choices are on display in a restaurant window. The other choices do not identify the location. Choice (A) uses another meaning of the word *dish*, as in *plate* rather than *menu item*. Choice (B) uses words associated with food: *produce* and *market*. Choice (D) uses words associated with a restaurant or with eating in general: *table, set for dinner*.

11. **(C)** A man has *glasses* or goggles on his hardhat. He is holding a paper cup in his right hand and is taking a drink. The other choices do not identify the action. Choice (A) uses the associated word *face*. Choice (B) tries to confuse by using the similar-sounding word *glasses* meaning *eyeglasses* and *glass* meaning a *cup*. Choice (D) tries to confuse by using the similar-sounding word *grass* for *glass*.

12. **(A)** The secretary in an office is holding the lid to the photocopy machine open. She is about to insert a document to be photocopied. The other choices do not identify the action. Choice (B) uses the associated word *opening*. Choice (C) uses a word associated with machines: *turn on*. Choice (D) also uses words associated with machines: *shut down*.

13. **(B)** Many bicycle riders (cyclists) are racing down the road. The other choices do not identify the photo or the location. Choice (A), the bicycles are *on the street*, but are not *parked*. Choice (C) uses a similar-sounding word, *motorcycles*, for *bicycles* and the associated word *trees*. Choice (D) uses the associated word *racers*.

14. **(D)** A man standing behind a counter is making a notation (writing) in a ledger. He has a pen in his right hand. The other choices do not identify the action. Choice (A) uses the associated word *pencil*. Choice (B) uses the word *shirt*, which the man is wearing. Choice (C) uses the similar-sounding word *reading* for *writing*.

15. **(A)** Guests at a banquet are about to eat a feast. None of the dishes have been touched. The food has been placed on the round table. The other choices do not identify the action. Choice (B) uses the associated word *dishes*. Choice (C) uses the associated word *food*. Choice (D) uses the word that descibes the kind of table: *round*.

Part II

16. **(B)** *Thirty-five dollars* answers the question *How much?* Choice (A) answers *Where?* Choice (C) answers *When?*

17. **(A)** *She just left* means *No, she isn't in her office.* (B) answers *Where is her office?* (C) answers *When is she in her office?*

18. **(A)** *At 5:30* answers the question *What time?* Choice (B) answers *How?* Choice (C) answers *Where?*

19. **(B)** *He's the new manager* answers the question *Who?* Choice (A) answers a yes-no question. Choice (C) answers *Whose?*, confusing it with the similar-sounding *Who's?*

20. **(B)** *Next to the bank* answers the question *Where?* Choice (A) associates *stamps* with post office. Choice (C) repeats the word *office* out of context.

21. **(A)** *I don't mind* is an appropriate response to a polite question beginning with *Do you mind?* Choice (B) confuses the similar-sounding words *mine* and *mind*. Choice (C) confuses the similar-sounding words *clothes* and *close*.

22. **(B)** *Tomorrow before noon* answers the question *Where?* Choice (A) uses the word *call* out of context. Choice (C) confuses the similar-sounding words *taller* and *call*.

23. **(C)** *I met him yesterday* answers *Have you met....?* Choice (A) repeats *manage* (manager) out of context. Choice (B) confuses the similar-sounding words *get* and *met*.

24. **(B)** *They're Tom's* answers the question *Whose?* Choice (A) confuses the similar-sounding words *cooks* and *books*. Choice (C) associates *read* with *books*.

25. **(A)** *It was great* answers the question *How?* Choice (B) confuses the similar-sounding words *move* and *movie*. Choice (C) answers the question *How long?*

26. **(A)** *I'm tired* is an appropriate response to an offer to sit down. Choice (B) uses *like* out of context. Choice (C) confuses *down* with *downtown*.

27. **(C)** *3:30* answers the question *What time?* Choice (A) answers *Where?* Choice (B) confuses the meaning of *Do you know?* In this example, it is really used to introduce an indirect question, not to ask whether the listener knows a particular person.

28. **(B)** *I had an appointment* explains the speaker's reason for leaving early. Choice (A) uses the word *left* (leave) out of context. Choice (C) confuses the similar-sounding words *wide* and *why*.

29. **(A)** *I live in another city* explains where the speaker is from. Choices (B) and (C) repeat the word *here*. Choice (C) also confuses the similar-sounding words *car* and *are*.

30. **(B)** *A restaurant down the street* answers the question *Where?* Choice (A) confuses the similar-sounding words *wear* and *where*. Choice (C) answers the question *When?*

31. **(C)** *I'll tell him right now* answers the request *Tell Mr. Kim....* Choice (A) repeats the word *meeting* out of context. Choice (B) confuses the similar-sounding words *eating* and *meeting*.

32. **(C)** *This evening* answers the question *When?* Choice (A) confuses the similar-sounding words *drive* and *arrive*. Choice (B) answers *Where?*

33. **(B)** *Not very good* answers the question *How?* Choice (A) confuses the similar-sounding words *rest* and *restaurant*. Choice (C) associates *ate* with *food* and *restaurant*.

34. **(C)** *That's a great idea* is an appropriate response to a suggestion. Choice (A) associates *swimming* with beach. Choice (B) confuses the similar-sounding words *get* and *let's*.

35. **(A)** *A shoestore downtown* answers the question *Where?* Choice (B) confuses the similar-sounding words *pears* and *pair*. Choice (C) confuses the similar-sounding words *newspaper* and *new pair*.

Part III

36. **(A)** The woman says *Traffic was terrible*. Choice (B) repeats the word *car*. Choice (C) repeats the word *walk*. Choice (D) repeats the word *bus*.

37. **(C)** The name of the place is *Central Cinema*, it has shows, and it sells refreshments in the lobby. Choice (A) repeats the word travel (traveling) from the title

of the movie advertised. Choice (B) associates *travel agency* with *traveling*. Choice (D) associates *shows* with *television*.

38. **(C)** Both speakers mention the cold weather. Choice (A) is not mentioned. Choice (B) repeats the word *warm*. Choice (D) confuses the similar-sounding words *snowy* and *know*.

39. **(B)** The man says he wants to invite the woman to the movies. Choice (A) repeats the word *gym*, which is where the woman wants to go. Choice (B) repeats the word *home*. Choice (D) repeats the word *work*.

40. **(A)** This is the time the woman gives for her arrival. Choice (B) confuses the similar-sounding words *ten* and *then*. Choice (C) confuses *eight* with the similar-sounding words *great, wait*, and *gate*. Choice (D) is the time when the man will leave his house.

41. **(D)** The woman tells the waiter what she would like to eat. Choices (A), (B), and (C) associate *groceries, party*, and *meal* with the food the woman mentions.

42. **(B)** The woman plans to stay home and rest. Choice (A) confuses the similar-sounding words *game* and *same*. Choice (C) confuses the similar-sounding words *restaurant* and *rest*. Choice (D) repeats the word *work*.

43. **(D)** *Isn't it great?* and *I can't wait!* mean that the speakers are excited. Choice (A) associates *unhappy* with *won't be fun*. Choice (B) uses the word *tired* out of context. Choice (C) uses the word *troubled* out of context.

44. **(B)** The teacher is telling his class to get ready for an exam. Choice (A) associates *writer* with *books, pen*, and *pencil*. Choice (C) associates *doctor* with exam. Choice (D) associates *librarian* with books.

45. **(C)** The woman is parking her car and will pay 15 dollars to leave it in the parking lot all day. Choice (A) uses the word *park* out of context. Choice (B) repeats the word *car*. Choice (D) associates dollars with *bank*.

46. **(C)** The speaker warns that cars are moving slowly and that there is a lot of traffic on the bridge. Choice (A) associates *weather* with *rain*. Choice (B) repeats the word *travel* out of context. Choice (D) repeats the word *car*.

47. **(A)** The woman says that the party was boring and the man agrees by saying *I know*. Choice (B) is the opposite of what the man said: *I didn't meet any interesting people*. Choice (C) confuses the similar-sounding words *fun* and *one*. Choice (D) is the opposite of what the woman said about the food: *It tasted awful*.

48. **(B)** The woman asks the man to help her carry her package. Choice (A) associates *weigh* with *heavy*. Choice (C) associates *mail* with *post office*. Choice (D) repeats the word *deliver*.

49. **(B)** The man says that he wants to return a shirt that doesn't fit. Choice (A) uses the word *cash* out of context. Choice (C) uses the word *credit* out of context. Choice (D) associates *buy* with *cash* and *credit*.

50. **(B)** The ad says *Pay $20 for a two-course lunch*. Choices (A), (C), and (D) repeat other words mentioned in the ad.

ANSWER KEY FOR READING

Part IV—Vocabulary Building Activities

SPORTS

1. fast	7. referee	13. uniform	19. safety
2. cheered	8. goalie	14. safe	20. safely
3. basketball	9. scored	15. lose	21. safe
4. finish	10. field	16. winnings	22. loss
5. win	11. whistle	17. win	23. loser
6. coach	12. match	18. winner	24. lose

ENTERTAINMENT

1. funny	7. dance	13. curtains	19. musical
2. circus	8. theater	14. movie	20. music
3. film	9. applause	15. musician	21. musician
4. laugh	10. clapped	16. action	22. lighten
5. actor	11. set	17. actress	23. light
6. band	12. lighting	18. act	24. lighting

GROCERIES

1. cart	7. cheese	13. grocer	19. packed
2. juice	8. coupons	14. butcher	20. pack
3. pack	9. list	15. dairy	21. package
4. frozen	10. fruit	16. frozen	22. groceries
5. aisle	11. pick	17. freeze	23. grocery
6. bags	12. weigh	18. freezer	24. grocer

GEOGRAPHY

1. island	7. valley	13. altitude	19. globe
2. mountainous	8. distance	14. planet	20. globular
3. equator	9. far	15. atlas	21. Global
4. terrain	10. globe	16. equatorial	22. populated
5. continent	11. solar	17. equate	23. population
6. population	12. volcano	18. equator	24. populate

FURNITURE AND FURNISHINGS

1. lift	9. hang	17. painting
2. Plastic	10. lamp	18. paint
3. pillows	11. wooden	19. bed
4. fabric	12. tablecloth	20. bedroom
5. couch	13. sheets	21. bedding
6. paint	14. furnish	22. furnished
7. move	15. carpenter	23. furniture
8. carpet	16. painter	24. furnish

Part IV: Incomplete Sentences—Skill Building Activities

PARTS OF SPEECH

1. D	3. A	5. D	7. B	9. A
2. B	4. C	6. E	8. C	10. E

SINGULAR AND PLURAL NOUNS

1. B	3. C	5. A	7. B	9. B
2. C	4. D	6. D	8. B	10. A

ARTICLES

1. C	3. B	5. C	7. A	9. C
2. A	4. B	6. C	8. D	10. A

NOUNS—COUNT AND NON-COUNT

1. A	3. B	5. D	7. A	9. C
2. D	4. C	6. C	8. B	10. C

PRONOUNS

1. C	3. C	5. B	7. D	9. B
2. A	4. B	6. A	8. D	10. D

DEMONSTRATIVE ADJECTIVES

1. A	3. A	5. A	7. C	9. C
2. D	4. D	6. A	8. D	10. A

PREPOSITIONS OF TIME

1. A	3. D	5. A	7. C	9. B
2. B	4. A	6. B	8. D	10. C

PREPOSITIONS OF LOCATION

1. C	3. D	5. B	7. B	9. B
2. A	4. C	6. A	8. C	10. C

SUBJECTS AND VERBS

1. C	3. B	5. A	7. D	9. B
2. C	4. A	6. B	8. A	10. D

REDUNDANT SUBJECTS

1. B	3. A	5. B	7. A	9. A
2. B	4. D	6. C	8. B	10. B

SUBJECT-VERB AGREEMENT

1. B	3. C	5. C	7. D	9. A
2. A	4. C	6. C	8. B	10. C

PRESENT TENSE

1. C	3. B	5. D	7. B	9. D
2. A	4. A	6. C	8. A	10. B

PAST TENSE

1. C	3. D	5. B	7. A	9. D
2. A	4. B	6. C	8. B	10. C

FUTURE TENSE

1. B	3. A	5. B	7. B	9. A
2. C	4. D	6. A	8. D	10. C

STATIVE VERBS

1. D	3. B	5. C	7. D	9. A
2. A	4. B	6. A	8. C	10. B

GERUNDS AND INFINITIVES

1. C	3. A	5. A	7. D	9. B
2. D	4. C	6. B	8. A	10. B

VERBS PLUS PREPOSITIONS

1. A	3. D	5. A	7. C	9. D
2. B	4. B	6. C	8. B	10. C

CONDITIONALS

1. B	3. C	5. B	7. A	9. A
2. D	4. B	6. D	8. B	10. C

PASSIVE-ACTIVE MODES

1. A	3. B	5. A	7. B	9. B
2. C	4. A	6. C	8. D	10. A

ADJECTIVES AND ADVERBS

1. B	3. C	5. B	7. A	9. C
2. A	4. D	6. C	8. B	10. A

ADJECTIVES—COMPARATIVE AND SUPERLATIVE

1. C	3. C	5. B	7. D	9. C
2. A	4. B	6. A	8. B	10. A

ADJECTIVES—DESCRIPTIVE PHRASES

1. B	3. C	5. A	7. D	9. C
2. C	4. D	6. B	8. B	10. A

ADVERBS—DATE, TIME, SEQUENCE

1. C	3. D	5. B	7. A	9. B
2. C	4. B	6. C	8. D	10. C

ADVERBS OF FREQUENCY

1. B	3. D	5. A	7. C	9. C
2. A	4. C	6. B	8. A	10. A

CONJUNCTIONS

1. B	3. B	5. A	7. C	9. D
2. D	4. C	6. D	8. A	10. C

PARALLEL STRUCTURE

1. B	3. C	5. B	7. D	9. C
2. A	4. B	6. D	8. A	10. B

CAUSE AND EFFECT

1. B	3. A	5. D	7. C	9. A
2. C	4. D	6. C	8. B	10. C

PREFIXES

1. C	3. A	5. D	7. C	9. D
2. D	4. B	6. A	8. B	10. B

Part V: Reading Comprehension—Vocabulary Building Activities

DINING OUT

1. recommend	9. slice	17. bakery
2. spicy	10. specialty	18. bake
3. mild	11. prepare	19. fresh
4. meal	12. serving	20. freshly
5. fried	13. selection	21. freshness
6. baked	14. decor	22. specializes
7. fresh	15. tasty	23. specialty
8. vegetarians	16. baked	24. special

SCHOOL

1. deadline	9. payment	17. payment
2. require	10. submit	18. pay
3. semester	11. instructor	19. permissible
4. tuition	12. absent	20. permit
5. advanced	13. registration	21. permission
6. permission	14. schedule	22. requirement
7. accept	15. attendance	23. required
8. individual	16. payable	24. require

HOUSING

1. convenient	7. tenant	13. property	19. neighborhood
2. vacant	8. owner	14. neighbor	20. neighborly
3. beautify	9. occupied	15. current	21. neighbor
4. location	10. application	16. conveniently	22. residential
5. available	11. rental	17. convenient	23. resident
6. landlords	12. residents	18. convenience	24. reside

SHOPPING

1. shipping	7. guarantee	13. refund	19. refundable
2. items	8. satisfied	14. receipt	20. refund (noun)
3. quantity	9. customers	15. checkout	21. refund (verb)
4. discount	10. order	16. receive	22. satisfy
5. total	11. returns	17. receipt	23. satisfied
6. cashier	12. purchase	18. receptive	24. satisfaction

HEALTH

1. nourishing	7. fit	13. research	19. science
2. work out	8. symptom	14. patients	20. scientific
3. pharmacist	9. treatment	15. scientific	21. scientifically
4. physical	10. benefit	16. nourishment	22. treatable
5. cure	11. illness	17. nourishing	23. treat
6. prescription	12. emergency	18. nourish	24. treatment

Part V: Reading Comprehension—Skill Building Activities

ADVERTISEMENTS

1. B	4. A	7. A	10. A	13. B
2. B	5. D	8. D	11. C	14. D
3. C	6. B	9. B	12. B	

CHARTS, TABLES, AND GRAPHS

1. D	5. A	9. B	13. D	17. D
2. B	6. C	10. A	14. D	
3. D	7. B	11. C	15. A	
4. C	8. D	12. C	16. B	

FORMS

1. A	5. D	9. B	13. C	17. D
2. C	6. A	10. A	14. C	18. A
3. C	7. D	11. B	15. B	
4. C	8. C	12. D	16. B	

NOTICES AND SIGNS

1. B	4. A	7. C	10. A	13. C
2. A	5. A	8. D	11. B	14. A
3. D	6. C	9. A	12. C	

PASSAGES AND ARTICLES

1. B	5. A	9. A	13. C
2. A	6. B	10. C	14. B
3. D	7. C	11. B	15. B
4. C	8. B	12. A	16. C

CORRESPONDENCE

1. C	5. D	9. B	13. B
2. A	6. A	10. A	14. B
3. D	7. A	11. B	15. C
4. B	8. C	12. D	16. C

ANSWER KEY FOR MINI-TEST FOR READING REVIEW— PARTS IV AND V

Part IV: Incomplete Sentences

51. **(C)** is the correct noun meaning *teacher*. Choice (A) is a noun meaning *directions from a teacher*. Choice (B) is a gerund. Choice (D) is the third-person present form of the verb.

52. **(C)** is the correct determiner meaning *the required amount*. Choice (A) is not used with a non-count noun. Choices (B) and (D) are adverbs.

53. **(B)** is the present perfect, used to express actions that started in the past and continue in the future. Choice (A) is the past form of the verb *do*. Choice (C) is used for future tense. Choice (D) is used in unreal conditional sentences.

54. **(A)** is the correct preposition used for specific time. Choice (B) is used for destinations. Choice (C) refers to specific days and dates. Choice (D) must be followed by a noun.

55. **(C)** completes the passive sentence with the correct past participle. Choices (A) and (B) are nouns. Choice (D) is a simple present verb.

56. **(B)** is the correct object pronoun. Choice (A) is a subject pronoun. Choice (C) is a possessive pronoun. Choice (D) is a subject plus future tense verb.

57. **(D)** completes the infinitive with the correct base form of the verb. Choice (A) indicates *a place above* and is not a verb. Choices (B) and (C) are adjectives.

58. **(D)** is the correct adjective used with a plural noun. Choice (A) is an article used with singular count nouns. Choice (B) is a demonstrative adjective used to identify singular nouns. Choice (C) is an adjective that cannot be used with plural nouns.

59. (**B**) is the correct word choice meaning *requires* or *uses up*. Choice (A) means *constructs*. Choice (C) means *moves from one place to another*. Choice (D) means *requires help*.

60. (**C**) is the correct verb that precedes the gerund. Choice (A) is an incorrect verb because it requires an object. Choices (B) and (D) are adjectives.

61. (**A**) completes the "if" clause in the conditional sentence. Choice (B) is a conjunction used in a result clause. Choice (C) is a relative pronoun. Choice (D) is a conjunction used to show contrast.

62. (**D**) is the correct adjective preceded by an adverb. Choice (A) is the simple present form of the verb. Choice (B) is the past participle. Choice (C) is a noun.

63. (**B**) is the correct adverb meaning *up to now*. Choices (A) and (C) are illogical because the verb form is present perfect. Choice (D) is used with simple present negative sentences.

64. (**D**) completes the cause and effect sentence. Choice (A) is illogical and is not a cause. Choice (B) shows contrast and must be followed by a noun. Choice (C) introduces an effect.

65. (**A**) is the correct simple past form of the verb. Choice (B) is a noun meaning *knowledge*. Choice (C) is the simple present. Choice (D) is a noun meaning *someone who gives people information*.

66. (**C**) is the correct simple past verb meaning *exhibited*. Choice (A) is the simple past of *look* but is illogical and requires a preposition such as *at*. *(We looked at the pictures)*. Choice (B) is the simple past form of see and is also illogical. *(We saw their pictures)*. Choice (D) is the simple past form of the verb *picture* meaning to *imagine something (I pictured your house much bigger)*.

67. (**B**) is the correct preposition that completes the phrase. Choice (A) is a preposition of time meaning *on or before*. Choice (C) is used to indicate destination. Choice (D) is an adverb that describes *when something begins*.

68. (**A**) is the simple past first-person form of the verb. Choice (B) is the simple present. Choice (C) is the past participle. Choice (D) is the gerund.

69. (**A**) is the correct adverb meaning *possibly*. Choice (B) is an adjective. Choice (C) is a modal that must be preceded by a subject unless in a question. Choice (D) is an illogical adverb because of the reference to *tonight*.

70. (**B**) is the correct adverb meaning *at the same time*. Choice (A) is an illogical adverb meaning *even now*. Choice (C) is used to show result. Choice (D) must precede a noun.

71. **(D)** is the correct adjective meaning *extending far*. Choice (A) is a noun that cannot directly follow an adverb. Choice (B) does not form a description of a river. Choice (C) is an adjective used to describe *thickness*.

72. **(D)** is the correct noun preceded by an article. Choice (A) is an illogical adjective. Choice (B) must be followed by a plural noun. Choice (C) is an adjective used to compare other adjectives.

73. **(C)** is the correct adjective meaning *causing other people to be entertained*. Choices (A) and (B) are nouns and cannot be preceded by *very*. Choice (D) is the past participle.

74. **(C)** forms the correct phrasal verb meaning *remove*. Choice (A) means *depart from*. Choice (B) means *delay*. (Let's *put off* the meeting until tomorrow.) Choice (D) means *emit*. (The perfume *gives off* a vanilla scent.)

75. **(A)** is the correct adverb meaning *more than necessary*. Choices (B) and (C) are determiners used with non-count nouns. Choice (D) is an adjective meaning as much as required or an adverb that follows an adjective (*Are you warm enough?*).

76. **(D)** is the correct adjective meaning *complete*. Choices (A), (B), and (C) are simple present verb forms.

77. **(C)** is the correct possessive pronoun. Choice (A) is the contracted subject and verb. Choice (B) is a redundant subject. Choice (D) is an object pronoun.

78. **(A)** completes the infinitive. Choice (B) is the past tense form of the verb. Choice (C) is the present tense. Choice (D) is the gerund.

79. **(B)** is the correct demonstrative adjective referring to a plural noun that is close to you. Choice (A) is an adverb referring to a place or position (*I put the keys there.*). Choice (C) is an adverb meaning *next* or *afterwards*. Choice (D) is a demonstrative adjective referring to a singular noun.

80. **(D)** is the correct superlative adjective proceeded by the article *the*. Choices (A) and (B) are not superlative adjectives. Choice (C) is a simple present verb.

Part V: Reading Comprehension

81. **(D)** *A guarantee* is needed only if a customer is unsatisfied and wants to return a product. Choice (A) is given but is not the purpose. Choice (B) is not mentioned but confuses *repair* with *replace*. Choice (C), A customer service department, deals with returns but also has other functions.

82. **(C)** The company will replace the product free of charge. Choice (A) is not mentioned. Choice (B) confuses *return address* with *a letter*. Choice (D) confuses *call our Customer Service Office* with *get a phone call*.

83. **(C)** The office is open from 9 A.M.–5 P.M. Choices (A) and (B) are too early to call. Choice (D) is incorrect because the offices are only open during certain times.

84. **(C)** Shirts are 2 for the price of one; one usually costs 25 dollars. Choice (A) confuses *one dollar* and two for the price of *one*. Choice (B) is how many days the sale is on. Choice (D) was the cost of two shirts before the sale.

85. **(C)** 7 days is equal to one week. Choices (A) and (B) are contradicted by *seven days*. Choice (D) associates *summer shirts* with *all summer*.

86. **(A)** The parking garage is closed for repairs. Choice (B) associates *9 P.M.* with *night*. Choice (C) is not mentioned. Choice (D) confuses *the lot at the bus station* with *it is for buses only*.

87. **(C)** Two other garages are suggested as alternatives. Choice (A) associates Second Avenue with *street*. Choice (B) associates *bus station* with *take the bus*. Choice (D) is not mentioned.

88. **(D)** The memo asks staff members to *eat their lunch in the break room only*. Choice (A) This is not an invitation; it is a memo. Choice (B) confuses *don't take food into the conference room* with *announce a conference*. Choice (C) confuses *keep the office clean* with *how the offices are cleaned*.

89. **(A)** The memo is from Bill Jones, Director. Choice (B) confuses *cooperation* with *coordinator*. Choice (C) associates *keep the office clean* with *office cleaner*. Choice (D) *Lunch* is the subject of the memo but a *server* is not mentioned.

90. **(C)** The memo asks staff not to bring food into the conference room. Choice (A) is what staff members are not supposed to do. Choice (B) confuses *dining table* and *clean the table*. Choice (D) confuses *store food* (keep food in a closed area) with *a store* where you buy food.

91. **(D)** 300 students were enrolled in 2003. Choice (A) is how many were enrolled in the year 2000, Choice (B) in 2001, Choice (C) in 2002.

92. **(B)** 100 students were enrolled in 2001. Choices (A), (C), and (D) are contradicted by how many were enrolled in 2001.

93. **(A)** 50 was the lowest amount of students enrolled. Choices (B), (C), and (D) show higher enrollment.

94. **(A)** The number of students has increased from 2000 to 2003. Choices (B), (C), and (D) are not shown in the graph.

95. **(C)** The bill indicates that there were 3 customers. Each of them ordered a drink, a meal, and a dessert. Choices (A), (B), and (D) are contradicted by the number of customers and items ordered.

96. **(B)** 1 juice costs $2.25. Choice (A) costs $1.50. Choice (C) costs $3.00. Choice (D) Hamburgers or chicken sandwiches cost more than 6 dollars each.

97. **(C)** $13.00 divided by two equals $6.50. Choice (A) is the cost of a coffee. Choice (B) is the cost of a chicken sandwich. Choice (D) is the cost of two hamburgers.

98. **(D)** The bill says *please pay cashier*. Choice (A) confuses cash (money) with cashier (person who takes money). Choices (B) and (C) are not mentioned.

99. **(A)** The advertisement says *at my home*. Choice (B) confuses *student's home* with the teacher's home. Choice (C) confuses *near bus lines* with *bus station*. Choice (D) associates *lessons* with *school*.

100. **(C)** Lessons are for ages 5–15. Choices (A) and (D) are contradicted by ages 5–15. Choice (B) confuses *experienced teacher* with *experienced student*.

Appendix B—Audioscripts

AUDIOSCRIPTS FOR LISTENING COMPREHENSION

Part I: Photographs

LISTENING PRACTICE: LOCATION

[Narrator]   Number 1. Look at the picture marked number 1 in your test book.
[Man A]

(A)	[Woman A]	The boat is on the water.
(B)		The cruise ship is at the dock.
(C)		The sailboat is on the shore.
(D)		The canoe is in storage.

(Pause 5 seconds)

[Narrator]   Number 2. Look at the picture marked number 2 in your test book.
[Man A]

(A)	[Woman B]	They're ordering dinner at home.
(B)		They're buying food at a grocery store.
(C)		They're dining at an outdoor restaurant.
(D)		They're cooking in the kitchen.

(Pause 5 seconds)

| [Narrator] | Number 3. Look at the picture marked number 3 in your test book. |
| [Man A] | |

	(A)	[Man B]	The hikers are enjoying the country air.
	(B)		The roadway is closed to foot traffic.
	(C)		The cars are parked in the garage.
	(D)		The pedestrians are walking down the street.

(Pause 5 seconds)

| [Narrator] | Number 4. Look at the picture marked number 4 in your test book. |
| [Man A] | |

	(A)	[Woman B]	The paintings are stored on the shelves.
	(B)		The art is hung on the walls.
	(C)		The frames are across the floor.
	(D)		The pictures are placed in the album.

(Pause 5 seconds)

| [Narrator] | Number 5. Look at the picture marked number 5 in your test book. |
| [Man A] | |

	(A)	[Woman A]	The fly is buzzing around the ceiling.
	(B)		The climber is walking through the fog.
	(C)		The crane is gliding through the air.
	(D)		The plane is flying above the clouds.

(Pause 5 seconds)

LISTENING PRACTICE: PEOPLE

| [Narrator] | Number 1. Look at the picture marked number 1 in your test book. |
| [Man A] | |

	(A)	[Woman A]	The dentist is examining his patient.
	(B)		The plumber is opening the drain.
	(C)		The handyman is fixing his tools.
	(D)		The pediatrician is weighing the baby.

(Pause 5 seconds)

| [Narrator] | Number 2. Look at the picture marked number 2 in your test book. |
| [Man A] | |

	(A)	[Woman B]	The pilots are off course.
	(B)		The players are having tea.
	(C)		The golfers are on the course.
	(D)		The gophers are in the tunnel.

(Pause 5 seconds)

[Narrator]   Number 3. Look at the picture marked number 3 in your test book.
[Man A]

    (A)   [Man B]   The secretary is writing in the notebook.
    (B)   The passenger is riding on the bus.
    (C)   The patient is lying down.
    (D)   The doctor is talking with the patient.

(Pause 5 seconds)

[Narrator]   Number 4. Look at the picture marked number 4 in your test book.
[Man A]

    (A)   [Woman B] The attendant is cleaning the laboratory.
    (B)   The technician is looking through the microscope.
    (C)   The beautician is examining her nails.
    (D)   The librarian is checking the reference section.

(Pause 5 seconds)

[Narrator]   Number 5. Look at the picture marked number 5 in your test book.
[Man A]

    (A)   [Woman A] The pilot is standing in front of the helicopter.
    (B)   The cop is walking under the fan.
    (C)   The flight attendant is boarding the plane.
    (D)   The mechanic is repairing the engine.

(Pause 5 seconds)

LISTENING PRACTICE: ACTIONS

[Narrator]   Number 1. Look at the picture marked number 1 in your test book.
[Man A]

    (A)   [Woman A] The barber is cutting the boy's hair.
    (B)   The boy is talking to his teacher.
    (C)   The doctor is examining the patient.
    (D)   The father is feeding his son.

(Pause 5 seconds)

[Narrator]   Number 2. Look at the picture marked number 2 in your test book.
[Man A]

    (A)   [Woman B] They're running a race.
    (B)   They're rubbing their feet.
    (C)   They're standing in line.
    (D)   They're looking at the time.

(Pause 5 seconds)

[Narrator]   Number 3. Look at the picture marked number 3 in your test book.
[Man A]

     (A)   [Woman B]   The tourists are getting off the train.
     (B)   The travelers are climbing a ladder.
     (C)   The visitors are walking in the rain.
     (D)   The passengers are boarding the plane.

(Pause 5 seconds)

[Narrator]   Number 4. Look at the picture marked number 4 in your test book.
[Man A]

     (A)   [Woman B]   She's cutting her plants.
     (B)   She's arranging flowers.
     (C)   She's measuring the flour.
     (D)   She's admiring her garden.

(Pause 5 seconds)

[Narrator]   Number 5. Look at the picture marked number 5 in your test book.
[Man A]

     (A)   [Man B]   They're performing a duet.
     (B)   They're playing cards.
     (C)   They're singing around the piano.
     (D)   They're cleaning the keyboard.

(Pause 5 seconds)

Part II: Question-Response

LISTENING PRACTICE: WORDS REPEATED

1. Were there many students in the classroom?

   (A) Yes, it was near there.
   (B) Yes, the room was crowded.
   (C) Yes, we studied before class.

2. What time did you get home?

   (A) It was the last time.
   (B) I got it at home.
   (C) At about 9:30.

3. What did you do last night?

   (A) I played tennis.
   (B) It was late at night.
   (C) That's the last kite.

4. Whose books are those?

   (A) They belong to the teacher.
   (B) They're English books.
   (C) Those are new books.

5. What day is the tennis game?

   (A) Today is a very nice day.
   (B) It's next Saturday.
   (C) Tennis is a fun game.

6. How long was the movie?

   (A) It was long ago.
   (B) We stayed too long.
   (C) About two and a half hours.

7. What would you like to drink?

   (A) A cup of coffee, please.
   (B) I don't drink much.
   (C) Yes, I would.

8. When did you go to a concert?

   (A) It wasn't a very good concert.
   (B) It's time to go now.
   (C) I went last weekend.

9. How often do you play soccer?

   (A) I can teach you about soccer.
   (B) I play with my friends.
   (C) Two or three times a week.

10. What month is your vacation?

    (A) It's very cold this month.
    (B) It's in August.
    (C) I have a long vacation.

11. When will we see Mary?

    (A) She'll be here tomorrow.
    (B) It's too dark to see.
    (C) I know Mary quite well.

12. Did you study English last year?

    (A) Yes, and I learned a lot.
    (B) Yes, it lasted a year.
    (C) Yes, they speak English.

13. What time does the meeting begin?

    (A) It takes a long time.
    (B) It was a business meeting.
    (C) At ten o'clock.

14. Would you like to have a sandwich?

    (A) Yes, it's a sandwich.
    (B) Yes, I'm very hungry.
    (C) Yes, I like it.

15. When is your birthday?

    (A) It's my birthday.
    (B) It's next month.
    (C) It's a birthday party.

LISTENING PRACTICE: SIMILAR SOUNDS

1. It's raining today, isn't it?

   (A) Yes, take an umbrella.
   (B) Yes, the train is coming.
   (C) Yes, his plane leaves today.

2. Why did you close the window?

   (A) It's close to 4:00.
   (B) Because I feel cold.
   (C) My clothes are on the floor.

3. What date is the party?

   (A) I ate a lot at the party.
   (B) It's on December 10th.
   (C) It's getting late.

4. When did they leave?

   (A) I saw them then.
   (B) They live in New York.
   (C) About an hour ago.

5. When did his plane arrive?

   (A) He plans to drive.
   (B) Last night at 10:00.
   (C) The train will be late.

6. Did you wait for her long?

   (A) Only about five minutes.
   (B) It's very far away.
   (C) She wants to lose weight.

7. Do you work here?

   (A) Yes, this is my office.
   (B) Yes, they walked here today.
   (C) Yes, his work is hard.

8. Will it be cold tomorrow?

   (A) Yes, wear your coat.
   (B) Yes, I told them.
   (C) Yes, he's getting old.

9. Where is the store?

   (A) It opens at 4:00.
   (B) I can't wear it anymore.
   (C) It's on the corner.

10. How much time do you need?

    (A) I see just a few.
    (B) Everything's fine.
    (C) Just a few minutes.

11. How long did you stay there?

    (A) They went there today.
    (B) It's a long way to get there.
    (C) Just two days.

12. Would you like to take a walk?

    (A) Yes, I love to talk.
    (B) Yes, let's go to the park.
    (C) Yes, I need some work.

13. Did the train arrive late?

    (A) No, that's not the right date.
    (B) No, it was on time.
    (C) No, there were more than eight.

14. Did you spend much money?

    (A) No, just a few dollars.
    (B) No, I'll send it tomorrow.
    (C) No, there weren't very many.

15. How long was the class?

    (A) It's not very fast.
    (B) It doesn't last.
    (C) About an hour.

LISTENING PRACTICE: ASSOCIATED WORDS

1. What kind of flowers are those?

   (A) I like gardens.
   (B) They're roses.
   (C) Plant them in the spring.

2. Would you like some coffee?

   (A) No, thanks, I prefer tea.
   (B) That's not my cup.
   (C) I like hot drinks.

3. Where is the post office?

   (A) It's right across the street.
   (B) I sent the letter yesterday.
   (C) I need to buy some stamps.

4. Which desk is yours?

   (A) I need a bigger table.
   (B) That's a comfortable chair.
   (C) It's the one by the window.

5. Do you prefer movies or books?

   (A) Actually, I like television best.
   (B) There's a theater near here.
   (C) Let's go to the library.

6. Where do you work?

   (A) It's my first job.
   (B) At a store downtown.
   (C) It's a good profession.

7. How far is your school from here?

   (A) I have a very good teacher.
   (B) Class begins at 9:00.
   (C) It's about two miles from here.

8. May I use your telephone?

   (A) I'll call you tonight.
   (B) It's ringing.
   (C) Of course.

9. What do you study?

   (A) Yes, I'm a student.
   (B) At the University of California.
   (C) Math and science.

10. What time does the bank open?

    (A) I'd like to open an account.
    (B) I need some money.
    (C) At 8:30 on weekdays.

11. Is this your glass of water?

    (A) Yes, it's mine.
    (B) No, it's plastic.
    (C) It's too wet.

12. Do you know how to type?

    (A) This isn't my computer.
    (B) Yes, but I'm not very fast.
    (C) No, it's an old keyboard.

13. Where did you buy that sweater?

    (A) It didn't cost much.
    (B) It's cold today.
    (C) At a store downtown.

14. What time will his plane arrive?

    (A) At 10:15.
    (B) The airport isn't far.
    (C) Yes, he's a pilot.

15. This is your car, isn't it?

    (A) Yes, he knows how to drive.
    (B) No, it's my father's.
    (C) It's in the parking lot.

LISTENING PRACTICE: HOMONYMS

1. Would you like some more meat?

   (A) Yes, I'd like you to meet someone.
   (B) No, thanks, I've had enough.
   (C) No, we didn't have time to meet.

2. Does this store sell clothes?

   (A) We close at 9:30.
   (B) It's close to here.
   (C) Yes, women's wear.

3. Where is the bookstore?

   (A) It's downtown.
   (B) You can store them in here.
   (C) I booked a hotel room.

4. Will you be here next week?

   (A) No, I'm not feeling weak.
   (B) No, I didn't hear it.
   (C) No, I'll be on vacation.

5. Where does your son live?

   (A) There isn't much sun today.
   (B) In an apartment downtown.
   (C) He likes to wear jeans.

6. Did you get the right answer?

   (A) No, I answered wrong.
   (B) No, I didn't write the letter.
   (C) No, but I'll write to you soon.

7. When did you buy those shoes?

   (A) It's time to say good-bye.
   (B) There's a store close by.
   (C) I got them yesterday.

8. His plane leaves at eight, doesn't it?

   (A) We ate on the plane.
   (B) Yes, he already ate.
   (C) No, it leaves at nine.

9. Where did you get your new red dress?

   (A) I read that book.
   (B) I got it at a department store.
   (C) I knew him well.

10. What is that book for?

    (A) It's for my English class.
    (B) I bought four books.
    (C) It's four o'clock.

11. When is their party?

    (A) It's over there.
    (B) They said next Saturday.
    (C) They're usually on time.

12. Can I have two sandwiches?

    (A) Have as many as you want.
    (B) I like sandwiches too.
    (C) Give it to me.

13. How much is the taxi fare?

    (A) It's seven dollars.
    (B) The weather is fair.
    (C) We went to the fair.

14. Do you like my blue shirt?

    (A) The wind blew all day.
    (B) Yes, it's very nice.
    (C) No, they don't look alike.

15. Do you know how to sew?

    (A) He doesn't think so.
    (B) No, it wasn't so good.
    (C) Yes, I make my own clothes.

LISTENING PRACTICE: SAME SOUND AND SPELLING BUT DIFFERENT MEANING

1. How did John look yesterday?

    (A) I looked for him everywhere.
    (B) He didn't look well.
    (C) He looked it up in the directory.

2. How much does it cost to park here?

    (A) The fee is six dollars an hour.
    (B) No, Mrs. Park isn't here.
    (C) Yes, there's a park across the street.

3. Did you buy a first-class ticket?

    (A) No, English is my first class.
    (B) No, I fly business class.
    (C) No, they're not in this class.

4. He works very hard, doesn't he?

    (A) Yes, he never rests.
    (B) Yes, the chair is hard.
    (C) Yes, it was hard to understand.

5. What time was your class over?

    (A) I turned it over.
    (B) Put it over here, please.
    (C) It ended at 3:30.

6. How long is the trip to New York?

    (A) Don't trip on that rock.
    (B) I tripped on the stairs.
    (C) The flight is three hours.

7. Did you go running this morning?

    (A) Yes, and now I'm very tired.
    (B) No, I didn't go there.
    (C) It runs on electricity.

8. Did you enjoy the play last night?

    (A) It was very interesting.
    (B) I played the guitar.
    (C) I play soccer on weekends.

9. What kind of work does he do?

    (A) They worked out the problem.
    (B) My computer doesn't work.
    (C) He's a university professor.

10. Does Tom look like his father?

    (A) He likes ice cream.
    (B) Take a look around.
    (C) Yes, they are very similar.

11. Is there any coffee left?

    (A) Yes, I'll pour you a cup.
    (B) No, he left it there.
    (C) Take a left at the corner.

12. How many answers are right?

    (A) It looks all right to me.
    (B) All of them are correct.
    (C) It's on your right.

13. Can I turn off this radio?

    (A) No, they didn't turn up on time.
    (B) Turn in your work tomorrow.
    (C) No, but I'll turn the volume down.

14. How long did you rest?

    (A) The rest is for you.
    (B) I slept for about two hours.
    (C) They threw the rest away.

15. What did you get for lunch?

    (A) Just a sandwich.
    (B) Get off the bus here.
    (C) We'll get rid of it.

LISTENING PRACTICE: OPPOSITES

1. Laura hardly works at all.

   (A) She's a hard worker.
   (B) She always does all her work.
   (C) She's very lazy.

2. I've seen better movies than this.

   (A) Yes, it was excellent.
   (B) I agree. It was a boring movie.
   (C) You're right. It was the best.

3. Sam didn't look well today.

   (A) Yes, he's doing very well.
   (B) No, I think he's sick.
   (C) You're right. He's very healthy.

4. You didn't read the directions carefully.

   (A) I'm sorry. I'm very careless.
   (B) Thank you. I'm a very careful student.
   (C) Yes, I was very careful.

5. George isn't a very happy person, is he?

   (A) True. He's happy most of the time.
   (B) George is happy all day long.
   (C) No, he's usually unhappy.

6. This isn't an easy class.

   (A) You're right. It's very difficult.
   (B) Yes, it's quite easy.
   (C) I agree. The work is simple.

7. His new job isn't very important.

   (A) He's a very important man now.
   (B) True. He has an unimportant position.
   (C) Yes, it's quite important.

8. This hotel is very uncomfortable.

   (A) I don't feel comfortable here, either.
   (B) Yes, it's quite comfortable.
   (C) It's a nice place to stay, isn't it?

9. This restaurant is too noisy.

   (A) It's not very loud, is it?
   (B) Yes, let's look for a quieter place.
   (C) You're right. It's not very noisy.

10. Your car isn't big enough.

    (A) You're right. It's too small.
    (B) Yes, it's too big.
    (C) I agree. It's quite a big car.

11. It's an unusually cold day.

    (A) Yes, it's usual to have cold weather.
    (B) You're right. It isn't usually this cold.
    (C) Yes, it's often this cold.

12. Jim is not a safe driver.

    (A) I agree. He drives very dangerously.
    (B) Yes, I always feel safe with him.
    (C) You're right. He's a careful driver.

13. Martha is never on time.

    (A) You're right. She's very punctual.
    (B) No, she's always late.
    (C) True. She's usually on time.

14. This bus isn't very crowded, is it?

    (A) I agree. There are too many people.
    (B) Yes, it's very crowded.
    (C) No, it's quite empty.

15. The concert wasn't very long.

    (A) I agree. It was too long.
    (B) It was too short, wasn't it?
    (C) Yes, it was a long concert.

LISTENING PRACTICE: WORD ORDER

1. What a rainy day this is!

    (A) It's Tuesday today.
    (B) Yes, we need umbrellas.
    (C) I don't know what day it is.

2. How tall you are!

    (A) Yes, I've grown up.
    (B) I'm not interested at all.
    (C) I am five feet two.

3. This is the office where I work.

    (A) For a small company.
    (B) It's a nice office.
    (C) In that building.

4. No one can dance like Shirley.

    (A) You're right. She's a terrible dancer.
    (B) No, he doesn't like Shirley.
    (C) I agree. She's an excellent dancer.

5. Look how busy it is!

    (A) I thought it would be busier, too.
    (B) Yes, it will be hard to find parking.
    (C) No, it isn't busy here today.

6. Never have I seen a better movie.

    (A) No, I never go to the movies.
    (B) Me neither. I've never seen that movie.
    (C) You're right. It was very good.

7. What an expensive dress this is!

    (A) Yes, it costs too much.
    (B) It costs 750 dollars.
    (C) I don't know the price.

8. Look how fast he ate!

    (A) About four miles an hour.
    (B) Yes, he was in a hurry.
    (C) Three or four times a week.

9. What a boring time we had!

    (A) There's a clock on the wall.
    (B) My watch says 1:15.
    (C) You're right. It wasn't fun at all.

10. How rich can you be?

    (A) You can never be too rich.
    (B) About five feet.
    (C) My name is Richard.

11. Never have I eaten a worse dinner.

    (A) Yes, it was a delicious meal.
    (B) No, I never eat a big dinner.
    (C) You're right. The food wasn't very good.

12. No one can play tennis as well as Bob.

    (A) You're right. He doesn't play it well.
    (B) Yes, he's a professional player.
    (C) No, there are only ten of us.

13. How late it is!

    (A) Wow! It is late!
    (B) I think there are eight.
    (C) Yes, he's late.

14. This is the hotel where we spent our vacation.

    (A) It looks nice.
    (B) On the beach.
    (C) In a big city.

15. What an interesting job you have.

    (A) My wife works downtown.
    (B) It's interesting and it pays well.
    (C) No, I don't have a job.

MORE LISTENING PRACTICE

1. Where can I park my car?

   (A) You can park it across the street.
   (B) Let's walk in the park.
   (C) It isn't far to the car.

2. No one works as hard as Bob.

   (A) Yes, he walks very fast.
   (B) You're right. He's a very hard worker.
   (C) I agree. He hardly works.

3. How many students are in this class?

   (A) Yes, I'm a student in this class.
   (B) A first-class ticket is more expensive.
   (C) There are about 25, I think.

4. What kind of job does he have?

   (A) He's an engineer.
   (B) He works very hard.
   (C) He's a very kind person.

5. Do you work in this store?

   (A) Yes, I'm the manager.
   (B) No, you can't store that here.
   (C) Yes, we have some more.

6. Would you like something to drink?

   (A) Yes, it looks like wood.
   (B) Here are the glasses.
   (C) Just some water, please.

7. How far is the post office?

   (A) This is my office.
   (B) I'm going to mail a letter.
   (C) It's just down the street.

8. Math isn't an easy subject.

   (A) I agree. It's very difficult.
   (B) Yes, it's quite easy.
   (C) You're right. It's the easiest subject.

9. Where is your school?

   (A) We wear uniforms.
   (B) Yes, it's very cool.
   (C) It's close to my house.

10. Do you have plans for tomorrow?

    (A) Yes, his plane arrives soon.
    (B) At four o'clock tomorrow.
    (C) I might go to the movies.

11. When will her train arrive?

    (A) No, I don't plan to drive.
    (B) At two in the afternoon.
    (C) Yes, I think it will rain.

12. Do you play any sports?

    (A) Yes, I enjoyed the play.
    (B) Yes, soccer and basketball.
    (C) Yes, I wore shorts.

13. What day is today?

    (A) It's Monday.
    (B) It's a beautiful day.
    (C) It went away.

14. Did he have to work late?

    (A) No, he left the office early.
    (B) No, he already ate.
    (C) Yes, he was late to work.

15. Did you find your shoes?

    (A) He told me the news.
    (B) They are new shoes.
    (C) Yes, they were in the closet.

Audioscripts

Part III: Short Conversations and Short Talks

LISTENING PRACTICE: WORDS REPEATED

Answer the questions. Be careful of repeated words.

1. M: I'm making chicken and salad for
     dinner. OK?
    W: Chicken? Not steak?
    M: Sorry, I don't like steak.

2. Attention, please. There is a red car parked
    by the entrance. Its lights are on. Will the
    owner of the car please turn off the head-
    lights? Thank you.

3. Don't miss the end of season sale. All
    men's sports shirts are 25% off this week.
    Women's dress shoes are two pairs for the
    price of one. And we also have special
    discounts on children's jackets.

4. M: Is it comfortable taking the train to
     work?
    W: Well, the train's usually crowded, but
     it's more relaxing than driving.
    M: Yes, there's so much traffic these days,
     even walking is faster than driving.

5. W: Excuse me, does this bus go to the
     train station?
    M: I'm sorry, no. It goes downtown.
     The train station is that way, across
     the park.
    W: Just across the park? Then I'll walk.

6. W: I can't go to that soccer game tonight.
     I have to stay late at the office.
    M: But we already bought the tickets.
    W: I know, but I have a lot of work I
     need to finish.
    M: OK, I'll ask a friend to go to the game
     with me.

7. And now for this weekend's weather
    report. We'll have gray skies and lots of
    rain. Anyone who was planning a trip to
    the beach should forget about it. You will
    have to wait until next week to see some
    sun. The skies will clear up by the middle
    of the week and then we'll have some nice,
    hot, beach weather.

8. W: What's your favorite TV show?
    M: I don't really like TV. I'd rather read a
     book.
    W: Read a book? How boring! Don't you
     even like to watch movies?
    M: I'm always bored at the movies. Books
     are more interesting.

9. M: There's Jane over there, the one with
     long hair.
    W: But that woman has red hair. Jane's
     hair is black.
    M: No, the woman in the corner with
     long black hair.
    W: But she's not wearing glasses. Jane has
     glasses.

10. Hi John, it's Susan. I'm at the office now
    but I'll be leaving here in about 15 minutes,
    so I can meet you at the restaurant at 6:30.
    We'll have dinner there, right? Then let's go
    to the movies. Or would you rather just
    go home? Well, we'll talk about it at the
    restaurant. See you soon.

LISTENING PRACTICE: SIMILAR SOUNDS

1. M: What's that big ladder for?
   W: I'm going to help Gene paint his living room.
   M: That's a very long ladder. Be careful you don't fall.

2. M: Would you like some fruit? I have apples and pears.
   W: They all look so good. I don't know which to choose.
   M: Why not have one of each?
   W: I think I'll just have one of these pears.

3. M: What time is it?
   W: It's after 8.
   M: We'd better hurry. The movie starts before 9.
   W: It's too late now. We'll never get there on time.

4. Flight 17 for Miami is now boarding at Gate 10. All passengers with tickets please line up at Gate 10. The flight is full today so please pay attention to your seat number. In fact, we are overbooked.

5. M: I'm going downtown. Do you need anything?
   W: Yes. Could you go to the post office and mail this package for me?
   M: Sure. I'll pick up some stamps, too.

6. W1: Tell me about John. I don't know him at all.
   W2: Oh, he's a very nice person. And smart, too.
   W1: Is he good-looking?
   W2: I think so.

7. W: What's Mary's address?
   M: I don't recall. Why?
   W: I want to send her a card inviting her to our party.

8. M: This soup is delicious. You should try it.
   W: No, thanks. I'm not hungry.
   M: Not hungry? Oh, that's right, you already ate.

9. Next month the circus is coming to town. There will be clowns, acrobats, animals, and more to delight the whole family. Don't miss your fun day at the circus. The show begins on the first and will play every day for a week. Get your tickets today.

10. It's important to take good care of your pet bird. Birds need attention, so talk to your bird and play with it often. Your bird also needs fresh food in its dish and clean water to drink every day.

LISTENING PRACTICE: ASSOCIATED WORDS

Answer the questions. Be careful of associated words.

1. M: How much is this cookbook?
   W: It's just 18 dollars, and worth every penny. It has lots of delicious meals.
   M: Yes, I love cooking. Can I pay with a credit card?

2. W: Do you want to go to the tennis court this afternoon?
   M: It's too hot for tennis. This heat makes me feel tired.
   W: Then let's go swimming instead.
   M: Fine. I'll meet you after lunch.

3. Hi. Sorry to call so late. I know it's almost midnight, but my car broke down. I'm downtown near the City Garden Café. I need a ride. Can you pick me up please?

4. W: You look tired. Did you have trouble sleeping last night?
   M: No. I stayed out late at a party.
   W: And you had to come to the office early today. That's hard.

5. This is your movie hotline. We have three shows today at 3 o'clock, 5:30, and 8. The box office opens one hour before the first show. We have hot popcorn and cold soda for sale in the lobby.

6. This is one of the oldest buildings in our city. It was originally the house of our first president. Now it is our National History Museum. Don't forget to visit the museum gift shop where you can buy beautiful picture postcards of our city.

7. M: Sam's birthday is next week. I was thinking of giving him some tickets to a game.
   W: He's not really into sports. Why not get him a CD? He loves music.
   M: Music? Hmmm. No, he loves food more than music. I'll take him out for dinner.

8. W: Could you get me a glass of water? I'm really thirsty.
   M: Sure, but I'm all out of ice.
   W: That's OK. I'll drink it warm.

9. M: Is this your new office? It's huge.
   W: Yes, it's a good size and in a good place—right next to the elevator.
   M: And this is a nice-looking desk, but you should get a more comfortable chair.

10. W: What happened?
    M: I spilled this soup all over the floor. And look, I broke the plate, too.
    W: Oh, don't worry about it. I'll help you clean it up.

Audioscripts

LISTENING PRACTICE: HOMONYMS

Answer the questions. Be careful of homonyms.

1. M: Look at this great TV I got on sale.
   W: Wow! I need a new TV, too. Is the sale still on?
   M: Today's the last day, so you'd better hurry.
   W: I will. What time does the store close?

2. Come to the newest store in town. At Bob's Books we have books for children and adults. Our bookstore café is a great place to meet your friends or just to sit and read your new books. Bob's Books is located in the red brick building right by the City Bank.

3. M: That was some wind storm yesterday! It blew our big tree down.
   W: That tree is huge! How are you going to get it out of your yard?
   M: My son's going to cut it up for me and we'll use it for firewood.

4. M: Can you help me with this computer program?
   W: I can if you'll wait a while. I'm busy right now.
   M: That's okay. I'll ask George to help me. He knows a lot about computers.

5. Have you visited our city park recently? It's the perfect place to have fun with your family. Take a walk by the lake, have a picnic under the trees, relax by the fountain, or enjoy the swimming pool. Everything you need for fun is right here in our city park.

6. W: Did you meet any interesting people at the party?
   M: I ran into an old friend—Robert. We talked for a long time.
   W: Robert? Oh, you knew him in high school, right?

7. M: That's a very strong lock you have on your bicycle.
   W: I don't want anyone to steal it. You can never be too careful, you know.
   M: I'm sure your bicycle's safe now. Nobody could break that lock.

8. W: Didn't Janet go on vacation last week?
   M: She planned to, but she got the flu. She stayed home sick all week.
   W: I'm sorry to hear that. I know she wanted to get away and see new places.

9. M: We have to get this kitchen ready for dinner. Can you put the plates on the table?
   W: Sure. How many do we need?
   M: There'll be eight of us for dinner. Can you put these flowers on the table, too?

10. W: Look. Someone threw a ball at the window.
    M: What a mess. The floor is covered with glass.
    W: I know. Would you help me clean this mess up?

LISTENING PRACTICE: SAME SOUND AND SPELLING BUT DIFFERENT MEANING

Answer the questions. Be careful of words with the same sound and spelling but different meaning.

1. W: Could you check the car? It's been making a strange noise.
   M: I've noticed that too when the engine is running. I don't know what it is.
   W: I'll take it to the mechanic tomorrow morning.
   M: OK, then I'll pick it up after work.

2. W: I can't read this.
   M: What's the matter? Is that book too hard?
   W: No, there's not enough light in here.
   M: I'll bring a lamp from the other room.

3. M: Do you think this cake tastes funny?
   W: It's a little too sweet, isn't it?
   M: Yes, it's very rich.

4. W: Did you call to order the plane tickets?
   M: I forgot. I was so busy at work.
   W: Well, do it today. Please don't forget again.
   M: I'll call right now.

5. M: I need some exercise. Will you work out at the gym with me?
   W: I prefer walking.
   M: Walking sounds good. Let's go to the park.

6. M: How do you like to spend your free time?
   W: I play golf whenever I'm free. It's so relaxing.
   M: I enjoy golf too. I play almost every weekend.
   W: Me too. I hate to go back to the office after a weekend of golf.

7. W: Can you help me move the TV over there?
   M: It's too heavy to move. Let's just leave it here.
   W: OK. I guess we can watch it here.

8. Hi, honey. I forgot to water the plants before I left. Could you do that when you get home? Also, throw out those old, dry flowers on the kitchen table. They're a week old and they look it. Thanks.

9. Thank you for calling Sunshine Travel Agency. Please stay on the line and the first available agent will help you shortly. If you want to book a flight to Los Angeles, we're sorry, this week's flights to L.A. are sold out, but there are seats available to other destinations.

10. City College offers evening and weekend classes for people who work during the day. We have all kinds of classes to meet everyone's interests. Check out our catalog to find the type of classes and schedule you need. City College—the school for working people.

LISTENING PRACTICE: OPPOSITES

Answer the questions. Be careful of opposites.

1. W: What a mess.
   M: Don't tell me about it. It's not my responsibility to clean around here.
   W: Someone has to. This place is barely livable.

2. M: This book is useless.
   W: What's the matter? Don't you like it?
   M: Sure I like it, but it doesn't have the information I need to write my report.

3. All employees are requested to take their lunch break in the lounge. Please put your cups and plates in the trash when you are finished eating. Don't take drinks and food back to your desks. Please keep the office clean.

4. M: I can't say that was the best movie I've seen.
   W: You're not kidding. I've never seen a worse one.
   M: You're right. It really wasn't any good at all.

5. W: This hotel room doesn't have much space, does it?
   M: I've seen bigger. But we won't be here long.
   W: That's true. We can be crowded for one night.

6. M: That test wasn't so hard, was it?
   W: You're right. I've certainly taken more difficult tests.
   M: It wasn't a short test, but it didn't take long to finish it.

7. W: We had a wonderful drive to the beach. Very pretty scenery.
   M: And how was your day at the beach?
   W: Not so good. Such a gray sky. We - didn't see the sun all day.

8. Welcome to the State Street Theater. Food and soda are available in the lobby, but please don't bring food from the outside. Please turn off all cell phones, radios, and tape recorders before entering the theater, and don't talk during the show.

9. M: This restaurant's not so expensive.
   W: No, and the food's not bad either. I really like their desserts.
   M: But the service isn't very fast.

10. W: Wow. You painted the kitchen. It doesn't look bad.
    M: What do you mean? I worked really hard to do this.
    W: And you did a very nice job. It's much better than before.

LISTENING PRACTICE: INTONATION

Answer the questions. Be careful of intonation.

1. W: Me? Ride in that car? Are you out of your mind?
   M: What's the matter? Don't you think I can drive it?
   W: Oh, you can drive it, but don't think I'm riding in that thing. I'm staying home.

2. M: Susan's such a nice person.
   W: What's so nice about Susan?
   M: She lent me a dollar for my lunch.
   W: One dollar? Yeah, she's really generous. [in a sarcastic tone]

3. W: That trip was really fun. [sarcastically]
   M: Wasn't there one thing you liked about it? The food? Or what about the hotel?
   W: Yeah, sure and that great weather. The only good thing was the plane ride home.

4. M: You didn't eat all that!
   W: Well, actually, I did. Now I feel terrible.
   M: Overeating, that's a great idea. Why didn't you save some to eat later?

5. M: Look how rainy it is. There's so much rain you could swim down the street.
   W: So you're not going fishing?
   M: Of course I am. Do you think I want to stay home all day and watch TV?

6. W: You forgot to call Martha?
   M: No, I called her office and I left her a message.
   W: She never answers her messages, does she? Maybe you should try e-mail.

7. M: Thanks Lisa, that was a really funny joke.
   W: Oh, don't be mean. People usually love that joke. I thought it was funny.
   M: Ha ha. It was so funny I forgot to laugh.

8. W: Never have I tasted more delicious fish soup!
   M: Really? I was afraid you didn't like fish.
   W: Me? Not like fish? No, it's chicken I don't like. Fish soup with rice is the best.

9. M: This apartment isn't expensive, but it's not very big.
   W: You don't like the living room?
   M: Yes, but I want a bigger apartment.

10. M: Look at this great tie I got for my birthday.
    W: You're not wearing that ugly thing to the office? You should throw it away.
    M: Oh, it's not so bad. I'll wear it to work tomorrow with my new suit.

AUDIOSCRIPTS FOR MINI-TEST FOR LISTENING COMPREHENSION REVIEW—PARTS I, II, AND III

[Narrator]

Listening Comprehension

In this section of the test, you will have the chance to show how well you understand spoken English. There are three parts to this section, with special directions for each part.

PART I: PHOTOGRAPHS

Directions: For each question, you will see a picture in your test book and you will hear four short statements. The statements will be spoken just one time. They will not be printed in your test book, so you must listen carefully.

When you hear the four statements, look at the picture in your test book and choose the statement that best describes what you see in the picture. Then, on your answer sheet, find the number of the question and mark your answer. Look at the sample below.

[Narrator]	Now listen to the four statements.

[Man A]	(A)	[Woman A]	The boys are laughing.
	(B)		The boys are reading.
	(C)		The boys are fighting.
	(D)		The boys are painting.

[Narrator]	Statement (B), "The boys are reading," best describes what you see in the picture. Therefore, you should choose answer (B).

[Narrator]	Now, let us begin Part I with question number 1.

[Narrator]	Number 1. Look at the picture marked number 1 in your test book.
[Man A]	(A)	[Woman A]	This is a truck.
	(B)		This is a car.
	(C)		This is a duck.
	(D)		This is a bus.

(Pause 5 seconds)

[Narrator]	Number 2. Look at the picture marked number 2 in your test book.
[Man A]	(A)	[Woman B]	The shop closes at nine.
	(B)		The clothes are in the street.
	(C)		The road is not open to traffic.
	(D)		The rodeo is closed today.

(Pause 5 seconds)

[Narrator]   Number 3. Look at the picture marked number 3 in your test book.
[Man A]   (A)   [Man B]   He's putting red oil on the cart.
          (B)   He's filling his car with gas.
          (C)   He's painting his van white.
          (D)   He's waiting for a bus.

(Pause 5 seconds)

[Narrator]   Number 4. Look at the picture marked number 4 in your test book.
[Man A]   (A)   [Woman B]   The patient is taking his medicine.
          (B)   The pillow is on the rug.
          (C)   The farmer is tilling the soil.
          (D)   The pharmacist is holding medication.

(Pause 5 seconds)

[Narrator]   Number 5. Look at the picture marked number 5 in your test book.
[Man A]   (A)   [Man A]   They're fishing in a lake.
          (B)   They're swimming in a river.
          (C)   They're walking on the beach.
          (D)   They're sitting in a boat.

(Pause 5 seconds)

[Narrator]   Number 6. Look at the picture marked number 6 in your test book.
[Man A]   (A)   [Man B]   The trays are in the cabinet.
          (B)   The planes are on the runway.
          (C)   The trains are in the station.
          (D)   The taxis are by the tracks.

(Pause 5 seconds)

[Narrator]   Number 7. Look at the picture marked number 7 in your test book.
[Man A]   (A)   [Woman A]   The books are on the shelf.
          (B)   The students are at their desks.
          (C)   The pens are in the box.
          (D)   The papers are on the chair.

(Pause 5 seconds)

[Narrator]   Number 8. Look at the picture marked number 8 in your test book.
[Man A]   (A)   [Woman B]   He's crossing the street.
          (B)   He's driving home from work.
          (C)   He's entering the building.
          (D)   He's running across the finish line.

(Pause 5 seconds)

[Narrator]		Number 9. Look at the picture marked number 9 in your test book.
[Man A]	(A) [Man B]	The housekeeper is setting his watch.
	(B)	The scientist is observing the dials.
	(C)	The technician is watching TV.
	(D)	The pilot is at the controls of the plane.

(Pause 5 seconds)

[Narrator]		Number 10. Look at the picture marked number 10 in your test book.
[Man A]	(A) [Woman B]	The dishes are under the sink.
	(B)	The produce is in the market.
	(C)	The food is on display.
	(D)	The table is set for dinner.

(Pause 5 seconds)

[Narrator]		Number 11. Look at the picture marked number 11 in your test book.
[Man A]	(A) [Woman A]	He's washing his face.
	(B)	He's putting on his glasses.
	(C)	He's drinking from a cup.
	(D)	He's holding grass in his hand.

(Pause 5 seconds)

[Narrator]		Number 12. Look at the picture marked number 12 in your test book.
[Man A]	(A) [Man B]	She's making a photocopy.
	(B)	She's opening the closet.
	(C)	She's turning on the light.
	(D)	She's shutting the window.

(Pause 5 seconds)

[Narrator]		Number 13. Look at the picture marked number 13 in your test book.
[Man A]	(A) [Woman A]	The bicycles are parked on the street.
	(B)	The cyclists are racing down the road.
	(C)	The motorcycles are under the trees.
	(D)	The racers are taking a break.

(Pause 5 seconds)

[Narrator]		Number 14. Look at the picture marked number 14 in your test book.
[Man A]	(A) [Man B]	He's sharpening his pencil.
	(B)	He's changing his shirt.
	(C)	He's reading a magazine.
	(D)	He's writing in a book.

(Pause 5 seconds)

[Narrator]   Number 15. Look at the picture marked number 15 in your test book.

[Man A]   (A) [Woman B] They're ready to eat.

           (B)   They're cleaning the dishes.

           (C)   They're preparing the food.

           (D)   They're standing around the table.

(Pause 5 seconds)

[Narrator]

PART II: QUESTION-RESPONSE

> **Directions:** In this part of the test, you will hear a question or statement spoken in English, followed by three responses, also spoken in English. The question or statement and the responses will be spoken just one time. They will not be printed in your test book, so you must listen carefully. Choose the best response to each question.

[Narrator]   Now listen to a sample question.

[Narrator]   You will hear:

[Woman B]   Excuse me. Where is the bus stop?

[Narrator]   You will also hear:

[Man A]   (A)   It's across the street.

           (B)   It's underneath.

           (C)   It arrives in ten minutes.

[Narrator]   The best response to the question *Where is the bus stop?* is Choice (A), *It's across the street.* Therefore, you should choose answer (A).

[Narrator]   Now let us begin Part II with question number 16.

[Narrator]   Number 16.

[Woman A]   How much does a train ticket cost?

[Man B]   (A)   At the ticket counter.

           (B)   Thirty-five dollars.

           (C)   In ten minutes.

(Pause 5 seconds)

[Narrator]   Number 17.

[Man B]   Is Mrs. Black in her office?

[Woman B]   (A)   She just left.

           (B)   It's right across the hall.

           (C)   Usually around 9:30.

(Pause 5 seconds)

[Narrator]   Number 18.
[Woman A]   What time did you get home?

[Woman B]   (A)   At 5:30.
                   (B)   By bus.
                   (C)   In that building.

(Pause 5 seconds)

[Narrator]   Number 19.
[Man B]   Who's that man?

[Woman A]   (A)   Yes, he is.
                   (B)   He's the new manager.
                   (C)   It belongs to me.

(Pause 5 seconds)

[Narrator]   Number 20.
[Woman B]   Can you tell me where the post office is?

[Man B]   (A)   You can buy stamps there.
                   (B)   It's next to the bank.
                   (C)   This is my office.

(Pause 5 seconds)

[Narrator]   Number 21.
[Woman A]   Do you mind if I close the window?

[Man B]   (A)   No, I don't mind.
                   (B)   Yes, it's mine.
                   (C)   No, those aren't my clothes.

(Pause 5 seconds)

[Narrator]   Number 22.
[Woman B]   When can I call you?

[Woman A]   (A)   Just call me Mary.
                   (B)   Call tomorrow before noon.
                   (C)   You're taller than I am.

(Pause 5 seconds)

[Narrator]   Number 23.
[Woman B]   Have you met the new manager yet?

[Man B]   (A)   Yes, I can manage alone.
                        (B)   Yes, I'll get it tomorrow.
                        (C)   Yes, I met him yesterday.

(Pause 5 seconds)

[Narrator]   Number 24.
[Woman A]   Whose keys are those?

[Man B]   (A)   Certainly, I'd be glad to.
                        (B)   I think they're Tom's.
                        (C)   It was very nice, thank you.

(Pause 5 seconds)

[Narrator]   Number 25.
[Man B]   How was the movie?

[Woman B]   (A)   It was great.
                        (B)   It's too big to move.
                        (C)   It lasted about two hours.

(Pause 5 seconds)

[Narrator]   Number 26.
[Woman B]   Would you like to sit down?

[Woman A]   (A)   Yes, I'm very tired.
                        (B)   Yes, I really liked it.
                        (C)   Yes, let's go downtown.

(Pause 5 seconds)

[Narrator]   Number 27.
[Woman A]   Do you know what time it is?

[Man B]   (A)   I think he's in his office.
                        (B)   No, I've never met him.
                        (C)   It's 3:30.

(Pause 5 seconds)

[Narrator]   Number 28.
[Man B]   Why did you leave early yesterday?

[Woman B]   (A)   I left it on your desk.
                          (B)   I had an appointment.
                          (C)   It's too wide.

(Pause 5 seconds)

[Narrator]   Number 29.
[Woman B]   You aren't from here, are you?

[Man B]   (A)   No, I live in another city.
                          (B)   No, they didn't come here.
                          (C)   No, my car isn't here.

(Pause 5 seconds)

[Narrator]   Number 30.
[Woman A]   Where do you want to eat?

[Woman B]   (A)   I think I'll wear my sweater.
                          (B)   There's a nice restaurant down the street.
                          (C)   As soon as I finish this letter.

(Pause 5 seconds)

[Narrator]   Number 31.
[Woman A]   Don't forget to tell Mr. Lee about the meeting.

[Man B]   (A)   I'll get him one tomorrow.
                          (B)   He enjoys eating.
                          (C)   I'll tell him right now.

(Pause 5 seconds)

[Narrator]   Number 32.
[Man B]   When do you expect them to arrive?

[Woman A]   (A)   I don't think they'll drive.
                          (B)   At a hotel downtown.
                          (C)   They'll be here this evening.

(Pause 5 seconds)

[Narrator]   Number 33.
[Woman A]   How's the food at this restaurant?

[Man B]   (A)   We had a good rest.
                   (B)   It's not very good.
                   (C)   Yes, I ate a while ago.

(Pause 5 seconds)

[Narrator]   Number 34.
[Man B]   Why don't we go to the beach this weekend?

[Woman A]   (A)   They want to go swimming.
                   (B)   Because I'm not hungry.
                   (C)   That's a great idea.

(Pause 5 seconds)

[Narrator]   Number 35.
[Woman A]   Where can I buy a new pair of shoes?

[Woman B]   (A)   There's a good shoe store downtown.
                   (B)   Pears are my favorite fruit.
                   (C)   You can borrow my newspaper.

(Pause 5 seconds)

[Narrator]

PART III: SHORT CONVERSATIONS AND SHORT TALKS

Directions: In this part of the test, you will hear 15 short conversations or short talks only once, so you must listen carefully.

In your test book, you will read a question about each conversation or talk. The question will be followed by four short answers. Choose the best answer to each question and mark it on your answer sheet.

[Narrator]   Now let us begin Part III with question number 36.

[Narrator]   Number 36.
[Woman A]   I'm so sorry I'm late. The traffic was just terrible.
[Man B]   Well, you're not too late. Did you come by bus?
[Woman A]   No, in my car. But next time, I think I'll just walk.

(Pause 8 seconds)

[Narrator]	Number 37.
[Woman A]	Thank you for calling the Central Cinema. Today we are showing the hit comedy *Traveling with Charles*. We have shows at 1:30, 3:45, 6:00, and 8:30. Refreshments are available in the lobby.

(Pause 8 seconds)

[Narrator]	Number 38.
[Woman A]	I'm freezing cold.
[Woman B]	Why didn't you bring a sweater? Didn't you know it was cold?
[Woman A]	I thought the weather would warm up.

(Pause 8 seconds)

[Narrator]	Number 39.
[Man B]	Are you planning to go home right after work this evening?
[Woman A]	No, I'm going to the gym to work out.
[Man B]	Great idea. I was planning to go to the movies, but I think I'll join you at the gym instead.

(Pause 8 seconds)

[Narrator]	Number 40.
[Woman B]	My plane arrives at 1:30.
[Man A]	If I leave the house by 12:45, I can meet you at the airport then.
[Woman B]	Great. I'll wait for you by the gate.

(Pause 8 seconds)

[Narrator]	Number 41.
[Woman A]	I'll have the grilled fish, and could I get that with a salad on the side?
[Man B]	Certainly. Would you like something to drink?
[Woman A]	I'll have coffee later with my dessert.

(Pause 8 seconds)

[Narrator]	Number 42.
[Man A]	Do you have any plans for this Saturday?
[Woman B]	I've been working so hard lately, I'm just going to rest all weekend.
[Man A]	That sounds good. I think I'll do the same.

(Pause 8 seconds)

[Narrator]	Number 43.
Man B]	Isn't it great? The new office will be ready next week.
[Woman A]	I can't wait. I'm really tired of working in this small space.
[Man B]	Moving all our stuff won't be fun, but it'll be well worth the trouble.

(Pause 8 seconds)

[Narrator]   Number 44.

[Man B]   Good evening, class. I hope all of you are ready for the final exam. Please put all your books away now and take out a pen or pencil. Are there any questions before we begin?

(Pause 8 seconds)

[Narrator]   Number 45.

[Man B]   You can park over there by that red car.

[Woman A]   OK. How much does it cost to park here all day?

[Man B]   Just 15 dollars. You can pay when you leave.

(Pause 8 seconds)

[Narrator]   Number 46.

[Man B]   If you're traveling on Route 50 this morning, be careful. Last night's rain flooded several areas of the road and cars are moving very slowly. There is also heavy traffic on the Center City Bridge.

(Pause 8 seconds)

[Narrator]   Number 47.

[Woman B]   That party was the most boring one I have ever attended.

[Man B]   I know. I didn't meet any interesting people.

[Woman B]   And the food! It tasted awful.

(Pause 8 seconds)

[Narrator]   Number 48.

[Woman B]   Could you help me carry this package inside?

[Man B]   All right. Wow. It's heavy. What's inside?

[Woman B]   I don't know. I just picked it up at the post office and I haven't opened it yet.

(Pause 8 seconds)

[Narrator]   Number 49.

[Man B]   This shirt doesn't fit so I'd like to return it.

[Woman A]   Certainly. Would you prefer cash or store credit?

[Man B]   I'll take cash.

(Pause 8 seconds)

[Narrator]	Number 50.
[Man B]	Mo's Restaurant is now offering a business lunch special. Order a two-course meal from our special lunch menu and pay just 20 dollars. Dessert not included. We're also open for breakfast and dinner, so visit us soon.

(Pause 8 seconds)

[Narrator]	This is the end of the Listening Comprehension portion of the test. Turn to Part IV in your test book.

AUDIOSCRIPTS FOR TOEIC BRIDGE MODEL TEST 1

[Narrator]

Listening Comprehension

In this section of the test, you will have the chance to show how well you understand spoken English. There are three parts to this section, with special directions for each part.

PART I: PHOTOGRAPHS

Directions: For each question, you will see a picture in your test book and you will hear four short statements. The statements will be spoken just one time. They will not be printed in your test book, so you must listen carefully.

When you hear the four statements, look at the picture in your test book and choose the statement that best describes what you see in the picture. Then, on your answer sheet, find the number of the question and mark your answer. Look at the sample below.

[Narrator]	Now listen to the four statements.

[Man A]	(A)	[Woman A]	The boys are laughing.
	(B)		The boys are reading.
	(C)		The boys are fighting.
	(D)		The boys are painting.

[Narrator]	Statement (B), "The boys are reading," best describes what you see in the picture. Therefore, you should choose answer (B).

[Narrator]	Now, let us begin Part I with question number 1.

[Narrator]	Number 1. Look at the picture marked number 1 in your test book.
[Man A]	(A)	[Woman A]	They're eating breakfast.
	(B)		They're washing the dishes.
	(C)		They're waiting for a bus.
	(D)		They're shopping for food.

(Pause 5 seconds)

[Narrator]			Number 2. Look at the picture marked number 2 in your test book.
[Man A]	(A)	[Woman B]	The highway is under repair.
	(B)		The cars park on the street.
	(C)		The snow covers the ground.
	(D)		The road curves to the right.

(Pause 5 seconds)

[Narrator]			Number 3. Look at the picture marked number 3 in your test book.
[Man A]	(A)	[Man B]	She's taking out a loan.
	(B)		She's talking on the phone.
	(C)		She's walking alone.
	(D)		She's making a shawl.

(Pause 5 seconds)

[Narrator]			Number 4. Look at the picture marked number 4 in your test book.
[Man A]	(A)	[Woman B]	The bus driver is wearing a cap.
	(B)		The lawyer is carrying his briefcase.
	(C)		The student is waving his hand.
	(D)		The traveler is checking his bag.

(Pause 5 seconds)

[Narrator]			Number 5. Look at the picture marked number 5 in your test book.
[Man A]	(A)	[Woman A]	There are many cars in the lot.
	(B)		There are buses on the left.
	(C)		There are passengers in the van.
	(D)		There are motorcycles on the right.

(Pause 5 seconds)

[Narrator]			Number 6. Look at the picture marked number 6 in your test book.
[Man A]	(A)	[Man B]	The construction worker is repairing the road.
	(B)		The mechanic is fixing his engine.
	(C)		The plumber is looking for his tools.
	(D)		The carpenter is cutting a board.

(Pause 5 seconds)

[Narrator]			Number 7. Look at the picture marked number 7 in your test book.
[Man A]	(A)	[Woman A]	She's putting on her sweater.
	(B)		She's hanging a picture.
	(C)		She's closing the door.
	(D)		She's opening her purse.

(Pause 5 seconds)

[Narrator]	Number 8. Look at the picture marked number 8 in your test book.
[Man A]	(A) [Woman B] These are motorcycles.
	(B) These are bicycles.
	(C) These are motor parts.
	(D) These are skewers.

(Pause 5 seconds)

[Narrator]	Number 9. Look at the picture marked number 9 in your test book.
[Man A]	(A) [Man B] They're leaving the store.
	(B) They're cooking dinner.
	(C) They're buying food.
	(D) They're choosing a car.

(Pause 5 seconds)

[Narrator]	Number 10. Look at the picture marked number 10 in your test book.
[Man A]	(A) [Woman B] The taxi is on the street.
	(B) The train is near the station.
	(C) The plane is taking off.
	(D) The ship is in the harbor.

(Pause 5 seconds)

[Narrator]	Number 11. Look at the picture marked number 11 in your test book.
[Man A]	(A) [Woman A] He's pointing toward something.
	(B) He's building a house.
	(C) He's driving down the street.
	(D) He's drawing a map.

(Pause 5 seconds)

[Narrator]	Number 12. Look at the picture marked number 12 in your test book.
[Man A]	(A) [Man B] The librarian is reading the newspaper.
	(B) The secretary is filing a paper.
	(C) The cabinet maker is sanding the drawer.
	(D) The athlete is running a mile.

(Pause 5 seconds)

[Narrator]	Number 13. Look at the picture marked number 13 in your test book.
[Man A]	(A) [Woman A] The sheep are in the barn.
	(B) The toy boat is on the pond.
	(C) The sailboat is on the sea.
	(D) The ship is on the river.

(Pause 5 seconds)

[Narrator]   Number 14. Look at the picture marked number 14 in your test book.
[Man A]   (A)   [Man B]   He's painting the wall.
              (B)   He's lying in his hammock.
              (C)   He's putting a nail in the wall.
              (D)   He's walking down the hall.

(Pause 5 seconds)

[Narrator]   Number 15. Look at the picture marked number 15 in your test book.
[Man A]   (A)   [Man B]   The computer is on the desk.
              (B)   The commuter is at the station.
              (C)   The notebook is in the drawer.
              (D)   The computer is turned off.

(Pause 5 seconds)

[Narrator]

PART II: QUESTION-RESPONSE

Directions: In this part of the test, you will hear a question or statement spoken in English, followed by three responses, also spoken in English. The question or statement and the responses will be spoken just one time. They will not be printed in your test book, so you must listen carefully. Choose the best response to each question.

[Narrator]   Now listen to a sample question.

[Narrator]   You will hear:
[Woman B]   Excuse me. Where is the bus stop?

[Narrator]   You will also hear:
[Man A]   (A) It's across the street.
              (B) It's underneath.
              (C) It arrives in ten minutes.

[Narrator]   The best response to the question *Where is the bus stop?* is Choice (A),
               It's across the street. Therefore, you should choose answer (A).

[Narrator]   Now let us begin Part II with question number 16.

16. Woman 1:   When will the bicycles be ready?
      Woman 2:   (A) Tomorrow, after 3:00.
                   (B) They cost $20.
                   (C) We need two wheels.

Audioscripts

17. Woman: Take the train on Track 11.
    Man: (A)   The plane leaves now.
                         (B)   OK, thank you.
                         (C)   I don't think it will rain.

18. Man: Did you hear the phone message from Betsy?
    Woman: (A)   What message?
                         (B)   I don't know where she is.
                         (C)   She didn't hear you.

19. Woman: How many players do we need on each team?
    Man: (A)   About six teams.
                         (B)   The game ends at 9.
                         (C)   We always play with five.

20. Man: What's your first name?
    Woman: (A)   My surname is Pavel.
                         (B)   It's Helen.
                         (C)   Fine, thank you.

21. Man: Can you pass the salt?
    Woman: (A)   We're passing the bridge now.
                         (B)   Sure, here you are.
                         (C)   It's not my fault.

22. Woman 1:   Turn on the news. It begins in five minutes.
    Woman 2:   (A)   She talked for 30 minutes.
                         (B)   Are those new shoes?
                         (C)   O.K., what channel is it on?

23. Woman: How many people are going on the trip?
    Man: (A)   At least 45.
                         (B)   They're taking a bus.
                         (C)   The first stop is Indonesia.

24. Man 1:   Have you heard this band's new CD?
    Man 2:   (A)   Make it louder, please.
                         (B)   No, I don't like their music.
                         (C)   Let me give you a hand.

25. Man: Why don't we have lunch tomorrow?
    Woman: (A)   I never eat salad.
                         (B)   Sorry, I can't.
                         (C)   I'm hungry.

26. Man 1:   May I see your ticket, please?
    Man 2:
    (A) Didn't I show it to you?
    (B) Isn't the sea beautiful?
    (C) Where does it arrive?

27. Woman: It's almost 5:00. We have to hurry.
    Man:
    (A) You're right, or we'll be late.
    (B) You have the most.
    (C) You got there on time.

28. Woman 1:   What is the exchange rate?
    Woman 2:
    (A) I don't have any change.
    (B) Just go to the second counter.
    (C) Today, it is 1.7 to the dollar.

29. Man 1:   Will we make it to the 8 o'clock show?
    Man 2:
    (A) Sure, we have 20 minutes.
    (B) What did you eat?
    (C) She made one last year.

30. Man 1   What's the score of the game?
    Man 2:
    (A) At 7:00 P.M.
    (B) It's a basketball game.
    (C) We're winning, 50–35.

31. Woman: Would you like something to drink?
    Man:
    (A) Yes, a steak sandwich, please.
    (B) Just water.
    (C) There are five of us.

32. Man: Who's coming to dinner?
    Woman:
    (A) Aren't Julie and John?
    (B) Is he a good cook?
    (C) It isn't mine.

33. Woman 1:   That is a beautiful purse.
    Woman 2:
    (A) They're ugly, aren't they?
    (B) No, it's this one.
    (C) Thanks, I bought it yesterday.

34. Woman: I have to get a package at the post office.
    Man:
    (A) It is outside the building.
    (B) I'll go with you, I want to mail a letter.
    (C) I haven't started packing.

35. Man: Hello, this is Jack.
    Woman:
    (A) Are we?
    (B) Hi, is Sarah there?
    (C) Can I go now?

PART III: SHORT CONVERSATIONS AND SHORT TALKS

> **Directions:** In this part of the test, you will hear 15 short conversations or short talks only once, so you must listen carefully.
>
> In your test book, you will read a question about each conversation or talk. The question will be followed by four short answers. Choose the best answer to each question and mark it on your answer sheet.

36. [Man A]   Did you finish your homework?
     [Woman A]   No, not yet. Can you help me?
     [Man A]   You know I'm not good at math.

37. [Woman A]   Can I help you find something?
     [Woman B]   Yes, I'm looking for a good mystery story.
     [Woman A]   Try aisle 6, between the cookbooks and the novels.

38. [Woman A]   How much are 12 potatoes?
     [Man A]   The white baking ones are $1.25 a pound.
     [Woman A]   No, I mean the small red potatoes.

39. [Man A]   Sam, I have tennis practice this afternoon.
     [Man B]   What time do you finish? I'll meet you at the court.
     [Man A]   At six. Just in time for dinner.

40. [Man A]   We have three weeks to do our project.
     [Woman A]   Actually, I want to finish it by Friday.
     [Man A]   We can't possibly do all of this in 5 days.

41. [Man A]   Welcome ladies and gentlemen! We are very lucky to have an award-winning author with us tonight. She is here to read a passage from her new book about famous actors and well-known painters entitled *Artists and Actors*.

42. [Man A]   Do you have these pants in a smaller size?
     [Woman A]   No, I'm sorry, that's all the trousers we have.
     [Man A]   These are so large I'd be lost in them.

43. [Woman A]   We should go inside the theater.
     [Woman B]   But the film doesn't start for 30 minutes.
     [Woman A]   I want to get a good seat. I don't like to sit too close to the screen.

44. [Man A]   I have a bad fever. I need to see the doctor.
     [Woman A]   The doctor can't see you until Tuesday.
     [Man A]   Tuesday? I can't wait until then.

45. [Man A]   We planted 40 acres of corn.
    [Man B]   I grew only wheat last year.
    [Man A]   I hope this is a better year for our crops.

46. [Woman A]   This year all students have to write one essay every week. You will write 10 essays during the 10-week course. The essays are due every Friday. Only five of these will be graded. In addition, your final exam will be an essay exam.

47. [Man A]   Today should be another hot day with temperatures in the 90's. Cooler temperatures are expected for the weekend and there is a chance of rain late Sunday evening.

48. [Woman A]   World Travel, how may I help you?
    [Man A]   Hi, I wanted to get information on flights to Paris.
    [Woman A]   When would you like to depart?

49. [Man A]   The Annual Car Show starts today. Doors open at 10:00 A.M. and admission is $5, $7 for couples. One lucky ticket holder will win a brand-new Mercedes 230 sedan.

50. [Woman A]   Due to increased airport security, parking is prohibited in front of the terminal. Parking is available for all passengers and bags may be checked in the parking garages. Thank you and have a pleasant flight.

AUDIOSCRIPTS FOR TOEIC BRIDGE MODEL TEST 2

[Narrator]

Listening Comprehension

In this section of the test, you will have the chance to show how well you understand spoken English. There are three parts to this section, with special directions for each part.

PART I: PHOTOGRAPHS

> **Directions:** For each question, you will see a picture in your test book and you will hear four short statements. The statements will be spoken just one time. They will not be printed in your test book, so you must listen carefully.
>
> When you hear the four statements, look at the picture in your test book and choose the statement that best describes what you see in the picture. Then, on your answer sheet, find the number of the question and mark your answer. Look at the sample below.

[Narrator]			Now listen to the four statements.
[Man A]	(A)	[Woman A]	The boys are laughing.
	(B)		The boys are reading.
	(C)		The boys are fighting.
	(D)		The boys are painting.

[Narrator]	Statement (B), "The boys are reading," best describes what you see in the picture. Therefore, you should choose answer (B).

[Narrator]	Now, let us begin Part I with question number 1.

[Narrator]	Number 1. Look at the picture marked number 1 in your test book.		
[Man A]	(A)	[Woman A]	She's washing the wall.
	(B)		She's cleaning the floor.
	(C)		She's dusting the furniture.
	(D)		She's wiping the counter.

(Pause 5 seconds)

[Narrator]	Number 2. Look at the picture marked number 2 in your test book.		
[Man A]	(A)	[Woman B]	The ship is at sea.
	(B)		The sheep are near me.
	(C)		The sailor is on shore.
	(D)		The tailor is in the water.

(Pause 5 seconds)

[Narrator]   Number 3. Look at the picture marked number 3 in your test book.
[Man A]   (A)   [Man B]   The baby is playing alone.
            (B)   The father is putting his son to bed.
            (C)   The mother is holding her baby in her arms.
            (D)   The man carries a baby on his back.

(Pause 5 seconds)

[Narrator]   Number 4. Look at the picture marked number 4 in your test book.
[Man A]   (A)   [Woman B]   The driver is washing the truck.
            (B)   The homeowner is painting his house.
            (C)   The firefighter is putting out a fire.
            (D)   The gardener is watering the lawn.

(Pause 5 seconds)

[Narrator]   Number 5. Look at the picture marked number 5 in your test book.
[Man A]   (A)   [Woman A]   She's walking next to the train.
            (B)   She's sitting on the platform.
            (C)   She's running for a bus.
            (D)   She's reading a sign.

(Pause 5 seconds)

[Narrator]   Number 6. Look at the picture marked number 6 in your test book.
[Man A]   (A)   [Man B]   They're watching the news.
            (B)   They're sitting on a park bench.
            (C)   They're throwing a paper.
            (D)   They're taking a nap.

(Pause 5 seconds)

[Narrator]   Number 7. Look at the picture marked number 7 in your test book.
[Man A]   (A)   [Woman A]   The pharmacist is labeling a prescription.
            (B)   The patient is taking medication.
            (C)   The doctor is signing his name.
            (D)   The nurse is naming a child.

(Pause 5 seconds)

[Narrator]   Number 8. Look at the picture marked number 8 in your test book.
[Man A]   (A)   [Woman B]   The plane is taking off.
            (B)   The taxi is starting to move.
            (C)   The trolley is speeding up.
            (D)   The model is on the runway.

(Pause 5 seconds)

[Narrator]			Number 9. Look at the picture marked number 9 in your test book.
[Man A]	(A)	[Man B]	The housekeeper is cleaning the kitchen.
	(B)		The girl is eating dessert.
	(C)		The waitress is carrying the trays.
	(D)		The chef is decorating the cake.

(Pause 5 seconds)

[Narrator]			Number 10. Look at the picture marked number 10 in your test book.
[Man A]	(A)	[Woman A]	She's catching a rat.
	(B)		She's petting her dog.
	(C)		She's holding a cat.
	(D)		She's knitting a sweater.

(Pause 5 seconds)

[Narrator]			Number 11. Look at the picture marked number 11 in your test book.
[Man A]	(A)	[Man B]	The girl is writing in her notebook.
	(B)		The children want to sit down.
	(C)		The teacher is helping the students.
	(D)		The boy has a microscope.

(Pause 5 seconds)

[Narrator]			Number 12. Look at the picture marked number 12 in your test book.
[Man A]	(A)	[Woman A]	They're skiing.
	(B)		They're playing golf.
	(C)		They're shoveling snow.
	(D)		They're waterskiing.

(Pause 5 seconds)

[Narrator]			Number 13. Look at the picture marked number 13 in your test book.
[Man A]	(A)	[Woman B]	There are only men on the street.
	(B)		There are a lot of people walking.
	(C)		There are a few peas in the dish.
	(D)		There are many workers at their desks.

(Pause 5 seconds)

[Narrator]			Number 14. Look at the picture marked number 14 in your test book.
[Man A]	(A)	[Man B]	He's reading the chart.
	(B)		He's sending a letter.
	(C)		He's waiting by the bed.
	(D)		He's writing on the board.

(Pause 5 seconds)

[Narrator]	Number 15. Look at the picture marked number 15 in your test book.

[Man A]	(A)	[Woman B]	She's feeding her kids.
	(B)		She's watching the birds.
	(C)		She's opening the cage.
	(D)		She's sitting on the lawn.

(Pause 5 seconds)

[Narrator]

PART II: QUESTION-RESPONSE

Directions: In this part of the test, you will hear a question or statement spoken in English, followed by three responses, also spoken in English. The question or statement and the responses will be spoken just one time. They will not be printed in your test book, so you must listen carefully. Choose the best response to each question.

[Narrator]	Now listen to a sample question.

[Narrator]	You will hear:
[Woman B]	Excuse me. Where is the bus stop?

[Narrator]	You will also hear:
[Man A]	(A) It's across the street.
	(B) It's underneath.
	(C) It arrives in ten minutes.

[Narrator]	The best response to the question *Where is the bus stop?* is Choice (A), *It's across the street.* Therefore, you should choose answer (A).

[Narrator]	Now let us begin Part II with question number 16.

16. Man: The train stops at Center City next.
       Woman: (A) Sit next to me.
                         (B) I usually ride in the last car.
                         (C) Great, that's where I get off.

17. Woman: Did you hear the news?
       Man: (A) Isn't it horrible?
                         (B) Did you leave it here?
                         (C) Is it old?

18. Man: Who is your supervisor?
       Woman: (A) Sam is going tomorrow.
                         (B) It's Mrs. Clark, now.
                         (C) Mr. Wilson is not very good.

19. Woman: Is the movie theater far from here?
    Man: (A) We moved here in 1996.
                     (B) It's around the corner.
                     (C) Yes, an actor lives near here.

20. Woman 1:   I went to the new Italian restaurant.
    Woman 2:   (A) How was the food?
                     (B) Do you want to rest?
                     (C) I don't speak Italian.

21. Man: Did you bring a jacket?
    Woman: (A) Yes, but I left it in the car.
                     (B) That's a nice coat.
                     (C) You have so many clothes.

22. Woman 1:   How much are the tickets?
    Woman 2:   (A) The bus is stopping.
                     (B) They're ten dollars each.
                     (C) I usually go by plane.

23. Woman: What is the name of your dentist?
    Man: (A) It's Martha Brown.
                     (B) Her office is on 3rd Street.
                     (C) She does excellent work.

24. Man 1:   Can you do me a favor?
    Man 2:   (A) Which flavor do you prefer?
                     (B) Where is the can?
                     (C) Sure, what do you need?

25. Man: Are you ready?
    Woman: (A) Yes, let's go.
                     (B) I can't read it.
                     (C) My name's not Freddy.

26. Woman: Tonight is our school's election.
    Man: (A) This store has a good selection.
                     (B) We finished our homework.
                     (C) I hope you win!

27. Woman: Is it going to rain?
    Man: (A) No, this isn't our train.
                     (B) Yes, take an umbrella.
                     (C) I prefer to go by plane.

28. Woman 1:   Where were you born?
    Woman 2:   (A) A little baby girl.
                     (B) On May 15th.
                     (C) At University Hospital.

29. Man: State Bank Customer Service, may I help you?
    Woman: (A) I don't know the customs here.
                  (B) Yes, I would like to open a checking account.
                  (C) Yes, do you serve lunch?

30. Man 1:   Is the flight on time?
    Man 2:   (A) No, it's 30 minutes late.
                 (B) No, it's not a big plane.
                 (C) No, it's not very light.

31. Man 1:   We went to the concert last night.
    Man 2:   (A) It is very late.
                 (B) You did? So did we.
                 (C) She's singing now.

32. Man: When are you going on vacation?
    Woman: (A) I leave in two weeks.
                  (B) I'm going for one month.
                  (C) I'll spend it at the lake.

33. Woman 1:   Doesn't your brother have a pet dog?
    Woman 2:   (A) No, he has a cat.
                     (B) She has a sister too.
                     (C) I don't like animals.

34. Woman: Do you want to go on a bicycle ride?
    Man: (A) It's a 30-kilometer race.
               (B) Sure, I can ride a horse.
               (C) I can't. I don't have a bike.

35. Man 1:   Where is the meeting?
    Man 2:   (A) Next year's budget.
                 (B) At 8 o'clock.
                 (C) In Room 401.

PART III: SHORT CONVERSATIONS AND SHORT TALKS

Directions: In this part of the test, you will hear 15 short conversations or short talks only once, so you must listen carefully.

In your test book, you will read a question about each conversation or talk. The question will be followed by four short answers. Choose the best answer to each question and mark it on your answer sheet.

[Narrator]   Now let us begin Part III with question number 36.

36. (Man)   How do I get to the library?
    (Woman)   It's just around the corner.
    (Man)   I hope it's still open.

37. (Woman)   Coming up next is sports. Randy Schaffer will report the latest soccer and basketball news. You'll want to hear if your teams won, so keep listening for the latest results.

38. (Man)   Do you love music? If so and if you have a few extra hours every week, you can help the City Opera House. We need volunteers for our new season. In the process, you can hear famous opera singers perform.

39. (Woman)   It will be a beautiful and sunny day with temperatures ranging between 70–75 degrees with light winds from the southwest.

40. (Man)   Attention please. The bus for the City Tour will leave in 10 minutes. Please put all luggage on the bus now. We will be leaving at 8:00 a.m. sharp! Don't be late.

41. (Woman)   I feel horrible. What can I do for my cold?
    (Man)   Take two aspirins and drink a lot of water.
    (Woman)   And some chicken soup… and rest. Thanks a lot.

42. (Woman)   Passenger Jenny Lau, please report immediately to Gate 9. The plane to Manila is now boarding. Passenger Lau, please report immediately.

43. (Woman)   I left my red wallet on the table. Did you see it?
    (Man)   Let me check in our lost and found.
    (Woman)   I looked everywhere for it. It was brand new.

44. (Man) Hi, Bella. I'm leaving work now.
    (Woman) Great, so you'll be home for dinner at 7:00?
    (Man) Yes, I'll pick up the kids from school and come straight home.

45. (Man) It's finally over! After seven long days of searching, six mountain climbers were found in the Alps. All six men are tired but safe and healthy.

46. (Woman) Thank you for inviting me this evening. I've been asked to speak about the economy of Japan. I will focus on banks and their influence on the Japanese economy.

47. (Man) Prices are so high!
    (Woman) I know, but we really need a new car.
    (Man) They're only going to go up. We'd better start shopping today.

48. (Man) Add one spoonful of coffee for each cup of water.
    (Woman) I always add more. I like my coffee strong.
    (Man) OK, but don't make it too strong.

49. (Man) I'll see you tomorrow at the airport.
    (Woman) Great, the plane arrives at 11:15 A.M.
    (Man) If you change your reservation, let me know.

50. (Woman) The Clarksburg Housing Group announces the opening of 25 new family homes. Each home has three bedrooms and two bathrooms and a two-car garage. Come see the houses on Sunday, August 5 from 10 to 5.

CD1

CD2

MINI-TEST FOR LISTENING COMPREHENSION REVIEW—PARTS I, II, AND III

TOEIC BRIDGE MODEL TEST 1: LISTENING COMPREHENSION

TOEIC BRIDGE MODEL TEST 2: LISTENING COMPREHENSION